1841-1930 Pansy

Stephen Mitchell's Journey

1841-1930 Pansy

Stephen Mitchell's Journey

ISBN/EAN: 9783744761024

Printed in Europe, USA, Canada, Australia, Japan

Cover: Foto ©Andreas Hilbeck / pixelio.de

More available books at **www.hansebooks.com**

STEPHEN MITCHELL'S JOURNEY

BY

MRS. G. R. ALDEN (*Pansy*)

Author of

"Chrissy's Endeavor," "Her Associate Members," "The Little Card," "Twenty Minutes Late," etc., etc.

ILLUSTRATED

BOSTON
D. LOTHROP COMPANY
1893

CONTENTS.

Chapter		Page
I.	An Up-hill Start . . .	1
II.	On the Early Freight . .	14
III.	More than He Bargained For	27
IV.	The Afternoon Accommodation	39
V.	Making His Report . . .	51
VI.	Another Passenger . . .	62
VII.	The Down-hill Road Described	74
VIII.	Trying a New Road . . .	85
IX.	Becoming a Champion . .	98
X.	Obstructions	108
XI.	Intersecting Lines . . .	120
XII.	Side Tracks	132
XIII.	Plans for a Through Line .	144
XIV.	Stockholders in Council . .	156
XV.	More Passengers . . .	167
XVI.	Through a New Country . .	180
XVII.	Laying a Track . . .	193

CONTENTS.

XVIII.	Complications	206
XIX.	Progress	220
XX.	Trying to Catch Up	234
XXI.	Transferred	248
XXII.	A New Engineer	260
XXIII.	Blocking the Track	273
XXIV.	The Wrong Road	287
XXV.	Reviewing the Road	299
XXVI.	Other Travelers	313
XXVII.	Danger Signals	324
XXVIII.	The Through Line at Last	335

STEPHEN MITCHELL'S JOURNEY.

CHAPTER I.

AN UP-HILL START.

"NOW don't drive fast, Stephen. It looks as if it was going to be a warm day, and the horses had a hard pull of it yesterday. And mind you don't leave the things with anybody but Baker; he's the one I made the bargain with, and I want him there to see that it is all right."

"Suppose he isn't there?" said Stephen, laying one hand on the wheel of the large old-fashioned farm wagon and the other on his side, as he turned to look at the man in the gateway.

"He'll be there fast enough. He runs the place, he thinks, and there don't any potatoes or cabbages or anything of that sort come in without he tends to them; I don't know but he counts every one. Any way, you see that he's there before you deliver your goods. I ain't going to have any squabbles with him. He will as like as not say they never came at all, if he doesn't happen to see them unloaded. If he isn't on hand when you get there, you hang around till he comes, if you have to stay till night."

"And, Stephen, don't you forget to stop in the village and ask Mis' Bascome for that pattern she promised me. I should think she might have had a chance to send it out before this time; I know Sarah Jane is about tired waiting for it."

This direction came from a woman's voice in the doorway. While it was yet speaking, a small-paned sash from an upper window was raised, and a curly, reddish head appeared, whose owner shouted down her commission:

"Steve, you'll stop at the store, and get me that green braid, won't you?"

"O, land!" said Stephen gruffly, "I don't know a green braid from a blue one. How am I going to match a thing?"

"Why, they will match it for you; the clerk will, you know. All you have got to do is to take the piece out of your pocket and tell him you want one like it, and he will find it. I should think you might do that much, when you are the only one who gets a chance to go to town."

"You get it, Steve; it will be real mean if you don't. Sarah Jane has been waiting weeks for that braid." This from the mother in the doorway.

"Steve" looked sullen.

"I don't like to go to the store," he growled; "I don't mind the grocery, nor the shop, nor any of them things, but that dry-goods store I do despise. That fellow behind the counter is all watch-chain and finger-nails. He thinks he knows everything there is to know in life, and looks down on everybody that isn't behind a counter selling tape and braid and things; I wish Sarah Jane would do her own errands."

"She would in a minute if she had a chance," said the mother, "but you know just as well as we do that she doesn't get to town once in an age; it is a shame, too. I meant to have her get in this summer to pick out her own things. If there had been room with the load, she might have gone with you this morning."

"Well, there ain't room," said the man at the gate, speaking briskly; "it's a heavy up-hill road, and the horses are old, and Steve and the potatoes and cabbages and light truck of all sorts is about all they can manage. I guess Steve can get what Sarah Jane needs, if he tries. You tend to it, Steve, and show you know so much, anyhow. Keep track of your money; don't do no fooling with it. You will have to pay a quarter to get in at the gate, even if you don't stay half an hour. That is the cheating part of it. It is the way they make their money; can't go in to sell a few potatoes and things without paying for the privilege! I call that cheating, but there is no use in growling; poor folks have got to take what they find, in this world. It is a pretty enough place when you get in, and lots of nice trees that you can set under and eat your dinner, and there is plenty of good water to drink, so you will have a comfortable time, if you do have to wait. But don't you come home without seeing Baker; you won't get no money without he's there, and without the money I don't mean to have the things left. Come, get started; the sun is climbing higher every minute. It seems as though it took forever to get started anywhere from this house. I expect everything will go wrong because I can't be there to attend to it."

And with a long-drawn sigh the old, worn father turned and limped away toward the house, groaning with every step, and muttering in an undertone against the rheumatism which held him prisoner, instead of allowing him to attend to his own affairs.

You have now been introduced to the Mitchell family — father, mother, Sarah Jane and Stephen. As for the farmhouse, it would be easy enough to describe, if that were worth while — a long, rather low, old-fashioned, dilapidated building, gray with age and neglect, with a shutter here and there hanging by one hinge, and among the many small-paned windows was occasionally one which had lost a light of glass. It was a style of building which unfortunately is too common in some portions of our country — a broken-down, disheartened farmhouse, that might once have been pretty and bright, and full of life and cheer, but was now old and disappointed, and dropping daily into ruin; a place which had marked in distinct letters on every window and door, and even on the old pump at the back of the house, the word "failure."

The picture is much the same wherever found, though the causes vary: oftentimes it is shiftlessness, very often intemperance, occasionally ill-health, sometimes a want of that mysterious quality well understood and distinctly felt, but hard to describe, named "gumption," and sometimes it might almost seem, even in this Christian land and under the banner of our Christian ideas, that the words "ill luck" would best tell the story of some dismal failures. There is such unaccountable, heart-wearing misfortune about everything which their hands touch or their minds plan. It is to be feared that Mr. Mitchell, had he been interviewed, would have attributed much of his trouble to that cause.

"I have worked hard," he used to say, putting his hands together so that fingers and thumbs matched, and then looking down upon them reflectively, while he spoke in a half-tremulous, half-querulous tone: "I have worked hard, there ain't a neighbor around here but what will tell you that; I've worked early and late, and contrived, and planned, and struggled, if ever a man did, and what does it all amount to? A mortgage on the farm, the interest of which eats up every dollar we can raise; just a hand-to-mouth living from day to day, in expectation that to-morrow there will be an end to that. That's about the way it goes; everything run down, of course it is; house needs painting; barn needs painting, needs a new floor and a new door, and a new barn, any way, from beginning to end. The old wagon has to be tied together with ropes to keep it from going to pieces, and it will go, one of these days, and spill the truck over the road, I dare say; and now here's the rheumatism got hold of me right in the middle of summer. I am about tuckered out; an old man before my time. There's Jason Burke, he is three years older than I am, if he is a day, and look how smart he is! They call him in his prime; just as chirk as a young grasshopper, he is; wears his broadcloth, and his gold watch and chain, and I don't know what all. And here I am, limping along all weasened up with rheumatism — as gray as a rat, and more than half my teeth gone! Him and me was brought up on the same fodder, you may say; his father's farm and mine joined. My father's was the best, by a good sight; now he is Judge Burke, and I am — well, I'm nobody. His children are a dreadful smart lot, they say; Joe gone to college, and all that. His daughter plays the piano, and sings like a nightingale, and jabbers two or three different languages, though I don't know what good that does her, or her father, either; and there is our Sarah Jane, that has had no chance even of common schooling since she was a little girl twelve or thirteen years old; had to be kept at work, grind, grind, day in and day out! Her mother would have died if she hadn't had her help. There was no other way to do, in order to live. After a spell, I couldn't even afford the clothes that it would cost to fix her up for school. Then at last, when her mother took sick, Sarah Jane had to give up all hope of school. There's Steve, he didn't take to books, somehow — maybe he would if he'd had a chance — he went to school one whole winter, and didn't learn enough to pay for the shoe leather that he wore out in walking there; three miles' walk from our place, anyhow. But he had the meanest kind of a teacher; I have always thought if he had had a different one, he wouldn't have hated his books so much as he appeared to. But then, maybe it was lucky he didn't care to go on; I don't know what we would have done with him if he had wanted to study. I don't know what Steve does want to do, I'm sure. He hates the farm, and he hasn't got any gumption about a farm; it is hard work to get him at it; I would rather do a good stiff day's work myself, any time, than to keep him at it half a day. Here he is, a great strong fellow, nineteen years old, and what does he know about farming? I done my best to teach him, too."

Such was the style of talk in which Farmer Mitchell would often indulge, of a summer evening, perhaps, as he sat tilted back in his arm-chair, his gray head against the wall, his eyes fixed contemplatively on his great, bony, wrinkled hands. Mrs. Mitchell, sitting not far away from him in a little, old-fashioned, flag-bottomed rocker, engaged, generally, either in darning with careful hand some glaring rent in Steve's limited wardrobe, or in setting a huge patch somewhere, would answer, first with a sorrowful little sigh, and then, generally, with a patient attempt at comfort:

"Oh! well, father, things ain't so bad with us but they might be worse. The farm is mortgaged, I know, and the crops are a failure this year, but maybe they won't be next; and as for the children, what if Steve ain't no farmer? He don't go loafing round the village, or spend his time in the saloon, playing cards, and smoking and drinking and such things. See how them Lucas boys spend their time! Steve hasn't got any bad habits, if he isn't a farmer, or didn't take to books. He hadn't any books to take to, you know, Josiah."

"Smokes enough!" would Mr. Mitchell respond, grimly, to these crumbs of comfort. Then would come again a gentle sigh from the mother's heart.

"Yes; I know he smokes, and I am dreadful

sorry. I always did hope that I would have a boy who didn't smoke; I hated it when I was a girl, somehow; but then I don't know as it is strange; everybody around here smokes, and you know you do yourself, Josiah, and why shouldn't he, when you come to think of it? I wish he did take more to farming, but he don't, so what's the use? But as for Sarah Jane, there ain't a smarter girl to do housework in the country around; she turns off more work in a day, I do believe, than I ever could. I wish Sarah Jane could have a chance; she is young and strong, and real quick about things. It 'pears to me if she could have had a chance, she might have done something. I tell you, Josiah, if we could only go to church regular, there would be some hope of things. That is the thing I worry about most."

"I know it," would Josiah respond, still in that half-sullen voice, which covered an undercurrent of disappointment. "I know all about it, Phebe, but how can I help it? The horses are old and broken down, just like their master; they are tuckered out with week-day work, and the roads is awful heavy and hilly; when the going is bad, you know it is almost impossible to get back and forth; and it seems to me the going is bad just two thirds of the time in this country."

"I know you do your best, Josiah," would the mother reply in cheery tones, "and there ain't no use in worrying about any of it. You just chirk up; something will happen next spring, or next fall, or some time; things will get brighter."

The encouraging words always ended with that soft undertone sigh, but they were always spoken; and Father Mitchell, though he smiled at them with the superior air of one who knew better, was, nevertheless, more upheld by them than he himself dreamed, and would have missed them, oh! so sorely, if the voice which spoke them had been hushed.

As for Sarah Jane, during this interchange of confidences, she was generally upstairs in her own tucked-up, low-ceiled room; at work, nearly always—for Sarah Jane was industrious, and as "contrivin'," as her mother used to say, with a sort of sad admiration, "as contrivin' as the next one!" So Sarah Jane's leisure moments were spent in "contrivin'" something out of nothing, or so near to nothing that those who have plenty to do with would have considered that word just the name for her resources. Sometimes it was a skirt that had been ripped carefully apart, all the stitches picked out, and the material sponged and pressed, over which Sarah Jane bent laboriously hour after hour, contriving and cutting, without pattern or picture, save that which was evolved from her own busy brain, and the glimpse she had had of the Bascome girls the last time she went to church. Perhaps they had fluttered in, dressed in their pretty muslins, or percales, or some other rare and exquisite material whose name was unknown to Sarah Jane; and their draperies had shaped themselves in a different manner from any which Sarah Jane had worn. Her quick eyes would study details while they all stood, during the opening hymn. While the morning lesson was read — wonderful words from the grand old Book — alas! alas! Sarah Jane would be wondering if the skirt of her blue dress couldn't be cut over to look something like theirs.

Why did Sarah Jane care whether her dress looked something like theirs or like its old-fashioned self? Who was to see it, save the hens that she fed every morning, and the turkeys, who nearly always sickened and died before Thanksgiving came around, and a stray peddler now and then, and, on very rare occasions, a country neighbor, who came to sit for an hour, on a leisure afternoon? But the loneliness of her life seemed never to be a reason to Sarah Jane why she should not remodel her scant wardrobe to the very best of her abilities. The truth is, Sarah Jane Mitchell tingled to her fingers' ends with energy, and actually had not enough in her stunted life to exhaust its power. She washed, and ironed, and baked, and boiled, and brewed; she was a marvel of strength and skill in the eyes of her frail, always-tired mother; yet, at the close of a busy day, in which there had been farm hands to feed, and farm kitchens to scrub, and when the mother, who had been permitted to shoulder only the lesser share of the burden, quivered in every nerve in her body with weariness, Sarah Jane dashed off the tea dishes with eager fingers, her busy brain the while engaged in planning an assault upon some waist, or skirt, or sack, or bonnet, which she intended to "make over."

If she had had books, it is possible she would have read them; if she had had neighbors, it is altogether probable she would have gone to visit them, but there were no near neighbors, and the horses were always tired; and "Steve" hated neighbors, any way; so there could be almost no social interchange of life, and there were no newspapers except the "Weekly Agricultural," which, aside from the articles on carrots, beets and potatoes, and all the other belongings of farm life, was *weakly* as well.

There were almost no books at all, save the Bible, at which Sarah Jane looked reverently; respecting it always, because it was a book they read out of at church, and because it was — well, of course, it was the Bible, and every decent-minded person did respect it; but it was a perfectly sealed book to her, and was literally not opened by her fingers from one year's end to another; though she dusted it carefully every time she made her weekly dash upon the "best room," and swept it furiously, and put it in its dreary order, to be undisturbed until her next assault. What was there left for Sarah Jane to do, but rip, and sponge, and press, and make over her clothes?

The result was amusing to the Bascome girls, and would have been bewildering to those still above their set; but to Sarah Jane it was satisfaction. Her "things" were different, at least; and she "did grow so tired of them, made in the same old way." And it was so impossible to have new ones, except when absolute necessity came. Her only relief was to put them into some other form.

CHAPTER II.

ON THE EARLY FREIGHT.

ON the morning in which Stephen Mitchell started on his journey into the great unknown world, Sarah Jane dashed about the kitchen "doing the dishes," and a score of other things besides; her mind, meanwhile, on the green braid which she had resolved at any sacrifice to secure.

"It won't cost but forty-five cents," she had told her mother, "and there is a bad spot in the waist and another in the sleeve that it will just cover. There is that money for the eggs — you said I could have it, you know, to buy something I needed; and I need this worse than anything. I can mend up my stockings and make them do; and I feel somehow as though I had got to have it."

"Well, I would," the mother had answered, in her patient, motherly voice. "The land knows you don't have very much; and if you would rather have green braid than new stockings, why, I say have it; though to my mind the dress looks nice enough, now you have got it fixed over, to wear to a party without any braid on it."

No matter if it did; Sarah Jane's heart had gone out after green braid. She had walked, one morning, four miles — to Farmer Bascome's place and back again — for the sake of getting the information she needed, and a scrap of the braid for Steve to match. It was really an event in her life to be looking forward to the possession of something quite new. She could not keep her thoughts away from it, as she made swift progress with the work.

"I do hope Steve won't be late to-night," she said. "It worries father so dreadfully to have him late getting home. I wonder what he thinks could happen to him between here and the village? To be sure Steve has never gone as long a trip as this before, and I can see father is dreadfully worried about it, but it isn't likely anything will happen."

"O, no!" said Mrs. Mitchell soothingly. The family did not realize it, but she was the one who had to speak most of the soothing words. "There is nothing for father to worry about. He mustn't expect Steve home early. It is a real long trip, and up hill a good part of the way. And then there is no telling how long he may have to wait. Father told him, you know, on no account to let anybody but that Mr. Baker have the things; and of course he might not be around when Steve gets there. Oh! he will get along all right; there is no cause to worry about Steve; we ought to be dreadful thankful for that, Sarah Jane; just suppose he was one of them boys who would stop at the saloon and drink up all the money he got for the garden truck. And then not know enough to come home at all! That Lucas boy was reeling from side to side when he went by a little while ago; just to think if you was his sister, Sarah Jane."

"O, my land!" said Sarah Jane, "I wouldn't want to be his sister, not if he sat up straight instead of reeling around. Of all the loafering, ugly, lop-sided fellows I ever saw, Jake Lucas beats! I wonder if Steve will bring my braid? Do you suppose he will?"

"I guess so, child. He doesn't like to go to the store, a mite. He grumbles a good deal, but Steve is accommodating, for all that; he wouldn't want to disappoint you, not if he understood how much you wanted it, and I guess he does. I hope it will be the right kind, and won't cost more than you think it will."

Mr. Mitchell's prophecy in regard to the morning came to pass. It was very warm. Stephen shielded himself from the August sun as well as he could, and let the tired old horses take their own gait up and down the long stony hills. The Mitchell horses were always tired, and never in a hurry. Stephen, as a general thing, had no difficulty in putting himself upon their level, so far as haste was concerned. "What is the use in hurrying?" If he had had a motto by which to live, perhaps that might have been it. Nothing that Stephen Mitchell had found in life, thus far, had seemed to him worth hurrying for. He was tall for his years; he was ungainly in form, and uncouth in manners. His clothes were not only old-fashioned, but much worn, and badly patched. Not that his mother did not understand patching, and not that she did not work patiently to do it neatly, but the quality of the patches have a great deal to do with their appearance when the work is done. And Mrs. Mitchell's resources, even in this respect, were so meager that she sometimes produced startling effects.

On the day in question, Stephen had done what he could to make himself respectable, with indifferent success. It had been much too warm to think of wearing other than his linen coat, which was short-waisted, and short-sleeved, and much faded by many washings. Moreover, it was ornamented with long, zigzag streaks of grass stains. His trousers were of the coarsest gray cloth, and had a patch of bright new gray, set in a very conspicuous place; they were carefully turned up at the bottom, not because they were too long, but because they were badly frayed; and Stephen, considering it with more thought than he generally gave to dress, had decided that the least disreputable arrangement was to have them turned up, as if he were afraid of soiling them. He wore a loose gray shirt, with a turn-down collar made of the same material, and no necktie whatever.

In this attire, seated on the board which was laid across the farm-wagon for a seat, and accompanied by potatoes, cabbages, onions, apples, beets, and, indeed, a little of everything which grows in an ordinary farm garden, he was making his laborious way — whistling the while to pass the time — not only to the village which lay eight miles away, but nearly four miles farther than that, to the summer encampment ground.

Stephen Mitchell was very much the sort of boy that his father was in the habit of describing to his mother on the twilight evenings before mentioned. Nearly nineteen, freckled, blue-eyed, rough and ungainly in every way; inclined to be gruff in manner, sometimes surly, perhaps almost sullen, yet never loud-voiced, or coarse; a little out of sorts with life in general, but utterly at a loss to know how he would have life differently arranged. Hating ploughing and hoeing with all his might, yet by no means sure of anything else which he would like to do instead. He sneered at the clerk in the dry-goods store, and declared repeatedly that he would rather " hoe turnips for a living till he was a hundred and one, than to stand behind that counter, with white fingers, and long nails, and measure tape and ribbon for giggling girls." He did not want to stay at home, and yet he could not be said to want to go away; where should he go? Moreover, he gruffly told himself it "wouldn't do no good to go anywhere;" he would have to stay on father's account. He was almost literally without education, the one entire winter which he had been enabled to spend in school having been simply wasted. He knew how to read, and, after a manner, to write, though he had ideas on orthography peculiar to himself. He knew a little about figures, enough to calculate with a good degree of certainty in regard to the "garden truck" which he sold from time to time; though very little of this part of the work had fallen to Stephen's lot. Mr. Mitchell, having a thorough distrust of his son's business abilities, generally transacted sales, and made change himself; but on the few occasions when Stephen had been allowed to do so, he had kept his accounts square; and though the father saw him depart on this particular morning with great misgivings, and gave many admonitions as to the price of the different articles, and the amount of money which they ought to bring, Stephen had no anxieties in that direction. He had made a memoranda of his entire load, and calculated the probable price, and was satisfied that nobody could cheat him. Therefore he could have given his mind to other thoughts if he had had anything to think about.

A more desolate life than that which Stephen Mitchell lived, it would seem hard to imagine.

As to the stony farm over which he struggled, a great deal of the time alone, for the poor father had often days when he could not drag his stiffened limbs about, there was not a corner in it for which Stephen did not have a fairly defined dislike; yet day after day, with something like patience, he puttered away at his distasteful work, and at night lumbered home, tired out, to sit drearily through the short evenings, and to get to bed almost with the chickens, from sheer weariness of sitting still and doing nothing. Yet there was nothing which he wanted to do.

A problem to a looker-on interested in human nature would Stephen Mitchell have been. To the surface looker-on he would have appeared like nothing so much as a lump of animated clay, rolling awkwardly around doing the work which a machine might have accomplished could it have been set in motion in those directions. Doing as little thinking, apparently, as the animals he drove so much. Nay, even that would have seemed a libel upon Doll and Dobbin, who had ideas of their own, and tried stubbornly at times to carry them out. For that matter, so had Stephen; the difference between him and them being that he knew better than to try to carry his out. But the great difficulty in the whole matter was, that no student of human nature came along, eager to study Stephen Mitchell, or to help him be other than the clod he was. His one teacher during the winter referred to, he distinctly remembered as one whom he had both despised and hated; therefore, of course, whatever influence he had upon him was for the worse. And his father's troubles growing thicker and heavier upon him at about that time, that one teacher had been the last, so far as Stephen was concerned.

He had no intimacies with boys and girls of his own age; he lived a perfectly isolated life; on the rare occasions, growing rarer with every passing week, when they drove eight miles to the church in the village, Stephen staid at home if he could; his father thought because he was too indolent to make the necessary effort to get himself ready to go; his mother feared it was because he had no interest in such things. She, poor mother, though a Christian at heart, was a very timid, unspoken one, and knew not how to help her boy to have any such desires; knew not even how to speak to her wide-awake, energetic daughter; and neither son nor daughter knew how often the pathetic little sigh which she gave so much was because of their manifest indifference to church and Sunday, or any such thing. Not one of the family knew that Stephen's real reason for absenting himself from church was because he recognized the infinite difference between himself and most of the other farmers' boys who would be together there. It was not so much the matter of dress, though to even Stephen Mitchell that was important, but there was a free-and-easy way about the other boys; they shook hands with one another, and made gay little speeches; they made dashing remarks to the girls, over which the girls laughed as though they were funny; they seemed to feel perfectly at home in one another's society, and to have plans to consider, and amusements to arrange. At all these ways Stephen Mitchell looked with amazement. How could a boy stand before a girl "all prinked out in finery" and say, "It's a pretty day," or give her a rose, maybe, or a pink, as he had seen boys no older than himself do? do it without stammering or blushing, or feeling as if he had seven pairs of hands instead of one, and as though his feet were a yard long, and as heavy as logs? Stephen Mitchell did not understand it, did not understand himself, and got rid of his puzzling thoughts by resolving to put them aside with his unanswerable "What's the use?"

There was within him a determination to hold himself aloof from church people, and from the few families who could be called neighbors. He met all Sarah Jane's suggestions in these directions with a shrug of his ungainly shoulders, and an indescribable grunt, which she knew must be be translated in the negative.

It was a boy of this stamp who paid his quarter at the gate of the great encampment ground, and drove his tired horses slowly in, staring about him on every side. He was filled with bewilderment, not to say dismay, over the unusual sights and sounds which presented themselves. A summer encampment, holding its sessions, first for four weeks, gradually lengthening its time, from summer to summer, until now it was nearer ten weeks than four, had been in progress for years, within twelve miles of his home; yet Stephen Mitchell looked upon the grounds this August day for the first time in his life. His father had, of late years, made pilgrimages to the place, sometimes as often as once in two or three weeks, carrying with him a load of what he called "garden truck;" as much as he could get ready from his worn-out and ill-tilled land; because he had discovered that here was a ready sale at fair prices for anything fresh which he could bring. But so unaccustomed was he to trusting any responsibility to Stephen, that it had not even entered his mind to send the boy in his stead, although the long, slow ride was irksome to him. But for the sudden attack of rheumatism which a few unusually rainy days had developed, the paradise which suddenly opened before Stephen would still have been unknown land to him. His father was a man of few words, and had never taken the trouble to describe to his family the wonders of those grounds; perhaps he could not have described them if he had tried; but perhaps he would have tried, had he imagined that either Stephen or Sarah Jane would feel any interest in such a story.

Very slowly the horses walked up the broad avenue; they were entirely willing to walk slowly at all times, and they found the smooth road and the lovely shade from the great trees, whose branches locked overhead, delightful to them; but for a warning cluck from Stephen's tongue, they would have stopped altogether. It was with some difficulty, and with much blushing, that Stephen succeeded in asking questions sufficient to direct him to the hotel, after the Mr. Baker whom he sought. It was so astonishing to be driving through what he thought would be woods, and find it a city, with broad avenues, and parks, and fountains, and many cottages gay with flowers, the piazzas bright with groups of young people, and the streets alive with men and women and children, hurrying to and fro. Not that he realized that it was in the least like a city, not that he knew parks, and avenues, and fountains, and grottos by sight.

Stephen Mitchell was as far from his home this morning as he had ever been. No knowledge of the hum and whirl of life had penetrated the stony hillside farm where he had been reared; so that you will find it very difficult to understand what a strange sensation the surroundings gave him. Had he been familiar with the Bible, and the story of Eden, I think the grounds through which he was passing might have suggested to him that far-away, bright garden, which faded from human sight so many years ago. Nay, had he been familiar with the Revelation, and the language of the Seer of Patmos, I do not know but the golden city of the new Jerusalem might almost have seemed to him to have taken shape for earthly eyes. But he knew neither of those pictures sufficiently well to have them in mind, and at first was simply dazed, even panic-stricken. His first desire was to get away; there were so many people. What an army of young men! Hundreds of them, it seemed to him, fully as well dressed as the detested clerk behind the counter of the one store in the village. And girls — hosts of girls! those creatures who had been the terror of his bashful boyhood. He felt himself ill-treated, deceived. Why had not his father told him what he would have to endure? He looked down at his patched knees, and his turned-up trousers, and blushed a deeper red than even the August sun had succeeded in producing. He was sorely tempted to turn his horses then and there, and go back to town, dispose of his potatoes and cabbage for what he could get at the village store, and make all speed homeward, his mind in its first stage of actual rebellion against his father's authority.

His second mood was calmer. "What's the use?" he asked himself, resorting to his one philosophical sentence; "there ain't a fellow here who ever saw me before, or will ever see me again; as for the girls, what do I care? Let them laugh, if they want to. Laughing won't kill me; if it would, I would have been dead long ago. I have seen Fanny Bascome snicker right out in church when I came in. I'll just go right on, and find that Mr. Baker, and get rid of my load, and get out; and I'll act as though I didn't care a red cent for none of them."

CHAPTER III.

MORE THAN HE BARGAINED FOR.

SO thinking, he held up his head, and gave most decided orders to Doll and Dobbin to "go on fast!" To the best of their energies they obeyed; at least, they went according to their own ideas of fast; but the speed was not too great to allow Stephen a chance to give furtive glances at the piazzas as he passed, and at the people who passed him. A good deal to his surprise, he seemed to attract no attention whatever. Most of the groups were busy with their books, or with one another, and seldom even glanced his way; or, if they did, turned their eyes at once, as if he were not of sufficient importance to arrest their attention; nobody laughed, so far as he could discover; and two or three men, as they passed, actually nodded in a friendly way. After this experience, it almost seemed to Stephen as if the reddish brown hair on the top of his head stood up. Strangers bowing to him! Gentlemen, dressed better than the minister! "Dressed enough sight better than that jackanapes at the store," he muttered to his astonished self.

No courteous recognition from strangers had ever before been given to Stephen Mitchell; it gave him such a sensation as only a shy and heretofore utterly neglected country boy, or one who has sometime in his life occupied that position, can understand.

Mr. Baker was not at home; would not be until the two o'clock boat came in; that was the earliest hour in which Stephen could hope to see him, and it was now eleven. Three hours to wait. He was not so appalled as he would have been on his first entrance within the gate. The people he had seen on every side, during that brisk drive through the grounds, had roused within him a strong desire to discover what was going on; or, as he phrased it to himself, "what all these people were about! What this thing was, anyhow." It was a great point with him, that, so far, his appearance had not awakened a laugh. If the truth must be told, poor Stephen dreaded a laugh worse than he dreaded a pistol shot, a great deal. Perhaps they were too busy to laugh at him, or to notice him in any way; he would find a nice place for his horses, give them their dinner, and then saunter around and see what there was to be seen. What companies of girls there were to look at!

"If Sarah Jane were here," he muttered, " she

could find out ways enough to pucker her clothes over to last her into next summer. She would be taking the tablecloth to make a rig like that white one. It is funny, that's a fact. I'd just like Fanny Bascome to see it; I wonder if the Bascomes come here? If I should meet them, I should sink into the ground."

He looked about him immediately, in a frightened way, with a longing desire to be outside the gates, safe in the road again. Anything but to meet the Bascomes. However, they were nowhere to be seen, nor was any other human being that he had ever seen before; and Stephen, having settled his horses, began a stroll through the grounds.

He came, presently, to an immense, semicircular building, or, rather, roof supported on pillars, and filled with seats, which descended the hill in regular terraces; he stopped before it in amazement.

"It ain't a tent," he soliloquized, "and it can't be a circus; you can peek in all around; and there ain't any ring, either. There couldn't any ponies perform around there. But maybe they don't use ponies now, and maybe they don't shut up the sides any more; I don't know as they use tents; things keep changing."

The sentence closed with a sigh, as he realized his ignorance. Stephen Mitchell had not even been to a circus for the space of four years. The first reason being that their circumstances were growing more and more straitened, so that the necessary half-dollars required for even so mild a form of dissipation as this were difficult to secure. And the second reason lay in the fact that Stephen had discovered the fashion of the country to be for the boys to invite the girls, and pay their way, of course, and take care of them during an evening at the circus. His heart had almost ceased to beat at the thought of such a thing. He might compass paying for the tickets, he thought, just for once in a season, but as for taking care of a girl — going after her, and seeing her home again — he could never do it, never! Besides, there wasn't anybody to take; who would go with "Steve Mitchell?" And as likely as not they would laugh at him for going alone, since most all of them went with some girl. He might take Sarah Jane just once; but then, there didn't none of them take their sisters. Maybe that was a thing to be laughed at, too. And Stephen had resolved that he would stay at home. So now, for aught he knew, this strange wooden building, without sides, and with many seats, might be a new style of circus. If so, it was evidently popular; the seats all down the terraces were filled; only here and there a vacancy. A man on the broad platform was talking rapidly, while the eyes of all the multitude seemed to be leveled upon him.

"He ain't no clown," said Stephen to himself, stopping before one of the aisles, with his hands in his pockets, and forgetting even the crowd in his astonishment and desire to know what this thing was. "He ain't the manager of the thing, neither; and he ain't a preacher; or anyhow, he ain't preaching now — there's no Bible, nor hymn-book, nor nothing." And then he turned suddenly, for a neatly dressed man touched him on the shoulder and said respectfully, but with a great deal of firmness:

"You mustn't smoke here, my friend; it is against the rule."

And Stephen, very red-faced, threw away his cigar, which he had forgotten, because it was second nature to smoke, and stammered something to the effect that he didn't know the rules. Then, seeing that the man was indifferent to his words, so long as the cigar had been disposed of, he put on a bold face and asked a question:

"What do you have to pay to get in there?" pointing with his finger.

"Nothing," said the man.

"Nothing? Is it a free show?"

"Perfectly free, sir, after you are once inside the gates. Your gate ticket pays for all that goes on here during the day."

"O, my!" said Stephen; "does it, though?" Straightway his resolve was taken; the people were all so busy looking at the man on the platform, that they seemed to have no eyes for him; he saw not the slightest inclination toward laughter in any direction ; he would take one of those empty seats, and find out by his wits what this thing was, and why they all wanted to listen to it.

Down he went — down the incline plane, as he had seen others do, feeling every moment as though he were going to fall forward and strike on his nose ; but he didn't. Very red in the face, and with the perspiration standing in drops upon his forehead, he finally reached a seat, got out a handkerchief, much the worse for having been used for the same purpose many times during that August day, and mopped his face and neck thoroughly, then settled back, prepared to listen.

He had never heard any one speak in Latin, nor yet in Greek ; had he done so, he might, perhaps, have had a comparison by which to describe this speaker. He knew, however, that there were other languages than his own, and decided at first that this was one of them ; then he looked about upon the interested, even absorbed, audience. They were not all foreigners ; on the contrary, they were unmistakably Americans, most of them ; he was observing enough to be sure of that. Was it possible that they understood this unknown tongue? Was it possible that it was an unknown tongue? Did not he, himself, understand some of the words?

"It's English," he told himself, thoughtfully, after a few moments more of intense listening ; "but it's high and mighty English, I suppose ;

them kinds that scholars speak. Mr. Ransom himself uses some of the words, but he doesn't speak them so outrageous fast, like an express train. I wonder now, if all these folks do understand him?"

The feeling of curiosity with which Stephen gazed about him began to deepen into respect, almost into awe; presently into a strange heart-longing to be one of them; to understand what that man was saying; to like it as those folks evidently did. If he only could! It is the simple truth that then, for the first time in his life, Stephen Mitchell felt a longing to be other than he was. He had not been satisfied with himself, or at least had not been complacent over himself at any time. But so far, in his unfortunate life, the idea that he might be different had never seemed to enter his mind. It cannot be said that he had such an idea at this moment; there was simply a vague stirring of impulses at his heart. The only thought that took distinct form was the wish that he understood those words, and could have the look of interest upon his face which the audience around him wore.

The next thought was a step in advance, for it took almost the form of a resolve. What if he should write down some of the words, and try to find out what they meant? How would he go to work to find out, though? He thought of his father, and shook his head; Mr. Ransom, perhaps.

They said he had rows and rows of books on his library shelves; probably some of them told the meaning of words; but how would he ever get speech with Mr. Ransom?

He blushed violently at the thought of it; if he only had a dictionary, a big dictionary, such as he saw one day on the counter of the village bookstore; there were words enough in that, pages and pages. It made him dizzy to think of them; yet it would certainly be interesting to know the meaning of some of them.

"If I had had a dictionary," thought Stephen, ruefully, "and had been studying it all them long winter evenings, when I have not known what in life to do with myself, maybe I might have known most of the words that he is pouring out now; then, O, my! how I should feel. I just believe I'll write 'em down — just a few out of the crowd — and see what will come of it. It stands to reason that I might be able to get at the meaning of some of them, somehow; and it does seem kind of queer to have a lot of folks around you that all appear to know a thousand million things that you don't. I believe I'll try for it."

As he glanced around him, with a vague idea of finding something upon which to write, fortune favored him. Or was it a watching, over-ruling Providence? On the floor, just at his feet, lay a circular announcing the teachers, and hours and terms of the music school. It was a four-page affair, and one page was almost blank. Stephen seized upon it, picked up a forgotten text-book of some sort, which lay beside him on the seat, folded his paper, got out the stub of a pencil with which he had calculated the prospective returns from the cabbages and potatoes, and commenced business.

It was laborious work. He was unused to writing, and his orthography would have alarmed the speaker. But as he wrote he grew interested; it presently became his ambition to see how many of the words he could capture; they were being poured out in such a magnificent flood, that the very sound of them roused within him a strange recognition of power. Words became, for the time being, tangible things.

"S'pose they was apples," he inwardly chuckled, "and I was trying to catch them!" and his pencil fairly raced over the paper.

He was "catching them." A long row, reaching to the very edge of the foolscap sheet; a double row; a third one, and yet a fourth. He was reaching the end, his paper nearly exhausted, his brain in a whirl of excitement. Not a single word that he had written did he understand. Some of them were names, evidently, from the connection; names of persons of whom he had never heard in his life. Also there were names of places, but where those places were located he knew no more than did the seat on which he sat. Yet he had been roused, excited and absorbed for the first time in his life over words spoken from a public platform. He began to regret deeply that he had no more paper; the race after the "apples" being tossed hither and thither, was growing every moment more exciting; they had ceased, however, to be apples. His awakening imagination had named every one of them silver dollars. And in proportion as they grew in value his eagerness to secure them seemed to grow. It is a hint as to the real nature of the boy, that instead of stopping to exult over the quantity which he had secured, his heart was beginning to sink heavy within him because the material with which to secure was exhausting itself.

Suddenly the flow of words ceased. All unexpectedly to Stephen, the speaker had rounded out his closing period. Almost immediately the audience burst into song. The initiated knew that the "Gloria" was being sung; Stephen did not; he only knew that it was music — such as that he had never heard before. There was the roll of a great organ, and the sound of many voices, and the majesty of solemn yet jubilant words: "Glory be to the Father, and to the Son, and to the Holy Ghost. As it was in the beginning, is now and ever shall be, world without end. Amen."

It seems surprising, when one thinks of it, but it was a simple fact that Stephen Mitchell was listening to the "Gloria" for the first time; and the grandeur and power of the words settled themselves within his conscience, never to be forgotten. Something had awakened within him, some power which he did not understand; but he felt, as he bowed his head with the multitude, and listened to the words of benediction, that he, Stephen Mitchell, standing there, was in some mysterious way a different Stephen Mitchell from the one who had had much ado not to fall upon his face, as he came down the incline. He clutched at the paper in his hand, and muttered to his roused and inner self that he would "find out what some of the words meant, anyhow, before he was many days older."

"Look at that fellow," a gentleman had whispered to his companion during the progress of the lecture. He sat only three seats behind Stephen, and had been watching him intently for some minutes. "Look at that fellow, Myers; he is in the commonest farmer-boy's attire; nothing about him indicates intellect, yet he has been writing steadily since he first took his seat. That is an illustration of what I was telling you. The common mind is being gotten hold of by these summer encampments. They are permeating the country, educating the ploughman, who has, heretofore, done not much more thinking than have the clods he has turned over. Imagine a fellow dressed in that fashion listening to a lecture like what we have had this morning, taking notes of it! I should like to see his notes. He is a grand illustration of the progress of the times. Let us go forward and shake hands with him."

"He has a good head," said the other gentleman, as they moved slowly down among the surging mass, and stood presently close to Stephen's side. The first speaker laid his hand familiarly on the country boy's arm.

"How are you, my friend?" He held out his hand and grasped Stephen's rough red one in a cordial fashion. "Glad to see you here; grand lecture, was it not? I saw you taking notes; they are worth preserving, I am sure. It would really be a liberal education for a young man to understand thoroughly such a lecture as that."

Not a word had Stephen to say; he blushed to the roots of his hair; he opened his lips as if about to attempt a reply, but voice failed him altogether. The gentlemen, noticing and pitying his intense embarrassment, added a few more kindly words, and passed on.

"He is overwhelmed with confusion, poor fellow," one of them said; "he thinks a great deal more than he knows how to express, evidently. Never mind; men are made of such stuff as he. We may meet him on the lecture platform himself, yet."

CHAPTER IV.

THE AFTERNOON ACCOMMODATION.

ONE more experience had Stephen. This time with a young fellow of about his own age, but one very unlike him in appearance. Indeed, had Stephen but realized it, he was quite as faultlessly dressed as the clerk at the dry-goods store, who had so aroused his ire; but this young man wore his dress as though it occupied a subordinate place, and had no idea of demanding attention. He came down the aisle, where Stephen still stood as if rooted to the spot, and addressed him cordially.

"Did you get good notes? I saw you writing. I tried to take notes, but somehow I failed. He is such a rapid speaker. Do you write shorthand? No? Then I don't see how you succeeded so well; he pours out the words in such a torrent! But he is magnificent, isn't he? I tell you if I knew one third of what that man does, I am afraid I should be vain. Did you ever hear a lecture so full of historic reference? Why, he went all over the field of literature. Ever hear him before? He is a Chicago preacher; one of the finest, they say, in the city. I don't recall his name, but I know I should like to hear him preach. These are wonderful opportunities, are they not?" And the young man, whose voice and dress and manner all showed that he belonged to another world than Stephen's, smiled on him with an air of good fellowship before he sprang up the aisle, and was lost in the throng.

Who shall undertake to represent Stephen Mitchell's frame of mind? He to be shaken hands with by elegant gentlemen! To be congratulated on the notes he had taken! He to be asked if he wrote shorthand — whatever that was. It was a term quite new to him, but glancing down at his strong red hand when the question was asked, he had realized that whatever else that hand might be, it certainly was not short, therefore had answered in the negative.

"Shorthand," he said to himself; "I wonder what kind of writing it is? Easier than mine, I dare say, or his'n either, for that matter. He thought if I did, I could write more. I mean to find out what it is."

He drew a long quivering breath; the world had suddenly grown very large to him. There was a great deal to find out. He went mechanically through the duties which filled the next hour; found Mr. Baker, and made a satisfactory trade, less embarrassed than usual — less conscious of his feet and his hands, and the clumsiness of his tongue, than he had ever been before when trying to transact business. More alert, also, as regarded prices, and the money he received; so alert, in fact, that Mr. Baker, looking after him as he drove out of the grounds with his empty wagon, said, "That fellow knows more than he looks to at first sight; he has quite a head for business." Which remark would have astonished Stephen's father.

All the way to the village the boy was absorbed with the new thoughts which presented themselves in such whirls before him. It cannot strictly be said that he thought; there was too much chaos in his mind to dignify the process by that name. Still, he went over, in some fashion, the vivid scenes of the last two hours. He lingered with the notes, which had been carefully put away in an unused vest pocket. Since they had taken to his consciousness the form of dollars, he felt half-afraid, and wholly reverent before them. This feeling had been added to by some words he had overheard as he stood waiting for Mr. Baker to calculate the money due. Two gentlemen standing near had discussed the lecture of the morning, and then had made, one of them, this astonishing announcement:

"Gets a hundred dollars, I suppose, for that lecture?"

"I suppose so," said the other; "it is worth it. I would be willing to pay my share toward another hundred, for the sake of hearing it again."

"A hundred dollars!" Stephen Mitchell repeated under his breath the magic words. A hundred dollars paid to a man for standing on a platform for an hour and pouring out words. Then words were dollars—many dollars! For he had brains enough to know that the man could go on other platforms and repeat the same words. "Over and over again!" he said to himself; "there is no end to the money he can make by them." As he thought of this phase of the question he took out the precious paper, and began to count the words, while Doll and Dobbin, much refreshed by their long rest, trotted steadily down the hill toward the village. It filled Stephen with amusement to discover that he had a hundred and three words on his paper. "Three more dollars than he made," he chuckled. "Well, I never! I wonder what father would think of that? Ploughing, hoeing, digging, and the land knows what, from sunrise to sunset, day after day, week in and week out, to get a hundred dollars toward paying the interest on the mortgage, and buying the things we've got to have. And here's a man that stands up and talks off a lot of words just as fast as he can, and in about an hour makes his hundred dollars. It does beat all! I think I better learn the meaning of the words. That man said it would be an education to understand all they meant. I vow I mean to understand all of 'em. I will, so! I'll pitch into the things. He used a lot of words

I didn't get, to be sure; but after I understand a hundred and three, maybe some of the others will come to me. I shouldn't wonder. Anyhow, I'm going to try for it. There's a lot of chances for thinking and planning while I'm at work. I'm just going in. I won't tell no one a thing about it; but I'll take means somehow to learn that first word — the meaning of it, the different ways in which it can be used, and all. I don't care if they do find it out and laugh at me, I just mean to do it. Whoa!" For to his surprise Doll and Dobbin reached the village, and were passing the despised corner store, where the braid was to be matched, and the disagreeable clerk must be endured.

He was fully as disagreeable as usual. He had his hair parted nearly in the middle. He wore a very heavy watch-chain, which Stephen did not know was not pure gold. He had a superior smile on his face, and irritated his customer to the degree that when he turned to him and said, in a condescending tone, "Well, my good fellow, what can I do for you to-day?" the country boy felt like doubling up his strong red fist, and knocking him down. However, he did nothing of the kind, but with great meekness produced the bit of green, and struggled to bring his powers of discernment to bear upon the subject of matching it.

"It 'pears to me that that's it," he said at last, putting his strong forefinger, which was finished with a black and stubbed nail, on one of the rolls.

"O, no!" said the clerk, with a disagreeable simper, which sounded like an ill-suppressed sneer, "I assure you, you are utterly mistaken, my fine fellow. The ladies would go wild if they depended upon you for a match."

Then he laughed prodigiously over the smartness of his pun.

Stephen's red face grew redder, but he was not sufficiently sure of his ground to make reply, and the clerk went on glibly:

"Now, this is a much better match, and a finer article in every way. It is for your sister, I suppose? Well, you take my word for it, this is what she wants. And I hope you will explain to her that I rescued her from a very bad match indeed. How many yards did you say?"

And he shook off a quantity from the roll, preparatory to measuring it.

Just a little below him, selecting papers of pins of various sizes, stood a young woman, unknown to Stephen. She was of another world from that of the Bascome girls and their friends. A very quiet young woman—as regarded dress and movements.

Stephen Mitchell, being called upon some time afterward to tell how she was dressed, could say no more than that it was in "some pale, still stuff that looked as though it was made a purpose for her, and wasn't going to wear out."

Such was the impression made upon his senses

by her outer covering. Neither was he much more lucid in regard to the color of hair or eyes. Both, he thought, were brown, though the eyes, he admitted under cross-questioning, might be gray. They were big, he was sure of that, and "kind of searching looking, as though they saw lots of things that they didn't mean to tell anything about."

And her voice — but this part Stephen Mitchell always kept to himself. It would have been too absurd, he decided, to put into words; but her voice made him ever after think of that burst of music which began, "Glory be to God the Father." Yet the words which she said were commonplace enough.

She turned those gray eyes of hers at that particular moment, when the clerk was prepared to measure the green braid, fixed them for an instant on Stephen's face, then upon the clerk, and said quietly:

"I do not agree with you, Mr. Pettibone; I think the young man's judgment is correct; for his sister's sake, I hope you will let me suggest that the braid he selected first is the proper shade for his sample, and I am glad to learn that you do not consider it of so good a quality as the other. I supposed it was higher priced; of course it is not so expensive, then?"

It was Mr. Pettibone's turn to blush.

"There is no accounting for the taste of the

ladies," he said, with an attempt at nonchalance; "I think myself this is the better match."

"And I am quite sure the sister will be pleased with her brother's selection. I hope he will insist upon it," fixing her eyes in calm penetration on Mr. Pettibone's blushing face.

"I will, so," said Stephen, gathering voice. "Give me the other, three yards of it, and be just as quick as you can, for I'm in a hurry."

Then he wondered if the young woman ought to be thanked for her help, and earnestly hoped she ought not, for certainly he could never do it. Meantime he gave outward attention to the clerk.

"You told me this was fifteen cents a yard," he said, picking up the discarded braid, "and that it was better than the other. How much cheaper is that?"

There was the faintest gleam of satisfaction in the eyes of the young woman as she paid for her pins and moved from the store. It amused her to discover that the awkward country boy, whom she had saved from making a grievous mistake, had been quick-witted enough to take advantage of the clerk's glib statements, and demand a lower price for the braid which had been pronounced of poorer quality. However, this was not quick-wittedness on Stephen Mitchell's part; it was simple honesty. He knew nothing about the quality of braids; he took the clerk's statement in good faith, and was astonished to find himself obliged to pay fifteen cents a yard for that which had been declared inferior. Neither did he know why Mr. Pettibone should have grown gruff very suddenly.

"He is sulking," he said to himself, as he pocketed the braid and went to his waiting horses, "because I didn't take the kind he picked out. Just as if I didn't know green when I saw it, and laid it beside another piece of green. I ain't worked alongside of rows of grass, and bushes, and all sorts of shades of trees all my life for nothing. I know green, I guess; anybody can see that it was a better match than the other. The thing I don't understand is, why I need have been so dumb foolish as to almost take the other green, when I knew better all the time. But then folks never know what a girl is going to call a match. Sarah Jane said the clerk would know; she depended on the clerk. A nice match it would have been, according to the other girl, if I had depended on him. I don't think he need to sulk over it, though."

If Stephen had known that Mr. Pettibone had been obliged to sell three yards of braid for fifteen cents a yard, which was distinctly marked twenty, and make up the difference out of his own pocket, he would have understood the sulks better.

One more errand, and one that he hated worse, if possible, than that at the corner store. Stephen could only earnestly hope that Fanny and Celia

Bascome were not at home; or at least that they would not be anywhere within speaking distance while he was waiting for the pattern.

"I don't see," he muttered, "what Sarah Jane finds in them Bascome girls. If she had seen some of the girls I have to-day, she would know better than that. They don't look no more like the Bascome girls than poppies and sunflowers look like roses and little white lilies; and they don't look no more like her than nothing in the world, or out of it."

Comparisons were exhausted when he remembered those grave, kind eyes, and the "pale, still stuff" in which their owner was dressed.

He was destined to be unfortunate. Fanny Bascome was at home — the one whom he disliked more, if possible, than he did Celia. She was not only at home, but it was her voice which greeted him from the piazza.

"Why, if here isn't Steve Mitchell! For pity's sake, Steve, where did you come from? I didn't know as you ever got so far from home nowadays. How's Sarah Jane? You want to see ma? Come in. Ma, here's Steve Mitchell; wants to see you for something."

"A pattern?" said Mrs. Bascome, waddling in from the great farm kitchen, looking heated and tired. "Land alive! there is no need to ask me for a pattern; it is some of Fanny's folderols that she wants. Why don't you tend to it yourself,

Fanny? What pattern is it that you promised Mis' Mitchell?"

"I didn't promise any pattern. O, my! yes, I remember; she asked me, coming out of church one day, if I couldn't lend Sarah Jane my skirt pattern. I forgot all about it; I was going to send it to her. But I never have a chance to send away out there. Dear me! I don't know where that pattern is. If you are in a hurry, Steve, you had better go on, and I will hunt it up and send it. Let me see, when can I send it? Won't your folks be out Sunday, some of them?"

"I ain't in any desperate hurry," said Stephen, with a dogged determination to have Sarah Jane pleased, and a dim idea that the skirt pattern was to go with the green braid, somehow. "I ain't in any desperate hurry; if you could look it up now I could wait. I've got a pretty good start toward home."

It was a long speech for Stephen Mitchell to make. It involved not a little self-sacrifice on his part, for he was most anxious to be on his way home, and out of sight of the Bascomes.

"Well," said Fanny, with a reluctant sigh, "I suppose I may as well go and hunt it now as any time. Only I am all dressed. I do hate to rummage through boxes and things after I get dressed. Don't you remember seeing it, ma?"

"No, I don't," said Mrs. Bascome shortly; "and I ain't going to leave the supper I am cooking to go upstairs and hunt it, either. When you promise to lend things to folks you ought to tend to it. I suppose they have been waiting for it for weeks. It must be four or five weeks, at least, since Mis' Mitchell spoke about it coming out of church. I never did see such a careless girl as you are in my life, Fanny Bascome. I would be ashamed not to be ready to do a little favor of that kind for a neighbor."

They were out in the wide hall now, and though their voices could be distinctly heard they did not seem to be aware of it, or else they cared nothing for Stephen Mitchell's ears. Fanny answered irritably:

"Neighbor! Ma, what a ridiculous idea! They live most five miles away. I don't care about lending my patterns, anyhow. Who wants the skirts of every country girl for ten miles around made exactly like yours? I have a great mind to tell him I can't find it."

"You will have to hunt a good while first," muttered Stephen, whose energies were now roused in the direction of the skirt pattern, and who resolved to doggedly stand his ground, and insist upon his ability to wait hours, if necessary, while it was being hunted. He was conscious of disliking Fanny Bascome more than ever before, but for some reason he was not so much afraid of her as usual.

CHAPTER V.

MAKING HIS REPORT.

"IT'S an awful nice match," said Sarah Jane, examining the green braid with interest some hours afterward; "just exactly the shade I wanted. I don't see how clerks learn how to match women's dresses as well as they do."

"The clerk didn't match it," said Stephen, with unusual energy; "I matched it myself. I didn't take the one he wanted me to, by a long sight! He picked out the meanest kind of a match."

"Land!" said Sarah Jane, surveying him with wonder, "how did you know what it ought to be?"

"I guess I've got eyes. If I don't know green, why, then I don't know nothing. Don't I work amongst green things all my days? That stuff of your dress is just the color of the grass that grows on the south meadow — a kind of sunshine green; it makes you think of daisies, and dandelions, and such things. Yet there ain't no yellow in it. I don't understand it exactly, but that's the kind of green it is, and the braid he was going to give me was that miserable pusley green that never looks nice by the side of the others. I knew better the minute I saw it."

Sarah Jane regarded her brother with a look of wonder, and finally burst into a laugh.

"If I ever heard the like!" she said. "Who s'posed you noticed what color the grass was, or anything else? But I know just what you mean; that blue green would look nice on some things, but it would look horrid on my dress. I declare for it, Steve, I believe you would make a good storekeeper yourself."

"I'll never be one," said Stephen, half-ashamed and half-angry.

Then he shuffled out to attend to Doll and Dobbin for the night.

Sarah Jane, as she reveled in the mysterious pattern, and fingered the green braid lovingly, trying to determine which of various ways of placing it would look the best, gave also puzzled thought to Stephen. There was a look in his face which she did not understand. A feeling had come to her that he was in some way a different person from the "Steve" who went to town that morning. She chuckled over his encounter with Mr. Pettibone.

"I don't see," she said to herself, "how he ever screwed up his courage to quarrel with that fellow about which color to take. It is too funny for anything."

Sarah Jane, it should be understood, was not herself an admirer of Mr. Pettibone. There was a sort of rugged good sense about her which recoiled from his affectation of superiority, and his patronizing way of nodding to her, together with the disagreeable tone in which he said "How d' do?" when she met him on the street, or when, on rare occasions, she entered the store. His manner always vexed her, she could not have told you why. She did not use the word "superiority" or "patronizing;" she did not understand such words. There was simply within her a shrinking from the man and his ways, and a feeling in connection with him which made her laugh at the idea of his being, as she expressed it, "come up with." She reverted to the subject again and again, and cross-questioned Stephen that evening while he was eating the supper which had been kept warm for him, and laughed so appreciatively over his description of the scene that he was more communicative than usual. Up to a certain point he said nothing about the strange young woman who had sustained his decision. At last he brought her forward.

"I see a girl, Sarah Jane, that had on a dress that to my mind went away ahead of anything Fanny Bascome ever wore in her life. I don't see why you want to shape your clothes after that girl's. I'd rather take a peacock strutting around the barnyard for a pattern than her."

Sarah Jane giggled.

"So would I, but the peacock is too fine for me; I can't ever find anything that will match his feathers. I take Fanny Bascome's patterns because I can get them, and I can't get no others. But she dresses nicer than any girl in the village, they say. Who was it you saw, Steve?"

"I don't know who it was; I saw her in the store. She ain't the Fanny Bascome kind, nor any others like her. She don't look like 'em, nor act like 'em, nor anything."

"How was she dressed? What did she have on?"

"How do I know? It was some pale, still stuff that slipped all around her; it didn't make no noise, and didn't look as though she had thought about it much, or remembered what she had on herself. But it was away ahead of anything I ever see on Fanny Bascome, or any of her kind."

Sarah Jane regarded him with superiority, and slight disdain.

"That is just like you, Steve. How am I going to tell anything about a dress that is made of some 'pale, still' stuff, and 'slips around' on anybody? If I could have seen the girl, or if ever I could see anybody that is worth seeing, I could make my clothes look something like; but I can't tell anything about it by any such account as that."

"No," said Stephen slowly; "I don't suppose you can."

There was no sarcasm in his voice; there was even an undertone of sadness. He watched Sarah Jane with the greatest interest while she moved about the kitchen putting away the remains of his evening meal, and reducing everything to neatness and order. He was coming to a realization of certain interesting facts. He was discovering that his sister did not look in the least like Fanny Bascome; neither did she look in the least like the young woman in the store; and two persons more unlike each other than Fanny Bascome and that young woman he could not imagine. Where, then, did Sarah Jane belong, if she had to do with neither of them?

Sarah Jane was short — some people would have called her dumpy, though Stephen did not use that word. She had reddish hair, and freckles, but her hair was soft and wavy, and reminded Stephen of sunshine, though he had never told her, nor anybody else, that such was the fact. Sarah Jane had a pleasant mouth, though Stephen did not phrase it in that way; he only knew that he liked the looks of it. As he studied her face he reflected that he had seen a great many girls that day, and all of them, without exception, were unlike Fanny Bascome. Yes; and they were unlike Sarah Jane; and certainly they were unlike the girl in the store. He felt puzzled and troubled. It was a very bewildering world.

Then he thought of his list of words. He had

thought of them more or less all the way home, and studied ways and means of beginning his discoveries concerning them. The very first word in the list had exhausted his energies, and he had as yet made nothing of it. He said it over to himself, looking dreamily at Sarah Jane the while. "Barbarian," that was the word. He had a vague impression that he had heard it used somewhere, somehow, before to-day; but how, or where, or what meaning it was intended to convey, he could not determine. What if Sarah Jane should happen to know something about it? She knew about dresses and braids, and a hundred things that were out of his line. And cramped and isolated as her life was, she saw more people than he did. She went oftener to church, and knew girls — by name, at least — that he did not. Might she not possibly have heard the word "barbarian?" What harm would it do to try her? He need not explain why he wanted to know; for that matter he couldn't explain. He had not yet settled that matter in his own mind.

"Sarah Jane," he said suddenly, speaking with such energy that she almost dropped the pan of potatoes she was carrying to the sink. She had forgotten he was present, and was once more absorbed in the green dress, trying to determine whether she would have three rows of braid on the sleeves, or be content with two, and let the pretty stuff go round the neck as well. "Sarah

Jane, do you happen to know what 'barbarian' means?"

"My patience!" said Sarah, "how you made me jump. I had forgotten you was here. 'Barbarian?' why, it means — barbarian, of course."

"Exactly so," said Stephen; "that is what I supposed myself."

Sarah Jane laughed.

"Well, I don't know as I can tell what it means; I can kind of think it, though; it appears as if I knew. Ain't it some kind of animal, Stephen?" She spoke timidly; she was on untried ground, and Stephen had been away all day; there was no telling just what he had learned.

"I shouldn't wonder," said Stephen, in a non-committal tone. "The question is, what kind of animal? That is what I want to know."

"What do you want to know for?"

Here came the question which he had intended to try to avoid.

"Well," he said reflectively, "I suppose the reason I want to know is — because I want to know." And he joined somewhat shamefacedly in Sarah Jane's laugh. After a moment's silence he added, "I heard a man use the word to-day."

"How did he use it?" asked Sarah Jane quickly. "If I had heard him, I could tell pretty near what it means. I have often noticed, if you pay attention to what goes before and comes after a thing, you can pretty nearly always find out what it means. The last time I was in the store at the village there was a parcel of girls in there talking about a new kind of trimming — 'chiffon,' they called it. They said the word over and over again, and I couldn't make head nor tail of it. 'Chiffon,' I said to myself; 'what in the world can it be? It is something to wear, that is plain to be seen.' One of them said, ' She had on the prettiest rig, all made of lace and chiffon.' Then the other one told about a hat that was made of 'chiffon,' and they kept having that word over, and putting it in different places, and describing its color, and one thing and another, till I made out pretty near what it was, or at least that it was something you bought by the yard; so when they had gone out I walked up to Mr. Pettibone and asked him to let me look at chiffon; and he went off and got the stuff right away. I didn't want any, you know, or that is, I didn't mean to buy any. It was real pretty stuff, and I would have liked some first-rate; but what I wanted was to find out just what it looked like, so that I would know it the next time I heard about it. Wasn't that cute?"

"Yes," said Stephen, again giving his sister a most thoughtful survey. This time there was a shade of respect in his thoughts for her, coupled with a dim realization of the fact that had she had his opportunity that day, she would have made more of it than he had done. However, he could not have imagined himself going up to the platform and telling the speaker that he wanted to look at some barbarians. How was he to find out the meaning of the word?

"So," said Sarah Jane, going back to the point of her illustration, "if I could have heard the word used, you know, I might have made something out of it. What was he saying about them, anyhow?"

"That is more than I know," said Stephen, humbly; "he was saying a lot of things that I did not understand, and that was one of them."

Sarah Jane washed her potatoes vigorously for a few moments, and spoke no words. Then she said, and the sentence was preceded by a little sigh, which in itself was startling, for Sarah Jane was not given to sighing:

"I suppose you saw and heard a lot of things to-day, Stephen, that you didn't understand. I wish we knew about things. I am dreadful sick of sticking here on this stony old farm and not knowing what is going on. I wish I could go to the circus; there is going to be one next week, and I would give most anything to go to it; but there! I don't suppose it is of any use."

"I should think not," said Stephen; "I guess you forget the interest on the mortgage."

"No, I don't; and ain't likely to. Father has groaned over it more than usual to-day; and I have wished as much as twenty times that I hadn't sent for no green braid. Though mother was kind of bent on my having it; she said it would cover up the spots, and it will, too; but I could have got along without it."

"I guess forty-five cents won't make no great difference one way or the other," said Stephen, in a voice which was meant to be encouraging. Then he arose with a weary yawn, and lumbered out of the room, no nearer to discovering the meaning of "barbarian" than he was when he heard it spoken from the platform.

No form of prayer closed the day in the Mitchell household. The mother was the only one of the family who prayed at all, and she was so shy and quiet about it that no one beside herself was sure of it. As for Stephen, he had discarded the habit of childhood when he grew too old in his estimation to say "Now I lay me down to sleep," though why one should ever be too old to repeat that simple statement of fact, and ask God's keeping power at the time when he voluntarily relinquishes all attempts at keeping himself, it might be difficult to explain.

Sarah Jane could not have told when she outgrew the habit; but to all practical purposes the Mitchell family, the mother excepted, were "barbarians," so far as religious life was concerned. Yet I like to think and believe that the watching Shepherd was looking down that night upon the poor foolish sheep — who had wandered out of the pasture even while he was a lamb, voluntarily giving up the Sabbath-school and the church service, and any attempt at being led and fed — and was calling after him, though the sheep had wandered so far away that he did not know the Shepherd's voice. There are depths of love in the great Shepherd's heart that we cannot comprehend. And there are ways of reaching wandering ones that are in themselves so simple, that because of their very simplicity we cannot comprehend them. The very reaching out of this blind heart after a something which he did not understand, and knew not where to look to find, may have been translated in Heaven as a cry for help.

But Stephen Mitchell did not know enough to connect the next morning's experiences with his own heart-cry. He was out in the field, steadily following the plough, trying to move along in exactly the same paths that he had moved two days before, and finding himself unable to do so. He would have been astonished, probably dismayed, had some seer told him that he could never again find that old well-trodden path, and plod on in it. As a matter of fact it was lost to him — the footprints covered over; but this he did not realize.

CHAPTER VI.

ANOTHER PASSENGER.

HIS father was engaged that morning with a visitor from a town about twenty miles away, who was in search of a certain breed of cattle, and Mr. Mitchell was the owner of two good cows, which he was very anxious to sell. As Doll and Dobbin moved with dignified steps down the long field, they came upon their master and his visitor. At sight of Stephen the stranger wished him a genial "good-morning," and the father called out some question with regard to the cattle, on a point where he expected Stephen to be better posted than himself.

"Is this your son?" asked the gentleman, as he drew nearer.

"Yes," said Mr. Mitchell, in a half-surprised tone. He had forgotten that there could be anybody who did not know that Stephen was his son. "This is Mr. Meadows, Steve."

"I am glad to meet you, sir," said Mr. Meadows; and he held out his hand and gave Stephen's red one a cordial grasp.

"You are rather isolated here, are you not, Mr. Mitchell? How many miles is it to the village?"

"Oh! it's eight good miles," said Mr. Mitchell, with a sigh. "Sometimes we think, when we drag up the hills, that it is ten or twelve. Yes; we're away back from everywhere, and have got a miserable piece of land. It's mortgaged for all it is worth. We are seeing hard times, Mr. Meadows."

"Eight miles from any market," Mr. Meadows said reflectively; "that must make your work pretty heavy. But you have neighbors, of course; some quite near you. That little shanty, shall I call it, within a mile of you is inhabited, I noticed — very much so."

"Neighbors!" echoed Mr. Mitchell, in a tone of intense scorn; "they are nobodies. The man is a miserable drunken scamp, and his sons are like him; they are as hard a lot as you can find out of State's prison, I guess. As for the women folks, I don't know much about them, except that they are a rough-looking lot. They can't be anything, living as they do."

"They are perfect barbarians, I am afraid," said Mr. Meadows; "I stopped at their gate to make some inquiries. I thought perhaps I had lost my way; your farm lies a little out of the main road, you know, and I interviewed three or four children there — I don't know but more. After I had settled as to my way, I asked a few questions about theirs; and I don't know that I ever before, in a civilized land, struck such dense ignorance. It seems a pity " —

But just at this point Mr. Meadows chanced to glance at Stephen Mitchell, and paused in bewilderment, to note the changed expression of his face. What did that sudden flash of his eyes mean? Could he be a friend of any member of that wild family back in the woods? Did he resent the very plain language in which they had been characterized? Yet the look was not one of indignation. Mr. Meadows was fairly puzzled. The father, meantime, had turned, and was looking toward the house.

"There is my neighbor Harding, from the corners," he said; "he has stopped at our gate. If you will excuse me a few minutes I will go and see what is wanted."

Now was Stephen's opportunity. The Lucas family, who lived in the cabin just a mile away from their house, whose children had been alternately the nuisance and the terror of his mother for the year and a half that they had occupied the cabin, were barbarians, it seemed. Why? That was the question. Because of their descent from some race of that name? Because of their poverty, or ignorance, or for what reason did they bear that name? Stephen did not put his thoughts into such language, but such is their translation. His question came upon Mr. Meadows almost as abruptly as it had upon Sarah Jane the night before.

"What does 'barbarian' mean, sir?"

"Oh!" began Mr. Meadows, in a somewhat embarrassed tone, his mind full of the thought that perhaps he had given offense by his reference to the family in the cabin. "I didn't mean exactly what I said, of course; the children struck me as uncouth, and singularly ignorant of some of the commonest proprieties of daily life. I suppose they have had no opportunity, poor things! I fear I spoke rather rudely, in your opinion. One cannot judge of all the members of a family by the children, you know."

Stephen was not making headway; he did not understand what Mr. Meadows was trying to accomplish.

"You said they were barbarians," he added, "and I was wondering why."

"Well," said Mr. Meadows, smiling, "I confess the children suggested a barbaric state."

"What do you mean by that?"

There was no indignation in the tone; the young man did not act as though he had taken offense, yet he acted as though he were intensely in earnest. Mr. Meadows was puzzled.

"I don't think I get your meaning," he said hesitatingly.

"Why, all I mean is that I want to get at the meaning of 'barbarian.'" There was a half-smile on Stephen's face; he could not help wondering whether all gentlemen who used large words found it so hard to explain them.

"You mean the derivation of the word."

And then Stephen stared; this was growing worse and worse.

"I do not know that I could go into the root-meaning to your satisfaction," continued Mr. Meadows, after waiting in vain for further suggestions; "I am not very well up on philology. Of course all I mean was a lack of civilization. The loose way we have of using our language, you know. It is true that even the most uncultured people we find in this country are very far from absolute barbarism; that all have more or less civilization. Schoolhouses and churches, and society in general, have done very much for them; how much we will probably never realize, unless we are isolated for a while from all such surroundings, and set down in absolutely barbarous regions."

Light was beginning to dawn upon Stephen's mind. It was true, as Sarah Jane had said, that you could give a shrewd surmise as to the meaning of a word if you watched carefully its immediate associates. Notwithstanding the fact that Mr. Meadows had used, in those short sentences, literally more than a dozen words the meaning of which Stephen did not understand, he yet, nevertheless, was beginning to have a fairly correct idea of the original meaning and present use of the word "barbarian," but he could not help letting a smile illumine his face over the thought that in struggling after the meaning of this first word in his list, he was getting deeper and deeper into mystery.

"I'd have as many as twenty to take hold of," he said to himself, "if I had pencil and paper, and time to catch these. I declare for it, if words were dollars, then everybody would get rich, at this rate, in a little while."

"Much obliged," he said aloud; and then, made aware by Mr. Meadows's peculiar look that he had been caught apparently laughing at him, his face crimsoned, and he looked about him hastily for some subject to arrest attention, and turn the gentleman's thoughts into another channel.

"I reckon this ragweed is a barbarian," he said, touching a lusty specimen of it with his foot, "and it doesn't get civilized, neither; and it is as hard to get rid of as the Lucas family. Father has been trying some way to have them get out of this neighborhood ever since they came into it, but that isn't near as long as he has been trying to get rid of ragweed; and here it is every season as regular as if it had been planted and hoed and cultivated according to order."

"But your analogy will not hold good," said Mr. Meadows, smiling in his turn. "Earnest work on the part of good men and women will make a great difference with the Lucas family in the course of a few seasons. Has it ever been tried?"

"Sir?" said Stephen, bewildered in his effort to follow this line of thought.

"Have you ever tried to get hold of any of the Lucas family, my friend? I judge from what your father said, that there are young men in the family. Have you given as much thought toward getting rid of the barbarism about them, as you have to get rid of the ragweed?"

Stephen shrugged his broad shoulders.

"Tough job!" he said briefly. "The ragweed is tough enough, but we can get it out of the way for a spell, at least. But the Lucases are on hand summer and winter, and you can't take a knife, nor a hoe, nor a plough to them."

"No; 'the weapons of our warfare are not carnal, but mighty through God,' nevertheless, you know. I wonder how tools named patience and kindness would work? Perhaps you have a barbarous nation all your own to get hold of, young man; to civilize and cultivate, until you make of them a people worthy to become citizens in the Royal City itself. Did you ever think of that?"

But Stephen could only stare, and wonder what extraordinary language the man was talking now.

"We talk a great deal about barbarism and civilization," began Mr. Meadows again, after the silence had lasted for several minutes; "but I sometimes think the only civilization worth caring for is that which fits us for companionship with the Lord Jesus Christ himself. We are all barbarians when it comes to that, unless we have the change which only he can give. I trust you are a servant of his, my friend?"

Stephen had taken up his hoe, and was working furiously; something about these last sentences bewildered, indeed, almost terrified him. What a strange man this was! He had never met his like before.

It will be remembered that he had heard very little talk from gentlemen; the minister, whom he would not go to hear preach, being almost the only educated gentleman he knew. This must be "religion," he reflected. At least, it was very different from anything which had ever been said to him before. Truth compels me to admit that this was the first time in his life that he had been asked whether he was a Christian. He was not even sure that this was what Mr. Meadows meant, though he had heard sermons enough to surmise that it was. He did not know how to answer the question, and was relieved from doing so by the return of his father. With a nod of his head, in response to Mr. Meadows's bow, he strode swiftly back to his work at the farther end of the lot. He had certainly received a good deal of information that morning, and gotten his brain into a whirl thereby.

"Sarah Jane," he said, pausing before that young woman, as she was washing the tea dishes, "I've found out what a 'barbarian' is."

"Have you, though?" said Sarah Jane, holding a dripping cup in her hand while she stopped to give him undivided attention. Anything new found out had its own charm for Sarah Jane. "What does it mean?"

"It means us," Stephen said, with a half-laugh. "I have made up my mind that I am a barbarian. I live in a country where a great many folks know lots of things, and I haven't learned any of them to speak of. Haven't got what they call 'civilized,' though there's schoolhouses and churches and them things round us. You ought to have heard Mr. Meadows go on."

"I'd like to have heard him," said Sarah Jane, emphatically. "He's the man who bought the cows, and paid money down for them—the nicest man I have heard of this long time. So he put all such ideas into your head, did he? Well, I' tell you what it is, I wish we could get civilized. I have thought this long time that it was too mean for you and me to be so different, somehow, from other folks. We don't go nowheres to learn things, nor have any company; we just have to blunder along. Can't we make things different, somehow?"

"Mr. Meadows thinks we ought to make things different for the Lucas family."

"The Lucas family!" Sarah Jane repeated, in amazement. "What in the world has the Lucas family got to do with us, or we with them?"

"He says we've got to civilize them; says we have been spending all our time on ragweed, that won't take on a decent character in spite of anything you can do with it; it stays ragweed to the end of the chapter. But he says the Lucases could be civilized, and he thinks the neighbors have something to do with it."

"Much he knows about it," said Sarah Jane. "What could we do for them, I should like to know? They will drink and swear, and be disgusting in every way they can think of, and who's going to help it? I can't, I know."

"I don't know as we ever tried," said Stephen, leaning against the window-seat, and watching the swift fingers, which were again manipulating the dishes. "I don't know as we know how to try. It is one of the things that we haven't learned, Sarah Jane."

"What started you?" said Sarah Jane, looking at him curiously. "It wasn't this Mr. Meadows, because you began at 'barbarian' before he came. Where did you get the word, anyhow? You told me you heard it yesterday; what else did you hear, Steve?"

"I heard a hundred and three words," said Stephen slowly, "and I wrote them down on a sheet of paper; and I don't know the meaning of one of them, except the first, which was 'barbarian;' I begin to understand a little about that."

"A hundred and three words," repeated Sarah Jane, in open-eyed wonder; "and you wrote them down — all of them? To think of your taking the trouble to write down a lot of words! What's some more of them?"

"The next one is 'emancipator,'" said Stephen, very gravely, "and the next one is 'champion;' and I don't know how to set to work to know what either of them mean. But I'm going to do it. I have made up my mind, Sarah Jane, to know the meaning of every word on that page before this winter is over."

"Good for you," said Sarah Jane, with emphasis. "Steve, wouldn't it be just splendid if you should turn out a scholar? I always thought I should like it so much. Fanny Bascome is always talking about her brother Ned being crazy over books; and I have wished a hundred times that you loved books more than Ned Bascome did, and knew more about them, too. He is awful silly. I don't believe he will ever be smart, if he is crazy over books; but I just believe, Steve Mitchell, that you could be smart."

"Of course," said Stephen, in slow sarcasm, "there is nothing in life to hinder. And I could go to school just as well as not. Suppose I start to-morrow morning, and leave the old farm, and the cows, and Doll and Dobbin, and all the rest, for father to look after? How would you like it?"

"O, my patience!" said Sarah Jane. "Of course

you couldn't, Steve; poor fellow! you are tied to this old farm and the mortgage. We all are. I just wish we could go and live in the village. I believe I could sew at the dressmaker's, and earn more money in one season than father does on the farm. Well, never mind; we will do something, you and I. Don't let us go on the same old way another day; let's be different. You have begun, haven't you? There is that list of a hundred and three words — that was awful cute in you, Steve — you know the meaning of one of them already; like as not you will get hold of another before long.

"Steve, suppose I try, too? I can keep my ears open, and get some of them. If you will make me a list of your words, I'll do it. Nobody likes to know things better than I do."

CHAPTER VII.

THE DOWN-HILL ROAD DESCRIBED.

WHILE the dishes were being put away, and the house set in order, Sarah Jane laid aside all thoughts of how she should fix the ruffles on her skirt, and said over, with a puzzled air: "'Emancipator,' 'champion'— seems as though I had heard that word before; 'champion' — I wonder if it has anything to do with horses? They champ. Maybe it is a horse's name; but it doesn't sound like that. I wish we had a dictionary. I wonder how much they be? Perhaps if"—

She did not finish her sentence, but the thought in her heart was, that perhaps if she had gone without the green braid and a few other trifles, such as her starved life had reached after and accomplished, she might have had enough money to buy a cheap dictionary; who could tell? And to such heights of self-abnegation did Sarah Jane reach, that she declared to herself, if she had thought about it before, she'd have gone without green braid, and also the roses her soul had craved for her summer bonnet — for the sake of accomplishing such a result as that.

Who shall say that there were not possibilities for martyrdom about Sarah Jane? It is an interesting fact, although she herself did not realize it, that from that moment things with her began to be "different." The making over of her old dresses became a secondary consideration. "Steve's" list of words took precedence of every other interest in life. Stephen's determination to know their meaning, and her determination to assist him in this effort, became the all-important work.

As the twilight deepened, Stephen came in from doing the "chores." Doll and Dobbin were settled for the night, and everything was done. On the side piazza, or "stoop," as the family called it, sat the father, much worn with his day's work, but in a more cheerful frame of mind than usual. The visit from Mr. Meadows, and, above all, the substantial reminder of that visit, in the shape of several crisp bills which Mr. Mitchell had in his pocket, was an event in his life. It cheered and encouraged him. Moreover, Stephen had done very well indeed with the load he had carried to the encampment ground the day before. A few weeks more of such "luck" as this, and he would be able to be prompt with the interest on the mortgage, which was the object for which Mr. Mitchell lived — to contrive to be ready for these semi-annual payments, and so keep in abeyance, at least, that terrible fear of being sold out of house and home.

Stephen took a seat on the step below him, and looked thoughtfully up at the worn and wrinkled face of his father. How little he knew concerning his father's early life. It had never surprised him before, but to-night, when he came to think of it, he wondered why he had not been told about it. Perhaps it was because he had asked no questions. Did his father work on a farm, he wondered, and did he hate it? Were there other things he thought he could have done if he had had a chance? Did he go to school when he was a boy? How much did he know, any way?

Stephen had never thought about it before, but he was suddenly struck with the fact that his father talked very well, and was apparently at ease with men like Mr. Meadows; yes, and with the minister himself. Perhaps he knew the meaning of a great many words; he might have learned them when he was a boy. It was barely possible that he might know the meaning of some of those on his list. What if he should try him? No sooner thought than he put the idea into language.

"Father, what is the meaning of 'emancipator?'"

"Emancipator?" repeated Mr. Mitchell, turning his eyes slowly away from the western sky and fixing them upon his son. "Why, one who emancipates. I don't know but what I call Mr.

Meadows an emancipator," he added, with a half-laugh. "Anyhow, he has emancipated me from the fear that I would fail altogether, this time, with the interest, and I feel about as pleased as a slave could with his freedom papers, I reckon. What did you want to know the word for, Steve?"

"I was thinking about it," said Stephen, an undertone of satisfaction in his voice. This was his first day's effort, and behold! two of the words which had looked so utterly bewildering to him yesterday, had suddenly been made plain; had been illustrated, indeed, one by the Lucas family, and the other by his father's own experience; both illustrations making the meaning stand out plainly. Might it not be possible that his father knew a great many things that he did not? Had Stephen Mitchell been asked at any time during the past years if he loved his father, he would have stared in astonishment on the questioner, and answered, "Of course!" But as he looked up at him this evening, he had, perhaps, the first dawning of a sense of respect for the old man who possibly knew a great deal, and yet plodded on, content to live, day by day, with those who knew little or nothing.

How astonished would Stephen Mitchell have been had he known his father's thoughts just then. A very strange remark had been made to the father that day — a remark which had staid with him; its only rival in interest being the fact that he had almost enough money in his pocket to meet the next payment due on the mortgage. The words were Mr. Meadows's — spoken as Stephen and his hoe had tramped hurriedly toward the far end of the lot.

"You have an interesting son, Mr. Mitchell, a thoughtful one for his years; he is studying philology, I take it; a valuable study for a young man, but somewhat unusual. Are you going to give him an education, sir?"

Strange words these to Mr. Mitchell, and about Stephen, of all persons. He a thoughtful young man — interested in the study of anything. The word 'philology' was quite beyond the father; he had wondered over it several times during the day.

He looked down at Stephen, as he sat on the piazza, with respectful curiosity; the boy impressed other people differently, then, from what he did him. A "good boy," he always called him; one to be proud of, every time the Lucas boys were thought of; but a student, or one who would have cared to be a student, had the opportunity been his — of such an idea the father had not dreamed. In his earlier days he had had dreams of having a son who would be "smart," and make amends for his own disastrous failure in life; but when Stephen made that miserable record in school, during his one winter, all such thoughts had been given up, and the bare struggle for existence had ground so heavily on both father and son as to give them little time or wish to think about such things. What if he had been unjust to his boy? What if Stephen had failed to be a student simply for lack of the right kind of help?

"What are you trying to do, Steve?" he asked, looking down at him with a touch of respect in his voice. "Mr. Meadows said he reckoned you was studying 'philology.' What's that?"

"More than I know," said Stephen, with a short laugh. "He used the same word to me, and I don't know what it means; and I don't know what I am doing; I am just trying to find out the meaning of a few words, that's all."

"Oh! that's a good thing to do; I wish you had a better chance to find them out; folks who know the meaning of words have got a pretty good education, as far as it goes. One of my troubles has been, Steve, that I couldn't give you and Sarah Jane any chances. I didn't think you cared, but Sarah Jane would have been a scholar, I guess, if she had had a chance; and I always kind of wanted one of you to turn out that way. There used to be scholars in my family; my great-grandfather was a real, thoroughgoing scholar — understood the Latin, and all that, and you are named for him; I used to have my notions when I was a young man and you was a little chap, but life went hard with me; things got wrong."

"How did they get wrong, father? I was thinking to-night how strange it was I had never heard anything much about you when you was a boy; what you did, and all that, and how you begun living, any way."

The shadows were growing deeper about the faded house; Stephen could not see the look of pain on his father's face, nor did he understand the long silence which ensued, nor the quiver in his father's voice when he spoke again.

"There isn't much to tell, Steve. A good deal of it had better be forgotten, instead of told. I went wrong in more ways than one; I threw away my chances, a good many of them; I had a great deal better than you ever had, when I was a boy, and threw them away. Then I married, and after that I went wrong again; I was a slave for a good while myself, Steve; I ought to understand what an 'emancipator' is, if anybody does. A man got hold of me, and set me free from the worst slavery any one can have. I used to get drunk, Steve; come reeling home to your mother, and pretty near break her heart. I have always been afraid you would inherit a taste for the stuff; I've kept you away from that the best I knew how. That's the reason I've kept you closer sometimes than you liked."

Stephen listened as one in a dream. His father a drunkard! This was the explanation, perhaps, of their poverty; and of the heavily mortgaged farm — the last explanation that had ever entered his mind. However vague and uncertain had been his teachings in other directions, they had been very pronounced on the question of rum. Both Stephen and Sarah Jane believed drunkenness to be the sin of sins. They looked down on the Lucas family with disgust and horror; and had never so much as dreamed that the curse of drunkenness had touched them. Poor, but respectable, they had prided themselves upon being.

Now, perhaps, but for some one of whom his father spoke as an emancipator, they would have been just another edition of the Lucas family themselves. So his father had been a "barbarian," and had been "emancipated." It was possible, then, to accomplish this. Ought not some one to accomplish it for the Lucas family? Stephen Mitchell's education was progressing; in point of fact, he was taking rapid strides along the journey which he had marked out for himself, though he did not know it. While hurried thoughts of this character crowded his brain, the father presently broke the silence again.

"I don't know as I ought to have told you about it so abrupt like, Steve; it is a hard thing for a father to have to say to his boy. Your mother, she couldn't bear to have you told, nohow; but when you talked about emancipation, it reminded me that there was more than one kind. And there's more than one kind of slavery. Yes; we have rum to thank for most of our troubles. I guess you could have had your chance like other boys if it hadn't been for that. I got free from it, but I had to twist and turn in every kind of a way to keep the old farm; heavily mortgaged at that. I had to begin life over again, you may say, and things have gone pretty hard with me ever since. I lost my health in the same way I did my money, and I have never got either of them back.

"No; the worst of my troubles was lived away from here. I deserted the old farm when I was young, and came back to it when I found I couldn't do anything else. Folks around here don't know that I ever drank. They think I'm shiftless, and all that, but they seem to have a notion that I have always kept kind of respectable. And your mother, she took care there shouldn't anybody hear about it. You see, the way it was, your mother, she came home to my father and mother, and lived here a whole year without me; she and you. That's the year you were born. Then my old mother died, and things were broken up here, and your mother came back to me, and I led her a life of it for a while, and then I got free from my curse — haven't tasted a drop of the stuff since — and we came back here and began life again; mother and father gone, and the farm mortgaged for all it was worth, to save me. That's about the story of it, Steve. Your mother didn't ever want me to tell you; she always talks as though she had forgotten it herself, but I know she hasn't. Sarah Jane doesn't know anything about it, of course, and I guess you had better keep still for your mother's sake; maybe you will make up, somehow, what has been lost to you. I don't know, I thought you didn't care about such things — about study and all that, but maybe I have been mistaken in you. I have been mistaken in most things in my life."

"Never mind about all that," said Stephen hoarsely; "it don't matter what I have lost. I haven't known enough to know that it was lost, anyhow, not till just now, at least; and I will make it up, as you say, maybe. I believe I have been a slave to something, I don't know what; I have been dumb-headed, anyhow. I will look around and see if I can find an 'emancipator';" and he laughed in an embarrassed way to cover feelings which he did not wish to show.

A small shadow came swiftly up the star-lighted path leading from the gate, and stood before them.

"Bless me!" said the father, startled; "who are you?"

"If you please, I'm Timmy Lucas, and I come to see if Mis' Mitchell wouldn't come over to our house? Ma is took very bad, and Melinda and Flora Ann don't know what to do; and Melinda said run and see if Mis' Mitchell wouldn't come, or something."

These sentences were jerked out in an eager, frightened voice, with gasps between.

"Dear me!" said Mr. Mitchell, rising and then

sitting down again in a helpless way; "I don't see as there is anything we can do. I guess you will have to run on somewhere else; Mis' Mitchell isn't very well herself, and couldn't walk that far, nohow, and she has gone to bed, I guess, anyhow."

"No; I haven't, Josiah."

Mrs. Mitchell's head was put out of an upper window, and her voice sounded down through the night.

"I haven't gone to bed yet; I was sitting here thinking. I wish I could do something for them, Josiah; people ought to be neighborly in sickness, anyhow. But I don't know as I could walk that far; my knee has been bad to-day."

"Of course you could not," began Josiah promptly; then up rose Stephen.

"Doll and Dobbin could, mother; I will harness them if you want to go."

CHAPTER VIII.

TRYING A NEW ROAD.

THIS announcement made Mr. Mitchell dumb with surprise. A patient, plodding boy had Stephen been since he had reached the years of responsibility, but there were times and occasions when he showed a dogged determination to do as he pleased; and one thing which he had sturdily held out against for the last two or three years, was the taking out of Doll and Dobbin, for anything under the sun, after their day's work was completed and they were safely housed in the barn. A great trial this had been to Sarah Jane, who knew there were days in which Doll and Dobbin had not very much to do; and felt that it would have been no trial to them to have marched to town, to the village store, to the post-office — anywhere, with Stephen and herself as companions. Truth to tell, Sarah Jane was so weary of staying at home that, though she expected no letter at the post-office, and had no money to make purchases at the store, it would have been a great relief to have driven to town for no purpose whatsoever but to see the lights from the windows, and the people walking cheerily along the streets. But Stephen would have none of it. His interests and sympathies, wherever else they were, certainly did not lie in that direction; and he had taken so decided a stand, and held to it with such grim determination, that his father, after a feeble attempt to take Sarah Jane's side, had retired from the combat, vanquished. In the privacy of their own room he confessed to his wife that he thought "Steve's" resolution not a bad one.

"He has streaks of being as obstinate as any balky horse, I ever tried to break," reflected the father, as he bent his stiffened joints to pull off another boot; "and balky horses, when they get going, sometimes go like possessed; since Steve has only balked about going out evenings anywhere, my notion is we had better let him be."

This decision he presently gave to Mrs. Mitchell, adding:

"If he should get a-going, there are lots of places to go to that could bring us no end of trouble."

Whereupon Mrs. Mitchell had sighed, as one who had understood life only too well, and had murmured:

"Yes, indeed!" Her husband's words having started within her such terrible memories of shadowed days, and, above all, shadowed nights, that she could not hear a suggestion thereafter in regard to the horses being used in the evening without trembling and turning pale. And Sarah Jane, vexed at Stephen, and astonished at them all, had been obliged to put aside her ambitions in that respect, as in many others, and go on in her humdrum ways.

No wonder, then, that father and mother were amazed when Stephen made his announcement. The mother was more than amazed — she was frightened.

"O, dear!" she said, "maybe we had better not. I guess it will do to wait till morning, Stephen; then I can walk it as well as not."

"It won't hurt Doll and Dobbin," said Stephen; "they haven't been working hard to-day; I will have them ready in five minutes, mother. I think we had better go to-night; the woman may be pretty sick, there is no telling."

Not a word said the father; he watched this innovation upon the established customs of his home in silence; not, it is true, without a foreboding of what "a balky horse might do when once he got started," but it was not so strong as it would have been but for Mr. Meadows's words that morning: "You have an unusual son, sir; a very thoughtful one." Perhaps Stephen was unusual, and he had never known it. There was something about him this evening which seemed new to the father's opening eyes.

As for Sarah Jane, she bustled into her mother's

room and helped her get on the black dress without which she never went abroad, and got out the old black straw bonnet which had seen years of service, and wrapped a much-worn black shawl about her with swift, skillful fingers, as she said :

"My land! What do you suppose started Steve? I thought it would take two yoke of oxen to get him out with Doll and Dobbin at night. Most ridiculous idea that was ever heard of, too. A boy like him sitting down in the chimney corner like an old man; he is older than father, sometimes, in his actions. I am glad he has got waked up, if it is only to get to the Lucases. Now, don't you stay and sit up, mother. Why, I wonder if I couldn't go instead of you? Maybe I would do just as well."

"O, no — O, dear, no, child!" said Mrs. Mitchell hastily; she felt as though the foundations of her home were being broken up; "I don't want you to go off among them Lucases; we don't know anything about them, remember, only that they are a set. If the mother is sick, I will try and do something for her, of course. They can't hurt me if they are bad. You stay and take care of your father; he won't know how to act with me out of the house. I haven't been out of the house without him for years, I do believe."

It was a desolate home upon which they entered. The father was stumbling around the kitchen in a dazed way, only partially sober, and his second son had just staggered in, much the worse for liquor. Two other grown sons were absent, presumably at the liquor saloon at "the corners," as the miserable place was called, situated three miles from them, where the roads forked. Miranda, a girl of about Sarah Jane's age, looking slatternly beyond description, appeared in the doorway with an exclamation of relief at sight of Mrs. Mitchell.

"O, my goodness! If I ever was glad to see anybody, I am you. Do come in, and tell me whatever I am to do. Ma's in an awful way. She just tosses about and groans the whole time; and she can't tell me nothing to do, and I am just at my wit's ends. I sent Timmy off, because I didn't know what else to do. Jim, get out of the way. You great loafer, standing there right in Mis' Mitchell's way. He's so drunk he don't know what he's about, Mis' Mitchell, and pa don't know any too much. They are a set, the whole of them. I am sure I dread the other boys coming home. I don't know what we will do with them to-night. Flora Ann, why don't you put Mime and Dele to bed? I should think you might do so much, instead of standing round here and wringing your hands. What good does that do? Now you come along with me."

This last to Mrs. Mitchell, who presently disappeared from Stephen's sight behind a door which, though hastily closed after her, revealed to him a form of poverty about which he had hitherto known nothing. The Mitchells were undoubtedly poor, but they were sober and clean.

Flora Ann, the other half-grown daughter, a girl of perhaps fifteen, whose dress was fully as slatternly as Miranda's, had been crying quietly while her sister talked. She was evidently not conscious that she was making an exhibition of herself; she did not even remember that she could be seen by any one. It was not a decorous, ladylike weeping behind a handkerchief held by a shapely hand; instead she had no handkerchief whatever; eyes and nose were red, and her large mouth was twisted into strange grimaces in the bitterness of her grief. But she wrung her red hands in such a pitiful way, that despite her frowzled head and her general uncouthness, Stephen's heart was touched.

"Is your mother so very bad?" he said to her, in a low voice, as he stood in doubt where to put himself.

"Oh! she's awful," said Flora Ann. "I never see her like this; she has been pretty bad a good many times, but never like this. And there wasn't nobody to do a thing; we can't get no doctor, nor nothing. Don't cry, Dele; you'll worry ma."

This to the little girl, who despite the warning set up a loud howl, evidently taking up the chorus where she had left off for a few minutes to stare at the strangers.

"Hush!" said Stephen sternly. "You mustn't make a noise; that will only make matters worse."

The loud howl stopped as suddenly as though the child's mouth had been sealed.

"O, dear!" said Flora Ann, "I am so glad you stopped her. She has been taking on just dreadful because she thought ma was going to die. Now, Mime, don't you begin; ma will be better, I reckon, now Mis' Mitchell has come to see her. She will do something for her right straight off. You and Dele go over there in the corner and get into your bed. Hurry, now, and be awful still, because I think I hear Jake coming."

The look of apprehension which both little girls wore at the mention of that name, and the way in which they turned their eyes toward the outer door, as if in fear of some one's entering, told volumes to those familiar with a drunkard's home. Jake was the elder brother, and was by no means so meek in disposition as the half-intoxicated Jim, who had settled himself in a rickety chair in the corner and already dropped into a drunken sleep. When Jake came home the little girls did not cry, unless, indeed, he extorted screams from them by some act of cruelty. Frightened as they were about their mother, curious as they were about the coming strangers, they were willing enough to be huddled off to the corner, into that miserable bundle of rags which they called bed, if there was any fear that Jake was coming.

Stephen retreated to the "stoop," and stood looking about him, busy with his own grave thoughts. What a day this had been to him. Into what strange positions was his list of words carrying him. These people were "barbarians." Whatever the word might mean to others, it had a sound which to Stephen's mind seemed to fit the Lucas family. He had always thought of his own family as very low in the scale of being. Were not he and Sarah Jane different from all the boys and girls who went to the village church, or gathered in the village Sunday-school, or sang in the village choir? As for the Lucases, he had thought nothing about them until their connection with the word "barbarian" had drawn him into their midst and given him a revelation. Here was poverty, indeed. Imagine Sarah Jane looking as that dreadful Flora Ann did. Sarah Jane, whose hair, even in the early morning, was always combed. Stephen had not appreciated that before; he felt sure that he would now, forever after. Sarah Jane, whose dress, no matter how little it cost a yard, nor how many times it had been washed and mended, always had a trim air about it; an air of what Stephen would have called "neatness," had he been familiar with people who were not neat. He contrasted his sister now with both Miranda and Flora Ann, to Sarah Jane's great advantage. He looked in at the blear-eyed, wizen-faced, altogether disreputable old man, who sat with his hat tilted back on his head, blinking at the smoking lamp, and contrasted him with his father. What if his father were such an one? In the light of the evening's revelation, how easily he might have been. Stephen Mitchell drew his breath hard, clinched his hands, and felt that there was work in the world to be done; that there was a stratum of society much lower than his own, and that because he was so different, because his surroundings were so much above those of the Lucas family, he was therefore bound to do something for them.

"Civilization will tell," he muttered to himself, going over Mr. Meadows's words of the morning. "I wonder if Sarah Jane and I haven't got enough to make a difference here, anyhow?"

Meantime, the father at home waited, with a great sinking of heart, over the thought that Steve had gone into the very midst of the family whose contamination he had dreaded as he would the small-pox. He would have been comforted if he had understood his son. It was good for Stephen to go to the depths below himself.

It was striking the hour of midnight when Doll and Dobbin drew up before their own gateway. Very much amazed were Doll and Dobbin; if they could have expressed themselves, they might not have had exalted views about emancipation. When before had they been called upon to do duty at the midnight hour? Mr. Mitchell had had an exciting time waiting for his family, and expressed himself with unhesitating tongue.

"For goodness' sake, Phebe; what did you stay

so for? I have been scared almost out of my wits for the last two hours. What happened?"

"Why, there didn't anything happen, Josiah; only there was a woman dreadful sick needing everything done for her, and nothing to do it with. I had to stay; there was no other way to do. Such a place as it is, Josiah; you never saw the like. The idea of human beings living in such a condition; it is enough to make one sick of life. Where is Sarah Jane? I want to take a look at the child, just to comfort me after seeing them two girls. Oh! such shiftlessness. You never saw anything like it, Josiah. I never did before, I am sure; but then, poor things, how can they help it? I thought their mother would die, sure, for the first hour. It did seem as though nothing that I did for her was going to do any good. But we got a hold of her at last. She quieted all down, and I shouldn't wonder if she should sleep pretty well. And we left them comfortable, compared to what we found them, and just as thankful! You have no idea; they have got hearts, anyhow. It does seem, Josiah, as though we ought to do something for them."

"I should think we had," said Mr. Mitchell. "Where was Steve all the while? Did you think of him, mother?"

"Think of him? I reckon I did; and had good reason to. Steve was everywhere. He made a fire in their rickety old stove; made some wood, in the first place — cut down a tree, or something; I don't know what. I know them girls said there wasn't one stick to make a fire with, and Steve told them that he would see about that; and it wasn't ten minutes before he had a fire roaring, and kept it up, too. Then he got a kettle and filled it with water from the land knows where. They don't have any water near the house — have to go off down the hill somewhere. There wasn't a drop for her to drink, even. O, well! Steve did everything. If you had seen him going around there giving his directions, you wouldn't have known the boy. You'd have forgot he was a boy, and thought that he was a grown man. He got that drunken Jim to go up a pair of rickety stairs somewhere, to bed. Then by and by that oldest one, Jake, came home swearing, just drunk enough to be ugly. Flora Ann, she wrung her hands and screamed, and Miranda, she just groaned, she was that scared. And I was scared myself, he knocked things about so — kicked over a chair, and swore, and told Flora Ann to shut up, or he would wring her neck. O, dear! I don't know what he didn't do. At last he took hold of the lamp, and was going to stalk off with it, and leave us all in the dark, with that woman sick, and maybe dying. Then says I, Josiah, you ought to have seen your son. He marched up to Jake, and spoke just as quiet and composed as though he was talking to me.

"'Jake,' said he, 'that's enough. Put down that lamp and go upstairs, quick! Don't you wait a minute.'

"'Who are you?' said Jake, staring at him as if he was too astonished to say any more.

"'That's no matter who I am,' said Steve. 'I'm somebody that you've got to mind. Put that lamp down on the table and go up those stairs. I won't give you more than a minute and a half to do it in.'

"Well, father, I never was so scared in my life. I just expected to see him throw that lamp right at Steve's head. He glared at him as though he meant to do it; and Steve looked back just as composed as if it was me looking at him. He didn't appear to be the least mite afraid. I was almost scared over that, for I have seen him turn all colors, and actually tremble, when a strange woman spoke to him coming out of church; but there he stood looking at that madman, perfectly composed. I suppose it was his steady gaze, maybe, kind of cowed Jake; anyhow, he set down the lamp, and swore that he didn't know what all this fuss was about; and then as true as you live he went stumbling up the stairs, Steve watching him till he got to the top; then he turned around and said to Flora Ann: 'I wouldn't cry any more if I was you; you might disturb your mother. Jake won't hurt anybody to-night; he will be asleep in a few minutes.'" And sure enough he was. What we would have done without Steve I don't know. I tell you, Josiah, there's a great difference in boys. When I saw that fellow there to-night raging around, swearing at us all, and then saw our Steve stand up so straight and strong and brave — O, my! but I thanked God that Steve was our boy, and not the other one. I don't know but we have got a good deal to be proud of, Josiah. Steve hasn't got education, such as you meant him to have, but he has got some other things that is worth having."

"That's a fact," said the father, with an emphatic nod of his head; "I don't know as we have done Steve justice; for he has always been a good boy."

CHAPTER IX.

BECOMING A CHAMPION.

THE next Sunday Stephen went to church. He could not have explained why it should seem in keeping with his new ideas, to do so. Certainly he was not in need of more words, nor could he hope to have light thrown on his present lesson by listening to the sermon, unless, indeed, Sarah Jane's idea in regard to watching for the connection between words might be put in practice.

Whatever the motive was, he astonished that young woman by making the kitchen fire for her nearly an hour earlier than usual, and announcing as he came from the cow house with a foaming pail of milk, that he was going to meeting, and she might go along if she wanted to.

"Going to meeting!" said Sarah Jane, setting down her pan of potatoes to stare at him. "Are you really? That is awful nice in you. It is such a pretty day. I was just wishing I could go, and wondering if I couldn't manage to coax you into it somehow; but I didn't expect to, because you have been dreadfully cranky lately about going to church, you know."

"The horses didn't have to work hard yesterday," said Stephen, "and I reckon it will be good for them to take a little tramp," which was the only explanation he gave to Sarah Jane.

However, she was in nowise disturbed. "Whatever took him," she explained to her mother, as she put herself with speed into the green dress, whose appearance did credit to her industry at least, and indeed to her skill, when one took into consideration her meager resources; "whatever took him to go, I am awful glad he did it; seems to me I should fly if I couldn't go somewheres today." Then she stopped in the middle of the delightful task of buttoning the green dress, and stared thoughtfully at her mother. "Look here, mother," she said at last, "why don't you go with Steve, yourself? You ain't been to meeting in an age. I wonder I could be so dreadful mean as not to think of it before. I'll help you get ready in a jiffy, and then I'll stay and tend to the dinner."

"O, no!" Mrs. Mitchell hurried to say, "I can't go to-day, child; I'm all tuckered out with the extra baking and things yesterday, and don't feel equal to it. I don't, honest, child, and I wouldn't have you miss it for anything in the world. Father and I will see to the dinner, and have everything comfortable when you come home; he likes the notion of your going off together to church, like other folks, as well as I do, though he doesn't say much about such things. Sarah Jane, that dress is as pretty as a picture. I declare! you do beat all for fixing over things. I wish Stephen had a better looking coat to wear."

"So do I," declared Sarah Jane earnestly, " but don't say a word, mother, or he will get a fit at the last moment not to go. It isn't so dreadful looking; I ironed it as though it had been a satin coat, instead of an old faded-out linen, and I turned over the collar deeper so that the grass stains do not show so bad. I reckon I had a notion that he would go to church to-day, and that is what made me take the extra pains."

Mrs. Mitchell was at the window in Sarah Jane's room, watching Stephen as he brought Doll and Dobbin, harnessed to the little old spring wagon, around to the side door. His coat was very short waisted, and, for that matter, narrow chested. "It was too bad in it," the mother murmured, "to go and shrink like that." But then it had been washed so many times. And she could see, even from the window, that it was frayed at the wrists. Mrs. Mitchell had a distinct mental photograph of her Stephen as he should have been dressed, had her power been equal to her loving will. He never knew how hard it was for his mother to see him driving to church dressed as he was; yet that he would go to church at all, was surely something to be thankful for. And the tears which she brushed from her eyes as she finally turned away, after watching them down the road, were born partly of regret over the outgrown clothes, and partly of joy at the thought that they were "on their way to meeting, like respectable folks."

The church was small and plain, but was fairly well filled with people who were a marked contrast to the Mitchells. Even as uncultured an eye as Stephen's was able to discover that he was by far the worst dressed person there; and Sarah Jane felt by no means so fine in her made-over green dress as she had in her own room. It took but one swift glance at Fanny Bascome's new lavender suit to discover that the plaits of her dress were not in the right place; that the points of her basque were too long, and that her sleeves were not the correct shape. Her face grew red as she looked and thought, and she actually had some trouble to keep back the tears. She had worked so hard, and believed that she had done so well. What was the use in trying to look in the least like other folks? Poor Sarah Jane!

At that moment the minister was reading: "Why do ye spend your money for that which is not bread, and your labor for that which satisfieth not?" Why, indeed? Sarah Jane did not even hear the words, so absorbed was she in her own sorrow. Even the green braid had lost its power to comfort, for Fanny's went down the back as well as the front, and crossed in some bewildering fashion which she could not make out.

The service over, Stephen stood on the steps outside and waited for his sister. He had need of patience, for she was making her passage down the aisle as slow as possible. Her courage had already revived. Was she, who had overcome such mountains of difficulties in the past, to be vanquished by a bit of green braid? She resolved to conquer. If somebody would only detain Fanny Bascome in the aisle long enough for her to discover just where the braid crossed in the back, she felt that she could succeed. Fortune favored her. Fanny was halted just before she reached the door, by some one who was eager to make arrangements for a basket picnic, gotten up hastily in honor of some of their friends. Sarah Jane, while she studied the braid, heard snatches of the talk, and found time to give one little regretful thought to the fact that from all such interests she was counted out. How did it feel, she wondered, to be invited to a picnic? To be asked how they should manage this or that detail; to be consulted as to what she meant to take and to wear; to be, in short, one of them? The last picnic which Sarah Jane had attended, the girls had ignored her, and gone off on a stroll by themselves; and at lunch time she had been unable to find any one to share her lunch with her. It was a Sunday-school picnic, too. After that Sarah Jane had not wanted to go to picnics, nor to Sunday-school.

Stephen knew nothing about the disappointment connected with the green braid, and he stood with his hands in his pockets and wondered why Sarah Jane did not come.

"Good-morning," said a clear voice, just beside him, and he turned quickly to meet the woman who had "gray eyes, and wore some still, pale stuff." The description fitted her yet. But why should she say "good-morning" to him? In his surprise and embarrassment, he forget even to nod his head in reply. But the lady did not wait for a response.

"You are Mr. Mitchell, I believe?" I am Miss Ransom, the minister's sister; I have come to keep house for him, and I want to get acquainted with his people. You attend church here regularly, do you not?"

Stephen studied this problem for a minute, going back rapidly over his past, to discover that it was nearly two months since he had been inside the church.

"Not very regular, I reckon," he said at last, with an embarrassed laugh; "we live a long way from the church, and the roads are heavy."

"I know; but this is your church home, is it not? Therefore we ought to be acquainted. Do you know my brother?"

Stephen shook his head. Mr. Ransom was himself a stranger, having been in the neighborhood but a few months, and on the few occasions when Stephen honored him with his presence, he had slipped away before the new minister could see him; or rather, without giving any thought whatever to the matter, he had accomplished it as a matter of course. It had never occurred to him to wait and speak to his pastor, or give the pastor opportunity to speak with him. Why should he?

The church had been long pastorless, and the constant succession of "supplies" had not made the acquaintance of the Mitchell family.

"Then I hope you will wait," said Miss Ransom, "and let me introduce you to him. He wants to get acquainted with his people as rapidly as possible. Are there others in your neighborhood upon whom we could call when we come out to see you?"

Stephen was about to shake his head, but he held it quiet, and gave himself to bewildered thought instead. Why should he at this moment think of the Lucas family? They were the only ones in his immediate neighborhood, it is true; but who could imagine anything so absurd as that people like her and her brother should visit them? Yet they needed doing good to, if that was what she meant. "They need civilizing," he said to himself, with a grim smile; "and like enough she could do it faster than Sarah Jane and I can; but of course she won't. Them ain't the kind they go to see."

"There's folks," he said at last, speaking half-sullenly; "but they ain't the kind to be called on."

"Why not?" with a genial smile; "wouldn't they want to see us?"

"I don't know about that," said Stephen; "but they're low-down folks that nobody ever calls on. They don't go to church; it's out of their line. They're a hard set — 'barbarians,' a man called them the other day. But I don't know as they can help it; the women folks can't, anyhow. They're poor, and never had any chance, and the men folks drink; and what can you expect of such?"

"Not much, certainly," said Miss Ransom, in gentle voice, "unless they get acquainted with Jesus Christ. He is the great civilizer, you know. But do you not think such people need calling upon and helping? I am glad to find they have a champion in you."

She was as much surprised at the sudden flash in his eyes as Mr. Meadows had been. Here was his third word, which thus far had resisted his efforts to discover its meaning. Behold! there must be some sense in which he was a "champion." And the sentence connected him with the Lucas family. Life was certainly growing very full of mysteries for Stephen Mitchell.

Miss Ransom hesitated in the word she was

about to speak, when she saw that peculiar flash of Stephen's eyes. What had she said which had brought such a look of keen, wistful intelligence into them? While she hesitated and wondered, Sarah Jane appeared, and some one from the other door claimed Miss Ransom; she turned back to bow to Stephen, and assure him of her intention of coming with her brother to see them as soon as possible, but he had plunged forward into the little yard, and was already lost to sight.

"I just wonder who she is," said Sarah Jane, coming slowly after him with her eyes behind her. "I never did see such an elegant-looking lady in all my days."

"Who?" asked Stephen, shortly.

"Why, that woman who stood close by you when I came out. You don't say you didn't see her, Steve? That's too bad! Why, she looked just like a picture. And her dress — oh! my. Wasn't it lovely, though? Steve, I wish I knew such people; and could shake hands with them, and laugh and talk and be one of them. There doesn't seem to be any folks for us to belong to; isn't it queer?"

"Only the Lucases," Stephen said; "I suppose we might laugh and talk with them as much as we have a mind to."

"The Lucases," repeated Sarah Jane, in intense scorn; "I don't see why you keep talking about them, Steve. We are poor, I know, and don't have company, nor chances, nor anything; but we are decent, and clean, and all that; and I think there is a big difference between us and them."

Then Stephen, who had already gone deeper into the problems of life than his sister had thought of doing, reflected that Sarah Jane, from her standpoint, looked down upon those below her with even more vehemence, perhaps, than those who were above her looked down upon her.

" But *she's* above us, high enough," he told himself, with the peculiar emphasis on the pronoun which distinguished one person in his mind from all others; "and she wasn't scornful nor lofty. I guess she would have been nice to Sarah Jane. I might have introduced her, I suppose. If it had been anybody but me, he would."

So, in much humility of spirit, he climbed into the old spring-wagon, and was unusually silent, even for him, during all the long homeward drive.

CHAPTER X.

OBSTRUCTIONS.

MISS RANSOM sat opposite her brother at the breakfast table. She studied his thoughtful, somewhat sad face, critically before she asked her question. During the Sabbath she had carefully refrained from questions of all sorts, and had soothed and ministered to the young pastor, who she felt was her special charge, to her heart's content. But now it was Monday morning, and there were certain things which Helen Ransom meant to accomplish that week if possible. Moreover, she felt that if there was any one thing which her brother needed more than another, it was to be aroused to a sense of his duties and responsibilities in certain directions, and to be drawn away from his brooding thoughts in certain other directions. The question she advanced was one of her means toward these ends.

"Maxwell, have you done any calling in the direction of Hilton Hill?"

The minister shook his head, and his sister could see that he winced at the question.

After a moment's hesitation he said :

"I have not done much calling in the country in any direction, as yet; but there are very few people to reach on the Hilton Hill road. Mr. Bascome told me he did not know of any who could be said to belong to us; and he lives where the road forks, and knows all that neighborhood."

"I met one from that region yesterday morning; he was in church with his sister. And he told me of others — one family in particular, in which he has evidently become interested. From what he said, they need to have others interest themselves in their welfare. Perhaps Mr. Bascome is not entirely reliable as regards people in whom you would be interested, Max. He impresses me as a man who might gauge the importance of people by their standing in society, or their bank account. I promised that young fellow that we would come out and call, this week if we could. It is going to be very pleasant to-day, I think. Couldn't we go this afternoon?"

"I am afraid you will find it hard driving, Helen. The roads are what people in the country call 'heavy'; it must be all up and down hill, and through a stony part of the country."

"Ah, but I want to ride. Mr. Dunlap told me of a beautiful riding horse to be had, and I am just longing to get into the saddle again."

The minister was silent for so long that his sister, who had purposely refrained from looking at him while she was speaking, turned, presently, anxious eyes in his direction. His own were bent upon his plate, though nothing on it seemed to be claiming his attention. He looked up at last with a faint smile, seeming to feel the anxiety in his sister's eyes, which were bent upon him.

"Aren't you rather hard on me?" he asked deprecatingly.

She shook her head. "You are hard on yourself, Max; yes, and hard on me. Is it fair to keep me from an exercise of which I am so fond, and which has been urged upon us both, because" — There she came to a sudden pause.

"No," he said firmly, after a longer silence than before, "it is not fair. I do not mean to do it; I fully intend to rise above this feeling. But it did not seem to me that I could just yet."

"But you can," she said, with the feeling which possesses a surgeon who has resolved upon the importance of probing a wound at whatever cost of pain, rather than with the air of a blunderer who did not know he was giving pain. "Max, I know by experience that when you allow such things to trammel you, they have power to grow harder and harder. I do not believe that you intend to let this sorrow hamper your life, or retard your work in any way, and I long to see you take hold of it with the strength of will which you possess. It does not seem to me that I can wait any longer."

But she had to wait some minutes again before she was answered. It was certainly not the minister's breakfast which was claiming his attention this morning. He cut his steak with exceeding care, as if he were preparing it for a delicate child, but he left it untasted, and proceeded to stirring his coffee mechanically.

"I sometimes think," he said at last, clearing his voice, for its huskiness was very perceptible, "that Gertrude was right; that it was all a mistake, and I am not fit for the ministry. There is work on every hand that ought to be done, but I cannot tell you how I shrink from it. In my study and in the pulpit I can forget myself, but this mingling with people is something for which I feel totally unfit. The eternal round of calls which seems to be necessary, the saying over the same inane sentences from house to house, and the beginning again when one has gotten through it alive, and doing it over. The very thought of all this weighs me to the ground. Sometimes, as I say, I feel that Gertrude was right, and that I am not called to the work."

If he had expected to shock his sister, he was mistaken. She turned her eyes away from his face, and looked out upon the lawn. So far from being shocked was she, that, if she had not feared to pain her brother, she could have smiled over the exceeding morbidness of such a confession. Helen Ransom was the minister's twin sister, and felt herself almost a part of him — his "other self," he used fondly to call her. Through babyhood, childhood, early youth, up to the time when the brother entered the theological seminary, they had not been separated for a day, scarcely for an hour. Even through his theological course, his sister kept such steady pace with his mental development — reading the books which he read, and, so far as possible, studying the books which he studied — that it hardly seemed a separation. She felt that she knew him thoroughly. She believed in him thoroughly. She believed that if ever a man was called of God to the work of the gospel ministry, Maxwell Ransom was that man. She knew that when his system had rallied thoroughly from the shock of a heavy sorrow which had fallen upon him, he would realize his call again, as he had in the past. In the meantime she must wait patiently, and plan as skillfully as she could.

"It is not surprising that you shrink from calls," she said quietly, "if that is your conception of them. 'Going from house to house, saying nothings,' month after month and year after year, must indeed be a dreary prospect. But, Max what if you go from house to house reaching consciences, turning wayward footsteps, holding out helping hands?"

He shook his head, the look of pain upon his face growing deeper. "I do not know," he said at last, "I do not understand myself. I seem to have lost interest in humanity. I used to have an ambition, as you very well know, to reach people — help them, lift them up, as you say — but I seem to have lost it. Sometimes it almost seems to me that I do not care whether people advance or not. It is this condition of mind which leads me occasionally to feel what I have just confessed to you, that I have mistaken my calling."

"Maxwell, do you care for Jesus Christ?" There was no mistaking the intense earnestness of the questioner, nor her tenderness. Her voice was as sweet as a chime of bells, yet she threw all the strength of her nature into that one brief question, and waited. He looked at her then, with a startled, searching look, as if he wished to get behind the question and see what prompted it.

"Yes," he said, after a moment. "I have not lapsed to that degree. I do care for Jesus Christ. But for him, it seems to me, there are times when I could not live."

"That is all," said his sister; "I was sure of it, but I wanted you to remind yourself, and then to think, in connection with it, of what you have been saying. Caring for Him, you are bound to care for his interests. You would be under just as strong obligations, you know, if you were a lawyer, or a bricklayer. He cared for people, and you must, because you are his servant, his steward, his lover. I am not in the least afraid for you, Maxwell, eventually; but I am troubled, often, to think how your conscience will upbraid you, one of these days, when you rouse to the fact that you are wasting time. Can not we go to the Hilton neighborhood this afternoon?"

"Yes," he said, looking at her again, and this time breaking into a smile which a wife might have envied; "we will go to the Hilton neighborhood, or anywhere else you please. And we will ride there. I will make inquiries in regard to the horse you spoke of. Did you say Mr. Dunlap told you? And, Helen, thank you. I don't know how it is, but you seem to know just what to say, and just the right moment in which to say it. I have not really meant to shirk, though I have felt my unfitness, utterly, of late. I believe you did not come to me too soon." After which, he left his scarcely tasted breakfast, and went to his study. His sister waited until the door had fairly closed after him, before she drew a long, quivering sigh — a sort of escape-valve for a great deal of pent-up anxiety — and murmured, under her breath: "Poor fellow! No, I did not come too soon."

You are not to understand that Maxwell Ransom was a sentimentalist, or a misanthrope; on the contrary, he was a strong-souled, strong-nerved young man, who had given himself utterly and gladly to the work of the gospel ministry. The years of preparation had been joyful ones; the preparation itself conscientious in the extreme. Nor was he one of those who, in their zeal to furnish the soul and mind, forget the needs of the body. It had been a joy to him to realize that he would be able to bring to the work a well-disciplined body, prepared by intelligent training to serve faithfully. There was really not a morbid streak in this young man's nature. And yet I am aware that I have presented him to you in a picture which suggests weakness, oversensitiveness and disappointment. It becomes necessary to make an explanation. Although, in order to understand it, you would need to do what one can never fully accomplish — put yourself in another's place, and think his thoughts. Also, I ought to be able to introduce to you Gertrude Temple — a very beautiful girl, who, in addition to her beauty and grace, had about her an indescribable charm which attracted and held captive many besides Maxwell Ransom. Still, I am obliged to confess that he saw in her not herself, but what he imagined her to be. Have you never known a strong, pure nature, who out of his own inner consciousness had evolved an ideal friend, and then at some period of his life had selected a very faulty, and it might be, in your eyes, very commonplace, creature, and said to his heart: "This is she! my ideal; the human embodiment of all that I have dreamed?" This he does, not willfully, but with a stupidity that to those who do not understand, seems inexcusable; and he walks with blinded eyes by her side, seeing nothing whatever of the imperfections which are perfectly plain to the eyes of others. If you know any such persons, you understand to a degree what Maxwell Ransom did. Not that he was one of those unreasonable mortals who expect to find perfection in human nature; not that he did not see what he supposed ought to be called faults in Gertrude Temple; but he saw less in her than in others, and the imperfections which she had were those which he fully believed time and grace could and would smooth away. And she was all the time, in his estimation, so fully above and beyond himself, that he often lost himself in amazement over her choice; for she made deliberate choice of the young theological student. She was a schoolgirl when he first met her, pursuing her studies in the same town where the theological seminary was located. Both were very busy; he with actual hard work, she with a thousand things which had nothing to do with her standing in class, yet with such a pretty way of imagining that it was geometry, and philosophy, and matters of like character, which hard pressed her, as to keep her student lover in a perpetual anxiety lest she should overstudy. He might have better feared that a butterfly would overtax its nerves. It would have been impossible in that stage of his career to have made young Ransom believe that he was happier in the brief spaces of time he was able to give to the lady of his choice, than he would have been had he been at leisure to know her better. As it was, he was satisfied and royally happy, and no more sincere prayer did he offer night and morning, than the one in which he thanked God for this last crowning gift — the love of a pure, true woman.

The first shadow which fell across their lives was during the Christmas holidays. Gertrude went home, of course, and the plan had been that Mr. Ransom, as soon as he had paid his respects to his own home, would follow her, and make the more intimate acquaintance of her family. But it came to pass that at home the theological student found work which held him. His father was the pastor of a large and important country church, and there was a revival in progress. Meetings were being held twice each day; and expected help had been detained by sickness. The father, overworked, and heavily burdened in several ways, was breaking under the strain, and hailed, as a father would, the relief which the coming of his son could bring. The path of duty was never plainer to Maxwell Ransom than during those three weeks when he was held steadily to the work in his father's parish. There was a sense, of course, in which it was a disappointment not to be able to make his promised visit. But there was another sense in which he gloried in the disappointment, and believed that Gertrude would join him in his joy. What a blessed opportunity had been given him for gathering experiences for his life-work.

"You can understand," he wrote to Gertrude, "how, in one sense, it is anything but a trial to be held here in this way. The meetings are wonderful, dear; every night, as I go over the day's record, I say to my heart, 'Oh! if Gertrude were only here; how she would enjoy these opportunities.' I sometimes feel as though the experience I am getting now will be worth more to me than a whole year at the theological seminary. And the interest, instead of abating, as it was supposed it would during the actual Christmas week, seems to be on the increase. Last night more than forty persons arose for prayers; many of them heads of families; and a number of them young men whose lives have been hard, and whose mothers wept and prayed over them, and felt at times that it was almost in vain.

"Think of it, Gertrude, what it was to see such rise for prayer, and to meet them afterward in the inquiry room. It was crowded to overflowing. My dear one, if you could only be with me during this blessed time, what a daily, hourly joy life would be to me. When, in addition to all that I have told you, I add that my poor father, who has been tempted all the early part of the winter to overwork, is really physically unable to carry on one entire meeting alone, and just at this point seems unable to secure other help, you will understand how impossible it is for me to get away even for a few days. There is a side to it, Gertrude, which makes me more sorry than the mere words placed on paper can tell. But I need not even try to explain ; you will understand ; it is blessed for me to remember that we are one in this, as in all other things."

CHAPTER XI.

INTERSECTING LINES.

IF he could have seen the frown on Gertrude's forehead deepening with every line she read, as she sat in becoming morning costume in her mother's room! If he could have heard the impatient exclamation caused by the sheet at which she sat fiercely scowling! If he could have heard the conversation which followed!

"Well," said Mrs. Temple, "when are we to see your theologue? It seems to me that he is very slow in coming. I wonder that you can tolerate such indifference to your charms."

"Mamma, if you can believe it, he is not coming at all! At least, that is what I should gather from his letter. Those poky old meetings, day and night! And his father is sick. I should think he would be, having meetings all the time! And Maxwell says I will understand how impossible it is for him to get away. I'm sure I don't understand it in the least."

"The idea!" said Mrs. Temple; "a three weeks' vacation, and he can't find time to come and see you in your own home I must say I consider that carrying things with a rather high hand. My dear, I am very much afraid that he is one of the fanatical sort, who will wear your life out with an eternal round of meetings, missionary societies, Sunday-schools and the like."

Said the young woman, who was so thoroughly to understand the letter which had fallen to the floor : "Mamma, do hush! You show that you do not know what you are talking about. Maxwell Ransom is the most brilliant young man in the seminary, by far; and he was the most brilliant one in college. There are a great many things that he has to learn, and a number of them I can teach him. I meant to give him some lessons during this vacation, but those poky meetings are distressing him. A 'sense of duty' is one of his strong points. But he will never be a country parson, mamma, and drag me off to missionary meetings and female prayer meetings, and things of that sort; you need not be in the least afraid. I am awfully sorry he cannot be here for New Year's. He has queer country notions, of course — he has been brought up in the country largely — and he needs to get them rubbed off. I could help him immensely in those ways. Oh! I don't mean that he is awkward, mamma, or anything of that sort; he is a perfectly exquisite gentleman everywhere; but I mean he has ideas, old-fashioned ones, you know, about dancing, and matters of that kind; and he is a bit fanatical on the temperance question, I suspect; not that I object to that in a man, only it would be awkward sometimes in city life. O, dear! I am too provoked for anything. I wanted to show him off to the girls. He is handsomer than any man in our set, mamma. He is, really. If it wasn't for those horrid meetings. I don't believe in having meetings day after day, wearing people's bodies all out. He shall never do it when he has a church of his own. I think people ought to be temperate in religion as well as in anything else, and I know I can coax him into thinking so, too. Oh! you needn't shake your head, mamma; I have a great deal of influence over him. Why, he thinks I'm perfection."

If he could have heard all this, it might have made a difference in his immediate future — we cannot tell. But he did not hear it; he went on with his eager work — though it was not the vacation which he and Gertrude had planned together — enjoying it as only one whose heart was in it could have done. He was ten days late at the seminary, because he had so taken hold of the work that it seemed not possible to get away before. The detention did not trouble Gertrude, for she was more than ten days late in getting back to school.

"Sister Kate has company, and I am sorely needed at home," she wrote Maxwell. "It really does not seem possible to leave just now. There are special reasons why mamma needs me; and she thinks that even a schoolgirl must not forget that she has some duties in her own home."

The young minister pondered over the sentences; wondered what the loving ministrations were, and wished his darling had been more explicit. He sympathized with her in her sacrifice of those two important weeks from school. He felt, and told her on paper, that it was just like her to think of others and not of herself.

She laughed over this added testimony to her power, and went on making out the list for the brilliant party which her mother was to give early in the following week; other engagements of the same nature having made it impossible for her to get hers in before. Certainly Gertrude was needed at home, for the party was to be the most elegant one of the season, planned with a special view to eclipsing all that preceded it; and Gertrude Temple was an excellent planner in all such directions.

They returned, both of them, at last, to the routine of study life. But they had met only two or three times before young Ransom began to feel that a change had come over Gertrude. She seemed ill at ease, and at times almost dissatisfied with her future prospects. She began to make suggestions, or perhaps they might more properly be called hints, concerning the trials and privations of ministerial life, and to ask Mr. Ransom if he felt very sure that he was called to that work and no other. What if he was theologically educated? So were college professors and authors, and men in political life; she had once heard a certain eminent lawyer say that he regarded the two years which he had spent in studying theology as two of the most valuable years of his preparation for his profession.

Gradually she grew more outspoken; she felt confident, she assured him, that he had made a mistake. She could not believe that a man of his talent was called upon to bury himself in a country village, and make an eternal round of calls upon people who could neither understand nor appreciate him. It was absurd for one so young as he to feel that because he had spent three years in a theological seminary, he was therefore called upon to spend his life in ministerial work. She had had a feeling for some time that he was called to a higher sphere; well, not higher, perhaps, she hastened to explain, noting his air of pained surprise; not in one sense of the word, of course, but different. Commonplace people, she believed, could preach the Gospel quite as well as highly cultured ones. What was there to do but point out the right road, and get men to walk in it if you could?

Young Ransom listened to her at first with a bewildered air; he even laughed a little over some of her bright speeches, believing that she must be trying to amuse him. It was not possible that such words as these could express Gertrude Temple's real convictions. For himself, he believed that life had no higher sphere to offer than opportunity to preach the Gospel. It was folly to talk about talents thrown away. Had it not been the joy of his life to feel that God had called him to such great honor; endowed him with powers which would enable him to be useful in that position?

"I do not understand Gertrude," he told himself wearily, and then his face brightened over a new thought. "Perhaps some one has been trying to make her believe that young men choose the ministry as a profession because they think it an opportunity to shine, and she wants my reply to such ideas to help her in proving how utterly mistaken they are."

So, when it became evident that treating the subject lightly was not to Gertrude's mind, he began patiently to explain his views, having all the time before his thoughts the caviler whom his imagination had erected, and trying to answer his supposed arguments in such form as Gertrude could repeat; going step by step over the ground, giving her occasional glimpses of the joy the future had in store for him, when he should discover that, because of his preaching and his teaching, some one had come to know Jesus Christ.

There came a time when Gertrude Temple said no more; not because she was satisfied, but because she had failed.

They were very busy, living their separate lives. The closing months of study were before them; they were looking forward, not only to the day when they should graduate, but one of them, at least, thought often of that important day in the future when they should be united to separate no more. They saw very little of each other during that last term. Young Ransom was away nearly every Sabbath preaching somewhere. His services seemed already in demand, and the time necessarily consumed in journeying to and from his appointments straitened him somewhat in his studies, and made it necessary for him to curtail his hours of rest and recreation. He thought Gertrude very patient, very wise and sympathetic over all these disappointments. He did not for one moment imagine that she was slowly reaching that state of mind when to visit with him was becoming embarrassing; and that she hailed each detention with a sense of relief. It was not until they were both graduated, and Gertrude had gone to her home, leaving Mr. Ransom in the full expectation of following her in a few weeks to perfect their arrangements for the future, that the blow fell upon him.

This, of course, was not only cruel, but cowardly. Gertrude Temple knew, weeks before she graduated, that she meant to tell this man to whom her hand was pledged, that she had discovered they were not suited to each other. But no hint of this determination passed her lips. She waited until miles had divided them, that she might be relieved of the embarrassment of being face to face with the misery she had wrought. She was very kind, indeed. Words failed, she assured him, to express her deep sorrow and regret. But she had felt for a long time, and mamma had fully agreed with her, that she was not fitted to be the wife of a minister; all her inclinations and tastes pointed in other directions. She did not know, she was sure, why she had allowed herself to be drawn into an engagement. She had always known perfectly well that she was a poor, worthless little creature, not at all suited to the dignity of such a station. She supposed it must have been that, in the enjoyment of his society, she really for the time being had forgotten the future, and had not realized but that the beautiful winter they had enjoyed together would always remain. Now that her eyes were really open, or that she had grown older and wiser, perhaps, she shrank from the future which he had planned, in inexpressible terror. He would bear her witness that she had tried to explain; had spoken very plainly, indeed, and done her utmost to induce him to give up the ministry, and devote himself to some profession in which she could hope to keep pace with him. He would remember, she was sure, how earnestly she had talked of this matter; and of course he would remember — certainly she would never forget — how solemnly he had assured her that nothing but the hand of God laid upon him, and the voice of God calling to him to give up his work, could possibly change his mind.

From that hour, she declared to him, she had given up all hope of their living their lives together; for of course she could not expect the Lord to work a miracle in her behalf, and it was nothing less than a miracle which he demanded.

Because of all her plain speaking in the past, she felt sure he must be prepared for the conclusion of the whole matter. They must just make up their minds that they had been foolish young people, who, because they enjoyed each other's society so much, and had had such royally pleasant times together for a few months, had blundered into the mistaken idea that they were suited to each other for life. People often made such mistakes, she believed. Mamma was engaged three times before she was finally married to papa. And as for gentlemen, she should think such experiences would be constantly happening to them. They had so many to choose from, and the choice was all in their hands; how did they ever reach the point of making a final decision?

For her part she should never forget the pleasant hours they had spent together, and the good that he had done her in many ways. She believed that her life would always be the better for having known so good and true and noble a man. She could even not help admiring him for holding so resolutely to his purpose to preach the Gospel, though she had thought for a time that it would break her silly little heart. But now that all was over between them, she presumed he was right. Probably he did have a special call to that work, and would do good service in it. It was only she who was utterly unfitted for it, and therefore it was eminently fitting that she should take herself out of his way. Perhaps she ought to have told him before she left college, but it seemed a pity to disturb those few last hurried minutes that they had together, by any disagreeable talk, and so she had resolved to wait until she had reached home and could put it all on paper, thus saving him a great deal of trouble.

And I shall always be interested in your welfare [the young girl's letter went on to say]. I think I should like to hear you preach better than almost any other person. I do hope you will get a church somewhere near where I live, or where I may live in the future. Who knows where that will be? Isn't life strange, Max? Oh! but I must call you Mr. Ransom now, must I not? How very queer! What if in years to come you should be my pastor, and call upon me — make pastoral calls, you know — and I should be "Mrs. Smith," or "Mrs. Jones," or something? Wouldn't that be too funny for anything? Well, just such strange things as that have happened. One of the professors in your own college was a very dear friend of mamma's once; was engaged to her for three whole months, and now he wouldn't have her for anything, I suppose. Any way, she wouldn't him. O, dear! how I am running on. I don't quite know how to finish this letter. It is such a strange letter, you know; different from any I ever wrote you. You won't be angry with the silly little girl, will you? I was always silly, Max, and was not worthy of you. I knew it all the time, but you never suspected it. That was because you were good; and because you are good, you will forgive me, won't you? And forget me, I dare say, in a month or two. So I will send you back the pretty ring you gave me, though I can not bear to part with it, but of course that is proper. I wonder who will wear it next? And now, wishing you a better and happier life than I could possibly have made for you, I close by signing myself,

Ever your sincere friend,
GERTRUDE TEMPLE.

You can imagine something of what such a letter as this was to Maxwell Ransom. A man who considered a pledge of any sort a sacred thing; a man who had thought long and thought carefully, and prayed for guidance, before offering his hand to this woman, and, once offering it, had surrendered himself as utterly as a true man can; had looked upon himself as, in the eyes of God, a married man, waiting only for the hour when it should become his right to consummate before the world the vows which had already been taken.

CHAPTER XII.

SIDE TRACKS.

"I DO not say," he had explained once in answer to a question which had been asked him by a friend in perplexity, "I do not say that engagements should never be broken. There are circumstances, perhaps, which make this not only right and proper, but I should go further, and make it the only right thing to be done ; but God grant that you and I may be delivered from any such experiences. I want to consider an engagement of marriage a holy thing, a pledge upon which my Master has smiled, and upon the consummation of which I have his blessing. Certainly such an engagement is not to be entered into lightly, nor for any common reason broken."

And these words were spoken but a few months before his engagement was thus rudely broken. How came he to be under engagement of marriage with a person who could write such a letter as has been described? Ah! the one who could answer such a question, and make the answer so plain that other young men and young women in the years to come would be open-eyed, and escape the bewilderments which have scarred some lives, would confer almost a priceless boon upon society. I suppose it would not be possible to make you see how altogether lovely in heart and mind and person Gertrude Temple had seemed to this young man. Childish he knew she was, and might well be — she was only nineteen; so young, that he had pledged himself to wait a year after he was graduated before he should claim her as his bride. So innocent, he thought she was, that he could read her very heart. So winning, that a heart of stone would have been drawn toward her; so earnest in her Christian life, that she was the only one of all the young ladies in her class who could be induced to take her turn in leading the young people's meetings; yet withal so shy and modest, that her voice had trembled like a frightened child's as she read the sacred Bible words, which had never before sounded so much like music in his ears.

Nor was Gertrude Temple playing a part at that time; she was sincere enough, or supposed she was. Had not the most talented young man in the seminary chosen her? She felt honored by his preference; she knew she was envied by a score of schoolgirls, and she imagined that she loved him. It is possible that had he been able to hold her steadily under his influence, she might not have discovered her mistake; but she went home to her gay world for vacations — a world as unlike her school life and the influences which surrounded her there as it was possible to make it. She frolicked and frittered away the days and nights in one continual round of parties and receptions and merry-makings of every sort, and awakened one day to the fact that this was her life; that it was altogether agreeable to her, and that prayer meetings and church societies and calls made from a sense of duty were distasteful in the extreme, and might grow intolerable. As for the mother, she had had other plans for her darling; she not only sighed, but shed tears, when she heard of the engagement, and told her confidential friend that "poor Gertrude was throwing herself away."

She did what she could in a ladylike way to foster the girl's sense of unrest, and her feeling of unfitness for the life which she had chosen. The first result, as you have seen, had been to lead her to attempt to turn the young minister from his set purpose in life. For a time she believed she could succeed; she was in the habit of succeeding in most of her undertakings. She had coaxed, wheedled and cried her way into the fulfillment of all plans which she had cared to carry out; why should she fail in this, the most important one which had touched her?

But she failed, and she could not but see this as the days went by. Mr. Ransom could not even understand her. He gave her credit for too much principle to suppose that she could be sincere in her suggestions. He succeeded in convincing her that he, too, had convictions, and that to move him from some of them was impossible. The only alternative left to her was to break her engagement. A minister's wife she could never be; she found that she shrank from it in horror. She spent some miserable weeks; sorry for Mr. Ransom every time she met him; sorry for herself whenever she heard his name mentioned — as she frequently did — in admiration and praise.

She did not deliberately plan to hold him as her attendant for the season, and then turn him off as worthless; she made it plain to herself that it would be cruel to desert him so near the close of his seminary course; it might seriously unnerve him. The wiser way was to wait, to say nothing about it until he should have graduated; people could write such things better than they could talk them. If she were a man, she would rather have information of this kind on paper than to try to meet face to face the one who was giving it. Yes; it was altogether the better way, the Christian way, indeed. So she kept her own counsel, and pressed moral science and intellectual philosophy, and every other high-sounding name she could, into the spaces where she might have been expected to have leisure for him, and bore with what gravity she could his earnest appeals to her not to over study.

So this was the letter which the young minister had taken to his room to read with locked doors; so that the joy of the next half-hour could by no possibility be interfered with. How utterly it had dashed to the ground, without a moment's warning, the cup which had seemed to him to be brimming with hope and happiness! He was not crushed outwardly; strong natures such as his rarely are. Within the hour he appeared at the family dinner-table much as usual; talked with his father concerning the news of the day; gave his usual thoughtful attention to his mother and sisters, and only his twin sister, Helen, knew that he was in any way different.

It was to her that he told the whole story, in course of time; at least, I mean he told his side of the whole story; he could not have told Gertrude Temple's side. Even after this experience he did not understand her. He had not admitted to his own heart that she was deliberately false; he had said that she was too humble, too distrustful of her own powers, and had been influenced by others to adopt the idea that she was not fitted to the life to which his profession called her.

"She has a worldly mother," he said, with a long-drawn sigh; "I have no doubt that her mother opposed our engagement; I felt it from the first. And Gertrude, of course, was influenced by her mother. Helen, she is not heartless; I will not have you think so. It is not necessary to wrong her, even in thought, because she is lost to me. She is very young, and less mature than girls of her age often are; she has depended upon her mother a great deal, I think. Of course, she did not care for me as I do for her; we are unlike in that respect; but undoubtedly she thought she did, and she is not to be condemned, so young as she is, and under such influences as she has been all her life, because she made a mistake."

Outwardly, after that, life moved on in about the same channel as before, for Maxwell Ransom. To his mother, who was a frail, suffering woman, to be shielded from all possible pain, and cared for and comforted in every way, he told only the extreme surface of his story. Of course, she knew that he had been engaged, and of course she must know that the engagement was broken.

"It seemed wisest, mother," he had said, with a grave smile; "I know I have held very strict views on that subject heretofore, but this is one of those rare instances in which it becomes right to break one's pledge. Do not worry about it, mother dear. 'All things work together,' you know."

And his mother, looking wistful, yet hesitating to question where he so manifestly did not care to tell, said presently:

"Well, my son, of course we are not sorry to have you all our own once more; only " —

"Only you don't want my heart broken," he

said, bending to kiss her, and trying to speak lightly; "it is not, mother, and you do not need, I think, to be assured that I have not been instrumental in breaking the heart of another."

It was impossible not to let his voice tremble over that sentence, and of course it told his mother a great deal. She asked no questions; but from that hour she had her own private opinion of Gertrude Temple.

It was only Helen, as I said, who knew all that her brother could tell; and she, who had been in some respects mother as well as sister, could not help watching him with some anxiety during the months which followed. His first step bewildered her. He declined, in a very positive manner, the unanimous call of a church in a distant city; a church in which she had supposed him to be deeply interested; one which, indeed, had apparently been waiting for him, and he had certainly given them some encouragement to feel that he would consider their call.

"I am distressed over that," he said, walking nervously about his room, while Helen sat at his desk; she had just been reading his emphatic refusal of the call, and reminded him that they would have reason to be disappointed.

"I am very sorry I gave them any encouragement; they will think that I have something better in mind."

"They cannot think that," said Helen, "because

you have been very plain in your explanation so far as all such points are concerned; but, Maxwell, there is a reason for your refusal; do you mind telling me what it is?"

"No," he said, after a moment's hesitation; "it is not worth while for me to mind telling you — my other self — anything, but it is a humiliating reason. Gertrude's uncle lives in that city, and attends that church, and Gertrude herself will be there a large portion of the season. I could not become the pastor of the church under such circumstances."

"No," she said, "you could not, of course; I understand." But she sighed as she spoke; it was a very flattering call to a beautiful, growing city, and she had ambitions for her brother.

Not only did he decline the call to the city church, but he accepted the very next opening which came, and it happened to be to serve the plain little church in the farming village, eight miles from where Stephen Mitchell lived.

So now we have gotten back to the breakfast-table at the manse, and to Helen's plans for the afternoon. Her plans had not been made without careful thought; she had only been installed about three weeks as mistress of her brother's home; but it had not taken three weeks for Helen Ransom to discover that the experience through which the brother had passed had not left him unscarred. He was certainly changed, and the change was one which made her anxious. He had been a genial young man, and one who was exceedingly interested in human nature, especially as it was exhibited in young people. Not alone was he interested in those of his own circle, but more particularly in the struggling ones, or those who were from any cause disheartened. She had often thought with pride of what a power he would be among young men.

It had not taken three weeks of careful study of her brother's congregation to discover that if there were not struggling and discouraged ones among them, there were certainly those who needed elevating; needed to have an influence come into their lives, different from any which had yet touched them. But she had discovered, also, that her brother had lost his interest, apparently, in humanity. He preached his sermons with energy and earnestness, it is true, and they were studied sermons — intellectual, cultured, wrought out with utmost care — and as cold as polished marble. They flowed smoothly over the heads of his hearers without touching the current of their thoughts. The truth is, the young minister was doing what he could to cover up the pain and disappointment of his life by losing himself in his books.

He was a born student, and books had a power to absorb him, so that he could forget himself, and his friends; yes, and, in a sense, his work. He shrank from society. He admitted it to himself; people, especially young people, became utterly distasteful to him; he felt out of sympathy with all their interests. His sister felt this, and knew the cause of it. She knew also that it would distress him some day to discover that he had let precious time run to waste. She had waited silently, but prayerfully, for the awakening, and had reached the conclusion that her brother should be roused. She had wondered during yesterday's service, as she looked frequently at Stephen Mitchell, whether possibly he were the one to help in this matter. There was something about the boy which greatly interested her, though she could not have explained why; and the reports she had received upon inquiry had not been calculated to deepen the interest.

"Oh! I know whom you mean," Fanny Bascome had said; "it is Steve Mitchell. He lives away out on one of the cross roads, on a farm that is all run down. It never was managed right, pa says, and is mortgaged for more than it is worth. They are dreadfully poor. Yes; there's a a father and mother. Steve is the only son, and there is one girl. She is an odd creature; always fussing with her clothes, trying to make them look like something; and it would just kill you to see her. She hasn't things to do with, you know, and she makes herself into a perfect fright — trying to follow the fashions. Why, yes; I know them just as you know people who have lived in the same neighborhood with you all their lives. They live on the old Mitchell place; Stephen's grandfather used to own it. He was a nice kind of a man; quite smart, they say. I wonder that none of his family took after him. But Josiah Mitchell, Stephen's father, has never been of any account; shiftless, I guess; anyhow, things have gone to wreck and ruin pretty generally around them. Oh! I never go out there. They don't have anything to do with other people; they can't, you know, they are so poor. Steve is a regular country bumpkin; the poor fellow will blush as red as a peony if a girl bows to him on the street; and as for coming to church, he doesn't do it once in an age. I suppose he is a hard sort of a boy. Ma thinks the mother has more to her; she went out there to see her once or twice, years ago. But she never comes to church, nor has anything to do with other people, and I don't suppose she is much better than the rest of them.

"It is a miserable kind of neighborhood, Miss Ransom; what few people there are scattered along that road don't appear to amount to any-thing. There is a Lucas set out there some-where. I have heard Ned talk about the Lucas boys; they are drunkards, every one of them, and I suppose they are just a terrible lot. O, well! as to doing anything for them, how can you? There is no way of getting hold of such people.

You can't mingle with them, of course, and they won't come to church, so you can't even preach at them. I don't know, I'm sure, whether the Lucases have ever been asked to come to church or not. I don't suppose anybody ever thought of such a thing. Dear me! they needn't wait to be asked. I don't know as anybody ever asked us to come," and Fanny Bascome finished the sentence with her usual little giggle.

CHAPTER XIII.

PLANS FOR A THROUGH LINE.

NEVERTHELESS, Helen Ransom continued to be interested in Stephen Mitchell. She had resolved, as we are aware, that his family should be called upon that very afternoon, and that she and her brother would ride there for that purpose, notwithstanding the fact that she knew he had not been on horseback since one bright day in the early spring, when he rode with Gertrude Temple.

Miss Ransom had never seen Gertrude Temple in her life, but she had a supreme contempt for that young woman, and resolved that by so much, at least, the power of association connected with her should be broken. Her brother should ride with her. She would urge it on the ground of her own enjoyment of that exercise, and let him understand that she considered it selfish in him to debar her from it. Those two arguments, she knew her brother well enough to realize, would be potent with him. He had no desire to nurse his disappointment at the expense of other people's pleasure.

"Oh! my sakes," said Sarah Jane Mitchell, gazing from her upper window away down the road, "what a cloud of dust! Look here, mother, quick! Here's a woman coming on horseback. My! doesn't she ride pretty, though? I declare, if it ain't Mr. Ransom with her, and she's that girl I see in church Sunday. I do wonder who she is. Don't they look nice together, mother? If I could ride a-horseback like that, wouldn't it be too splendid for anything? She's got a dark blue — mother, as true as you live and breathe, they are coming here. They have turned up our lane. O, good land! What will I do now? Say, mother, do go down and tend to them, won't you? It's the minister, you know, and he will have to see you. Just to think of his coming here to call on us! I'm all in a fluster. But I must put on my green dress before I can come down; this one ain't fit to be seen. O, good land of pity! Do hurry, mother. He's got her off her horse, and they're coming up the stoop together."

In the wildest excitement, Sarah Jane dashed like a great green grasshopper about her room, putting herself with frantic haste into her green dress, twice buttoning it wrong in her hurry, and at last, very red of face and almost breathless, made her way downstairs just as her mother was coming up to call her.

"I don't know how they did it," she explained to Stephen afterward, "but they hadn't been here three minutes before I felt as though I had known them all my life. They were just as nice and easy and pleasant as if we were old friends. Mother, she did it up real nice, too; you would have been proud of her, Steve. 'This is my daughter,' she said. And Miss Ransom got up and came over to me just like a queen;' oh! a great deal nicer than a queen, because she would have been stuck up; Miss Ransom wasn't a bit. She held out her hand and said: 'How do you do, Miss Mitchell? I saw you in church Sunday. I am so glad to know you,' and she kept hold of my hand, and turned to the minister, and said, 'My brother, Mr. Ransom, Miss Mitchell.' And then he shook hands as cordial as could be, and said he was glad to meet some of his flock away out here; that he hadn't known until to-day that his people were so far out. And then they both sat down and talked just as pleasant as if they were real glad to talk to us; and mother told them how far she was from church, and how much church was to her, and all that."

But one of Miss Ransom's remarks had astonished Sarah Jane.

"I hope your brother is at home, Miss Mitchell? We want especially to meet him, and ask him about some people of whom he was telling me yesterday. And my brother wants to make his acquaintance."

"Steve?" Sarah Jane had said in bewilderment, turning a rosier red than before, and looking over helplessly to her mother.

"Why, yes," said Mrs. Mitchell, who, in the days gone by had had knowledge of pastoral calls, and knew how to conduct herself, "Stephen is at home; he is digging potatoes. Sarah Jane, you run and find him, will you? And tell him the minister is here. I am sorry my husband isn't home," the mother had continued; "he has gone up the road a ways this afternoon; he'll be real sorry not to see you."

And then Sarah Jane had gotten herself out of the room, much astonished. How well her mother conducted the conversation. How nice it was for her to say that about father. But Steve, how was she going to manage about him? Ministerial calls, or any calls, for that matter, had been unknown quantities in the Mitchell family for years, and the idea of inducing Steve, with his horror of all womankind especially, to come in and receive a call, was not to be entertained for a moment. She followed him like one dazed, as, having received her astounding news, he dropped his hoe suddenly, and went toward the water trough to wash his hands.

"I don't look over and above respectable," he said, surveying himself ruefully; "but if you will slip up the back stairs, Sarah Jane, and get my coat, I reckon I'll do."

"Yes," said Sarah Jane, almost breathless, "I

will;" and as she dashed up the back stairs in eager haste, she wondered to herself if "barbarian," and "civilization," and "champion" could have anything to do with Steve's astonishing behavior.

While the minister interested himself in Stephen Sarah Jane was lifted to the seventh heaven of delight by the realization that Miss Ransom was actually giving the most of her attention to herself. She asked her innumerable questions about the farm, the animals, the garden, the woods in the vicinity, and the wild flowers that bloomed there, and seemed to be interested in her answers. Presently she roused to the fact that the minister was addressing her.

"I beg you pardon, Miss Mitchell; but may I interrupt you for a moment to ask my sister a question?"

"Helen, what would you think of waiting here for me while Mr. Mitchell pilots me to the Lucas home? He tells me that across lots it is a comparatively short walk; and I would like to be introduced by him to the family, if it can be arranged."

Miss Ransom expressed herself as entirely willing to remain as long as should be necessary, and Sarah Jane forgot to be overwhelmed with delight over this new plan, in her astonishment that "Steve" was actually going to pilot the minister across lots to the Lucases'. What could have made him willing to do it? She had never known Steve to act like that before in his life; she gazed on him with almost anxiety. A vague feeling that he might be going to die, and that this was some mysterious process of "getting ready," such as she had heard about, flitted through her mind. But Stephen looked exceedingly unlike a youth who was failing in health or strength; his cheeks had never been redder, and his eyes had a look in them such as she had never noticed before. He was evidently willing to take the minister across lots, else he would not have explained that there was any such route.

It was a charming September afternoon, not too warm for comfort. Part of the way across the fields led along the margin of a gurgling brook, which the minister, at least, admired very much. It had not occurred to Stephen Mitchell before this, that it was a subject for admiration.

"I know very little about farming," said the minister, looking around him with interest, and sending his eyes away across the level fields; "I have often wished that I had had opportunities in my boyhood days to study farm life. I like the country; everything about it interests me. I believe I should have made a good farmer if I had begun early enough. Do you like the work?"

"No," said Stephen frankly; "I hate it."

"Do you? I am sorry to hear that. It always seemed to me such clean, healthful, independent work. Then, too, it would be so interesting to watch the constant and marvelous changes, and to experiment and improve from year to year."

Stephen eyed him with a half-doubtful, half-cynical expression.

"I would like to know how!" he burst forth at last; "there ain't no changes about it, so far as I can see. It's just hoe, and dig, and plough, and harrow, and all them things, over and over and over again till you're sick and tired of the whole of it; at it early and late, day after day; just tugging along."

"Oh! but you forget the harvests. Think of the pleasure of seeing things grow that your own hands have planted; watching them develop from day to day, getting stronger, moving toward maturity, moving as steadily as they can toward that for which they were created. Then there is the experimenting to see what sort of seed will produce the best results; what sort of care such and such seeds need, and whether, by a little extra effort, you can produce a greater harvest, or one better in quality than was ever produced on that piece of ground before, and so create a demand for your work in the market. Oh! I should think it would be very fascinating work; the returns are so quick, and in a sense so sure."

Stephen was silent and very thoughtful. This was a phase of farm life which had never been presented to him before. There were little hints

MR. RANSOM PRESENTS A NEW PHASE OF FARM LIFE.

in it which held his admiring thoughts. He might like to do something of that kind. But he presently presented some of his objections.

"You can't do any of them things unless you are rich. Poor folks that ain't got anything to do with, must just plod along in the same old way, day in and day out; and fight with bugs and worms, and all kinds of pesky things that are doing their level best to upset what little harvest you can get. This land is all run out, anyhow."

"Then I should learn how to revive it," said the minister briskly. "There are ways of rejuvenating land, you know; making it young and fresh again. I have a friend who is studying in that line now; he is trying to find out just what changes to make in his field that will enrich the land. He has been reading and studying in that direction for some months — years, indeed, I may say. He has advanced some theories already which have upset the old ideas. And, what is better, has proved by his own experience that his theories are probably correct. No; I think you are wrong about its needing money. It is like most other things, my friend; it needs brains and perseverance, and pluck in the face of difficulties. Do you intend to be a farmer, Mr. Mitchell?"

It was certainly a simple enough question, yet there was something about it which made the blood flush to Stephen's very temples. Nobody had ever asked him before in his life what he meant to be. I am not sure that it had ever occurred to him that he ever could be anything in particular; he had just expected to live along somehow, getting through with days' works and getting to bed, only to get up in the morning to another day's work. This, until his ambition had been aroused about that curious list of words, and whereunto they were expected to lead, he had not planned. There had simply been born into his heart a desire to know the meaning of words. He looked up with a sudden accession of interest into the minister's face, and found that young man's keen gray eyes fixed upon him, studying him, apparently. He dropped his eyes under the gaze, and half-laughed as he said:

"I don't know, I'm sure. There ain't anything else for me to be. I don't know as I ever expected to be anything. I have to work on the farm, you see; we've got that, and we ain't got anything else; and father ain't able to do the work alone. I don't suppose I'd do it if I could help it; but I'm here, and have got to stay here. I ain't a farmer, though; I ain't anything, and I can't say that I have any notion of being."

"Why don't you take hold of the farm?" said the minister, speaking with eagerness; "put all your energies into it, and your knowledge and skill, and become such a farmer as people in this part of the country have never seen; become a farmer who will be quoted in agricultural papers

PLANS FOR A THROUGH LINE. 153

as one who knows, and whose opinion is to be received with all due respect. Lead off in new lines, and make yourself a power in all these directions; I believe you could do it."

Silence again on Stephen's part, and that peculiar thrill running through his veins which reached to the ends of his toes. Perhaps what Stephen Mitchell needed, more than anything else in life, was some one to believe in him; some one to think that he could be other than a blundering boy, who was barely trusted to go to the village on the weekly errands.

"The farm ain't ours," he said at last; "it's mortgaged — a big mortgage, I guess. I never asked how big, but I know it takes all the life out of father to think of it."

"Why don't you pay the mortgage?"

Mr. Ransom said the words as composedly as if they had been, "Why don't you kick that stone out of your way?"

Stephen caught his breath, and answered:

"That's what he's been struggling at 'most as many years as I am old, but he ain't got it done."

"No; I don't mean your father. He is getting to be an old man, and should be taken care of and treasured. I mean you. Why don't you take hold of that mortgage and get rid of it?"

"Me?"

"Certainly, you. You are just beginning life, with splendid health and strength, and with all your powers ready to develop in the direction in which you choose to push them. You are just the one to take hold of such a burden. It would take years, of course, but you have years to spare. If I were you, I would grapple with it."

"I don't know anything about it," said Stephen excitedly, and his voice was growing irritable — a sure sign that the minister had accomplished his object, and thoroughly roused the young man. He would not be likely to drop the subject again. His companion understood him, at least sufficiently well to answer wisely:

"Of course you don't. If I understand you correctly, you have not given the matter any thought, have not intended to accomplish. This being the case, you are not prepared with the ways of doing it most successfully. But there is such a thing as learning, my friend. Find out how. Take hold of it with the energy which any work worth doing deserves. Throw yourself into it, not as a life-work, but as a means toward an end."

"Not as a life-work." Stephen caught at that sentence. Suppose he should take hold of this farm. Given the possibility that he could find out how to do it, and make a success of it — even pay off in the end at least a part of the mortgage — it seemed to him that it would take a lifetime in which to do it. After he had accomplished that, what else would he be fit for in the world?

"Not as a life-work?" he said aloud, in an inquiring tone. What did the minister mean him to think about as a life-work? "Seems to me that a fellow who would do all that you have been telling of, would need a lifetime to do it in."

"Oh! I don't doubt that. I do not mean that I would not be a farmer all my life, if I considered that was my place in the world. It is a good, useful, healthful life; a grand life, if you make it such. But, after all, it is, as I have said, a means to an end. The true life-work, you know, Mitchell, is to get ready to graduate."

"Graduate!" Stephen could only repeat the words with a helpless stare.

"Yes, certainly. We are at school, you know, down here — just getting ready, educating our souls — and on graduation day we will receive our diplomas, and go home to do the work which has been planned for us. That's the real life. This life is such a little time; it takes all our powers to get ready for commencement."

CHAPTER XIV.

STOCKHOLDERS IN COUNCIL.

COULD the man mean dying? Stephen thought over the sentences with a strange awe in his heart. He knew that word "commencement." It was a sweet morsel on Fanny Bascome's tongue; she had a cousin who had graduated. But he had never heard the word used in this way before.

"Have you taken hold of that study yet?" asked the minister, after he thought the silence had lasted long enough.

"I ain't taken hold of nothing," answered Stephen, shortly.

"Then you have lost a good deal of time; if I were you, I would let no more wasted days pass. And about the farm work, though I am personally ignorant, I think I can put you in the way of getting started. This friend of whom I spoke has piles of agricultural papers, magazines, books — everything, indeed, which could be needed. He will be glad to lend them to me, and we might look over them together, and see if we find the starting point. Now, what about the Lucas family? How low down the scale are they, and what have you been trying to do for them? How did you first become interested in them?"

Was he interested in them? It seemed to be taken for granted that he was. In fact, he was their "champion." He remembered how those soft gray eyes had brightened as their owner used the word.

"They're as low down as they can get, I guess," he made answer; "I never see any folks as low before. Drink is the matter; the father and the three boys, all of them drink; get drunk, you know, and tear around and act like crazy folks. The women folks are afraid of them. They knock the little girls around some, I guess; and of course they're poor, and they live like pigs. We ain't had nothing to do with them; father had a horror of their coming around our place; he would hardly speak to them when they did come — even the little chap — so as not to get them used to coming, you know. Then the woman got sick, and they sent for my mother. That was last week; she did for them, and she has been there two or three times since. Folks, when they get sick, some way, want mother. And the girls were awful glad over what she done. That's about the whole of it; I went with mother, that's all I did. Oh! while I waited for her I done two or three little things, of course, that she wanted done; but I don't know how to do anything for such folks. Mr. Meadows said they needed civilizing. There's the cabin where they live, off there to the left; you can tell by the outside of it what the folks must be. It's the worst spot, by all odds, anywhere around us. The most of the other folks are kind of decent, at least; though they drink some, a good many of them."

"It is the old story," said the minister gravely. "Have you noticed how often rum is at the bottom of all sorts of troubles? Well, I am glad, as I said, that the Lucas family have found a friend in you. I think you are mistaken in your idea that you cannot help them. Living as near them as you do, you will probably be able to do more for them than others can. My sister told me I would find you especially interested in them, and ready to help."

Whereupon Stephen made what must have seemed to the minister a very irrelevant answer.

"What is the meaning of 'champion,' sir?"

Mr. Ransom turned his eyes away from the distant hills, which he had been studying as he walked, and studied the face of Stephen Mitchell.

"It's derivation, or, that is, its original meaning you refer to, of course; why, it comes from the Latin word *campus*, which means field, and used to have exclusive reference to field-battles, or, rather, to persons who took part in them."

"I reckon I ain't after any such meaning," said Stephen, bewildered; "ain't there a way in which folks use it now, different from that?"

"O, yes! for instance, I might use it in connection with yourself and the family about which we have been talking. We will say, for purposes of illustration, that the neighborhood looks down upon them, scoffs at any effort which may be made to better their condition, or to reach them morally, and you stand up as their champion, explaining that circumstances have been against them, and that they ought not to be left to poverty and misery; that people ought to take hold and help lift them. Such being the case, I might call you their champion, because you are prepared to engage in the contest that is going on about them. Do you get the idea?"

"Yes," said Stephen; and that peculiar gleam of satisfied intelligence shone for a moment on his face. This must have been what "she" meant when she called him the Lucas family's "champion." Was he? If it meant taking hold and lifting them up, what was there he could do? Undoubtedly they needed lifting, but so did he.

"Are you engaged in the study of words?" asked Mr. Ransom, watching with interest the changing expressions on his companion's face. "That is an excellent plan, and one that might be made to work two ways; if you should fall into the habit of asking questions of your friends as to the meaning of the words they use, they might learn to be more careful in their choice of words — try to fit them better to those with whom they converse. Is it proper to ask what suggested the word about which we have just been talking?"

"I heard a man use it one day," said Stephen evasively; then, after a moment's pause, he did what for him was a surprising thing; he began at the beginning, and told the minister the entire story of his experience at the encampment, and afterward. Not only of the long list of words, but in what surprising ways the meaning of some of them had been revealed to him; keeping silent only in regard to the portion of the story which referred to his father's past. Mr. Ransom listened with deep interest and ever-increasing surprise.

"That is certainly a very original idea," he said, when the story was finished.

His record completed, Stephen, with his face ablaze, had time to ask himself how it was possible that he had made such a revelation to a stranger. He had not even told Sarah Jane.

But the minister repeated his words: "An original idea, and an excellent one. Do you say you have a hundred and three words on your list? Undoubtedly, by the time you reach the end, you will have made a very fair start toward self-education. So you are engaged in watching people, to see how many of the words they use, eh? and what suggestion their connection gives as to the probable meaning? That is an exceedingly interesting plan. I would like to help you, and myself at the same time. Won't you give me a copy of your list of words, and let me see what ones among them will fit into my next sermon, and whether I can use them in a sensible manner, so that light will be thrown upon their meaning? We use a great many words so vaguely that it would probably be impossible for a listener to get a correct idea of their meaning, merely from our use of them. I think I have learned something this afternoon which will help my sermons in the future. I hope I may have a copy of the list?"

By this time they had reached the Lucas doorway, from which "Dele" and "Mime" ran like frightened deer as they saw the approach of strangers. Father and son, fortunately, were absent from home, but the frightened little woman, who had to pose as the head of the family, succeeded in answering the minister's questions only with "Yes, sir," and "No, sir," getting voice once, however, to say, in an expostulatory manner: "O, Mirandy! don't sweep now, for pity's sake. You'll choke us to death." For Miranda, overcome, apparently, by the magnitude of the situation, and filled with shame as to her surroundings, could find no better way to vent her feelings than to seize upon a stump of a broom, which occupied a conspicuous place leaning againt the front window, and begin to raise a whirl of dust not two feet away from where she had seated their guests.

"Well, I don't care," she said, in answer to her mother's petition; "it needs sweeping, if ever a room did. 'Tain't fit for nothing but a pigsty, anyhow, them young ones keep it in such a muss all the time. I thought I'd just dig out a place for his chair to set."

"Oh! do not mind me," said Mr. Ransom heartily; "I am seated all right, my friend. I would rather have a visit with you, just now, than to have the room swept."

And he prided himself upon maintaining his gravity, and rejoiced in the thought that his sister was a mile away. Had she been there to exchange glances with him, he felt that he must have laughed.

Thus seconded, the old lady renewed her petition, and Miranda was persuaded to put the broom in the corner. But the presence of the carefully dressed stranger had succeeded in awakening in her heart such a longing after respectability as would not be subdued. She seized upon "Dele," who, in an unfortunate moment, thrust her head in at the half-open door, and dragged her, an unwilling victim, into the room.

"Here, you Dele! Come along here, this minute. Flora Ann, hand me that comb up there on the shelf, behind the teacups. I'm going to have this young one's hair combed before she is a half an hour older. I never did see such a looking fright. And company come! I'm just ashamed of the whole set, anyhow."

Flora Ann handed the comb in silence, and there began a vigorous onslaught on the tangled locks of the unwilling "Dele." Flora Ann retreated to the doorway, and began an undertone conversation with Stephen, who felt utterly out of place, and bewildered.

"Who is he?"

"He's the minister down in the village — the new one, you know. He is round making calls, and getting acquainted with folks."

"What for?"

"Why," said Stephen, "that is the way they do, I suppose."

"I never heard of it," said Flora Ann emphatically; which was certainly a comment worthy the thought of Christian people, for Flora Ann had lived but a few miles away from a so-called Christian community all the fifteen years of her life.

Helen Ransom rode home, satisfied with the result of her afternoon's experiment. It had been pleasant to talk with the eager-eyed girl at the farmhouse, and watch the light of satisfaction in the mother's faded face while she did so. It had been pleasant to think of Stephen as having the benefit of a two hours' visit with her brother; but, after all, her special satisfaction was derived from the evident effect which the afternoon had had upon the minister. He rode home with a light in his eyes such as she had not seen for weeks, and with a certain ring in his voice which she recognized as belonging to the strong-souled, energetic young man she used to know. The very manner in which he sat his horse, told her of roused energy and interest.

"We must get hold of those people, Helen," he said; "there is great work to be done in this direction. That wretched home I visited — you have no idea of it. Children growing up there who are to go out in the world, and influence it for good or ill. It is only too evident that it will be for ill, unless they are rescued. Intelligent faces they have, too, some of them; especially the girl of fifteen or so, and, for that matter, 'Mirandy' has energy enough."

There followed an outburst of laughter; and he gave Helen a graphic account of the sweeping and hair-dressing scenes, turning almost immediately from its comic side to repeat with earnestness:

"They must be gotten hold of. I rely upon you, Helen, to study ways and means."

"Cannot Stephen get hold of them?" she asked; and then he laughed again.

"Poor Stephen," he said, "what a task he has undertaken. He is really an unusual boy. I am deeply interested in him. Yes; I do not know but he can, after he has learned how; but, in the first place, somebody must get a thorough hold of him. He is already roused; he will grow in some direction, and that rapidly, I think. He has started to grow in the most original way possible."

Then he told the story of the list of words, and the progress which had already been made in learning their meaning, and of the list which was to be made for him.

"I shall have rare assistance in the preparation of my next sermon," he said laughing. "I wonder how many of his words I can work in, and what ideas I can give him in connection with them?"

So, talking and planning, he forgot to think that his life was wrecked, and that henceforth for him there could be only a shadowed happiness. It was not that he had resolved to be unhappy, but that in his youth and inexperience he had supposed that unhappiness, or at least unhappiness in certain directions, was his heritage.

Helen, as she watched him, and saw the change in his face, and felt the healthful reawakening of his mental and moral nature, blessed not only Stephen and Sarah Jane in her heart, but the whole Lucas tribe as well. And she began that very afternoon her plans for getting a stronger hold upon them. She had her side of the story to tell at the tea-table, which was a brighter and pleasanter meal than she had enjoyed heretofore in her brother's home.

"You cannot think how interested I am in Sarah Jane. I had supposed that my interest would center on Stephen, but the sister has attracted me strongly. She is not slow or quiet in her movements, like her brother; she tingles to her fingers' ends with energy. I presume a great deal of it has been misdirected; yet, after all, she has done wonders. Did you notice how neat her dress was? And how clean and free from dust the large, dreary parlor was, with its pathetic attempts at ornament? How can I get hold of the girl, Max, and give her a chance to imitate things which are worth the trouble? She is by nature an imitator; quick to feel and see what others do. That elder Miss Bascome says she makes a fright of herself in trying to copy in dress the girls whom she sees in church, or on the street, and that she does it without patterns, or instruction. I think she does remarkably well. I studied her dress this afternoon, with a view to discovering how much talent she had probably spent on it; and really, when one thinks of the complications of the present style, it was a success. I was interested in it, too, for another reason — because I myself selected the braid with which it is trimmed."

"You selected it?" with wonder and incredulity in his voice. There followed a history of the scene at the corner store; and the minister laughed over Mr. Pettibone's probable discomfiture, for neither was Mr. Pettibone a favorite in this household.

CHAPTER XV.

MORE PASSENGERS.

"CANNOT you set her to sewing?" asked Mr. Ransom presently, going back to the question which he had been asked.

His sister's face brightened. "That is an idea; how quick you are at planning! I have ever so much sewing to be done this fall. Mamma was so distressed about your loneliness that she hurried me away before I was ready. I wonder if I could get her to come here and sew with me? That would be accomplishing two or three things at once. I should get my work done a great deal sooner than though I had to plod along alone, and I could teach her a hundred little things which she does not know now. Do you suppose it will do on such short acquaintance to ask her to come?"

"I should not think a long acquaintance would be necessary in order to secure help in the sewing-room; but I am afraid there is another difficulty in the way. Stephen mentioned the fact that his mother is not very well, and that Sarah Jane did what he called the 'heft' of the work, and shielded her all she could. I suspect the poor old lady needs shielding; and we could not begin by teaching her daughter selfishness."

"No, of course; but I wonder if there isn't a way to plan? What about that fifteen-year-old girl? She wasn't the sweeper, was she? What if it could be arranged so she could take Sarah Jane's place in the home for a week or two, to help the mother? Couldn't she learn neatness, and some lessons in cookery, from the mother, and save her drudgery, while Sarah Jane was learning other lessons here?"

"Possibly," said the minister. "That would certainly be accomplishing two or three things at once. If Mrs. Mitchell's consent to such a scheme can be secured, it is decidedly worth trying. As for the Lucas girl, the contrast between her abiding place and the Mitchell home is as strong as that between earth and Heaven to some of us. Her surroundings are simply terrible. But I am afraid she is so low down that she does not realize it."

"All the more need of helping her up," said Miss Ransom, with decision. They sat late at the tea-table discussing the two households, and the possible changes which might be made in the near future. The minister, on the point of leaving the room, turned back to say:

"I believe I will not study to-night, Helen. I

will go out and make some calls upon my young men. My ride has rested me so that I feel equal to it."

"I think that is an excellent plan," said his sister, quietly; but her eyes danced with triumph. For this particular minister to resolve not to study, but instead to mingle with his people, was a step in advance.

Two days thereafter Mr. Mitchell, who had been to town for some needed supplies, created a sensation at the supper-table. He set down his cup, and fumbled nervously in first one and then another pocket, for several minutes.

"I'm bound if I know what I did with the thing," he said at last. "I thought I put it away as careful as if it was made of gold. Ha! I've found it;" and he produced a dainty envelope of purest white, and held it between thumb and finger for careful study.

"A letter!" said Sarah Jane, her cheeks flushing with surprise and excitement.

"I call that a neat thing," said Mr. Mitchell. "Look at that handwriting now. Plain as print, yet full of pretty flourishes. I tell you what it is, Sarah Jane, if you could write like that, it would be something to be proud of."

"Where did you get it? Out of the post-office?"

"I got it from the new minister. He came up to me in the store, bowing as polite as though I had been the governor, and wanted to know if I was Mr. Mitchell, and if I would do his sister the kindness to take a note for her to my daughter."

"To me!" said Sarah Jane; and as she reached forth her hand, Helen Ransom ought to have seen her eyes.

"Yes, sir; them's the words he said; and a pleasant-spoken man he is, too. He didn't start off right straight, either; he stood and talked to me for as much as five minutes, I should think. The doctor and some high-up folks came in, too, while he was there — he just bowed to them pleasant, as if he was glad to see them, and said 'Good-day,' but he kept right on talking to me. Well, Sarah Jane, what have you got there? Read out. If it is as plain writing inside as it is out, you can do it."

But Sarah Jane's cheeks were glowing like damask roses, and she was apparently lost to sound, in the contents of that wonderful letter. She was seventeen, but a dainty note, written on perfumed paper, had never reached her hands before.

"Well, of all things in this world!" she said at last; "who would ever have thought that such a thing could have happened?"

"How can we tell?" answered Stephen, trying to hide his own intense interest under gruffness. "We can't find out what has happened."

"Why, she wants me to come there and stay,

to her house, and sew. She has got a lot of plain sewing, she says, and she saw by the way I fixed my own things that I knew how to sew, and she needs my help, and she will give me a dollar a day and my board. Only think of that, Steve. A dollar a day for just sitting and sewing! And, mother, she says if you can't spare me because the work is too hard for you — and she should think it would be — if you would let the Lucas girl come over in my place and help you for a week or two, it would be a real blessing to the girl. Not the oldest one, she says, but the next one to her; that is Flora Ann, ain't it? She says she would — well, here, I'll read the letter to you, and then you will know just what they all say."

There had rarely been such excitement in the Mitchell house as that letter produced. "Something different" had certainly come to them. Sarah Jane invited out to sew by the day, at the enormous price of a dollar a day and her board! She was particular to add that statement whenever the terms were mentioned; and not less bewildering was the suggestion to have Flora Ann Lucas come and work for them. The Mitchells keeping hired help!

"I would have to pay her," said Mrs. Mitchell, dubiously. She had never paid any one for working for her, except through one week of her sorrowful life, years ago.

"Yes," said Sarah Jane; "of course you would

have to pay her something. But, land! she would be tickled to death to work for a dollar a week. And just think, mother, I could earn six while she was doing it, and learn a lot of things, besides, that would help me through all the rest of my life. Mother, I do hope you can do it. And then, you know what she says about it's being a help to Flora Ann."

The minister had been wise in making that statement, and his sister had been as wise as a serpent in repeating it. Both of them saw deeper into the little worn-out mother's heart than her children had done. They knew that the thought that she could help some one would be a very powerful argument in Flora Ann's favor. Still, it must be confessed that she shrank from the ordeal with a dread which they also could not have understood.

"Well," she said, at last, after a period of utter silence, during which she sat with folded hands, looking straight before her at nothing at all — "well, if you would like to go, Sarah Jane, and he would like to have her come, why, I'll do my best about it; though I don't know as I can help her — that is, if your father thinks best."

It was a confused sentence certainly, but the Mitchell family understood it; and the children turned inquiring eyes toward their father.

"I don't know as we can do anything else," he said; "they appear to want it pretty bad, and have got it all planned. I did want to keep clear of that Lucas set. But then, the girl ain't so bad, maybe — I dare say she ain't so bad but she might be worse — and it will give Sarah Jane a start, if it is the kind of start she wants."

"Well," said Mrs. Mitchell again, "I'm agreed to it. Not but what I could get along better without Flora Ann than with her; but if he thinks I could help her to be more neat, why, maybe I'd better try."

And so the momentous question was settled, Stephen saying absolutely nothing. It was not until an hour afterward that Sarah Jane, as she dashed about the kitchen, putting it in order, realized this fact, and charged her brother with it when he came in from his good-night visit to the barn.

"Say, Steve, you didn't say one word about my going to the minister's. Ain't it a queer thing to happen to me? And what do you think of it, anyhow?"

"I don't know," said Stephen; "I can tell better when you come back. It's a good chance for Flora Ann, I think; she can learn lots of things from mother; but what you can learn from them will have to be found out."

Sarah Jane faced around upon him with a bewildered stare.

"Steve, what do you mean?" she asked; "if they ain't high enough up to learn from, I would like to know who is."

"That's just it," said Stephen slowly. "Maybe they're too high up. When I was at the village the other day, I saw a book lying on the counter that somebody had been looking at; and while I was waiting for the clerk to get my sugar, I took it up. Says I to myself, 'How do I know but what some of my words will be in this, with a meaning to them?' and I looked the thing through from beginning to end, and couldn't make head nor tail to it. There wasn't one word that I could understand; and come to find out, the thing was Latin. So I was thinking that maybe they live in Latin at the minister's house, and you and I couldn't understand them yet awhile."

"O, my!" said Sarah Jane; "if you don't have the queerest notions. If I don't learn a few things while I am there, whether it is Greek or Latin, or whatever it is, then you can set me down for a dunce. And I never believed I was one — in some things, anyhow."

But perhaps, after all, the most bewildered one of all concerned was Flora Ann Lucas.

Stephen's conceit about people living in Latin, and not being able to help those who lived in English, might have applied better to her, if he had but known it, than to his sister. Flora Ann was only fifteen, and her family had been reduced to the lowest dregs of poverty through all the years which her memory reached. An empty cupboard and a broken stove, with little or no fuel, was the basis on which the Lucas family did their housework. It is, perhaps, not to be wondered at that they had long ago fallen out of the habit, as a family, of sitting down to eat their daily portion, but ate it, rather, by snatches, standing in the doorway, or hiding sometimes in the corner closet, when Jake was heard coming; often, very often, going without food from early morning until late in the evening. Flora Ann, indeed, was more accustomed to this than were any of the other members of the family. Whether her heart was more tender than her sister's, or whether Miranda felt the need of more food, it was certainly Flora Ann who oftenest saved her portion to be divided between the hungry-looking little girls, who had never, in all their miserable lives, remembered the hour when they had all they wanted to eat.

It was Stephen who went to make the bewildering proposition to the Lucas family.

"I didn't mean he should go there," said his father, sitting at home and looking drearily into the darkening west after Stephen strode away. "I meant to keep them separate always; but I don't know what has come over the boy; he seems to be different, somehow, from what he was before. I've always told him things to do; but when he said, in that kind of positive way, 'I'll go over there, mother,' it seemed as if he was grown up all of a sudden, and there wasn't anything to be said."

"I don't feel exactly afraid of the Lucas boys' influence over Steve," said Mrs. Mitchell; "they're dreadful different from him, and he don't hanker after them; and besides " — there was a little pause, and then, in a lower key, she added — "besides, he has gone on a good errand — gone to try to help them, Josiah — and it's my notion that folks get took care of that go on such errands."

"Me go over to your house!" said Flora Ann, staring. "What for? What does she want of help? Ain't Sarah Jane there? And what in time can I do to help her? I don't know how to work; I ain't had no chance to learn."

Stephen could not help giving a significant glance around the hopelessly dirty room, with its small-paned windows so thickly set with cobwebs, and soot, and fly specks, that it was scarcely possible to see out of them. He was tempted to say that it looked to him as though "chances" were plenty; but he refrained, and presented, as briefly as possible, an explanation of the mystery.

"Well, I don't know," said the mother of the family, pausing in the work of bumping a bundle of rags back and forth, in a rickety chair without rockers, in a vain effort to get it to sleep. "I like to be accommodating to the neighbors, and Mrs. Mitchell was terrible good to me when I was sick; but Flora Ann ain't never been anywhere to do things, and I don't know as I could spare her very well, though I like to accommodate."

Stephen drew himself up, and his face flushed; evidently his sense of the fitness of things was jarred.

"It ain't exactly accommodation," he said, with dignity; "Sarah Jane is going away, and mother needs some help, because she ain't very strong, and is willing to pay for it. But of course if you don't want Flora Ann to come, then I can go somewhere else."

"Pay for it!" echoed mother and eldest daughter in the same breath, and Miranda added:

"Good land of pity! Ain't some folks getting big? I didn't know your mother could afford to keep hired help. Ma, do for pity's sake let her go; she ain't of no account here, only just to stand around in the way, and I'd like dreadful well to get hold of the sight of a little money again. How much is your mother going to pay, Steve?"

"She will give her a dollar a week," said Stephen.

"A dollar a week!" echoed Flora Ann, her tone expressing volumes. She had never as yet earned a cent.

"I say let her go," said Miranda, with emphasis; "dollars don't grow around on bushes, not that I ever found; and there's her eating, besides, that counts for a good deal. Flora Ann is as willing to eat as anybody, when she can get a chance."

The dollar seemed also to have a very happy effect upon Mrs. Lucas, and it was settled that

Flora Ann should come the next morning. She followed Stephen to the door, looking frightened.

"I ain't fit to go," she said deprecatingly; "your ma looks so terrible nice, Steve — clean dress, and her hair slick, and everything. I am afraid I will be scared out of my wits, yet I'd kind of like to try it. Say, Steve, is she cross?"

"No," said Stephen; "but she won't stand no dirt, that's a fact; and you want to wash up, and comb your hair, before you come."

"I can comb my hair," said Flora Ann timidly; "but I ain't got no dress but this, Steve, just as true as you live. And it's an awful-looking dress; it needs washing and mending, but how can I do it when I ain't got nothing else to put on? If I had as many dresses as Sarah Jane, you would see me looking different."

Stephen turned, and, surveying the forlorn object from head to foot, gave her the most compassionate look she had ever received in her life. Certainly she was very different in appearance from Sarah Jane. It emphasized once more his respect for his own family — Sarah Jane actually being envied because of her dresses. And how had she sighed over the poverty of her wardrobe.

"Never mind," he said to the shamefaced girl; "if you ain't got anything but that, you can't help it. Fix up your hair the best you can, and come along; mother will show you how to clean up, somehow, I dare say. She always contrives to make things clean; I don't know how."

Flora Ann looked after him until in the gathering darkness he was but a speck in the distance; then re-entered the house, to attack and conquer her rebellious hair. It had a reddish tint, and was very curly. Stephen little understood the terrible task he had set for her.

CHAPTER XVI.

THROUGH A NEW COUNTRY.

IT is worthy of record that Flora Ann accomplished it. When she presented herself before Mrs. Mitchell's dismayed eyes quite early the next morning, her dress was an accumulation of terrors, but face and hands were reasonably clean, and her tangled mass of hair had certainly been through a terrible ordeal, and must have been amazed at its own subjection.

The next few days were successions of bewilderments to Flora Ann; what they were to Mrs. Mitchell it would perhaps be hard to explain. The first time the girl set the table for the family meal, her mistress, who had been half-frightened and wholly dismayed over the thought that she was her mistress, lost self-control entirely when she came to survey the finished task, and sat down on the first chair which presented itself, to laugh. The tablecloth was still lying on its shelf in the closet; the table was against the side of the wall. Three plates were set in a row on one side of it, and a cup without a saucer stood at each plate.

"I'll go down cellar after the things, and you can set the table while I'm gone. Plates, and cups and saucers, you know." Such had been the directions; the last clause being added in response to Flora Ann's bewildered looks.

"For pity's sake!" said Mrs. Mitchell, "do you call that table set?"

"You said plates and cups," answered the puzzled girl, "and I got them out. There's three of you, ain't there?"

"Why, yes, four of us, for that matter. Don't you expect to eat nothing at all? Is that the way you fix the table at your house?"

"No," said Flora Ann promptly; "it ain't the way at all; we don't fix no table. We just stand round and eat something when we can get it. But you said put the dishes on the table; any way, that is what I thought you meant."

"You poor thing!" said Mrs. Mitchell, checking her laugh, and speaking in a more compassionate tone than she had yet used. The depths of Flora Ann's ignorance and desolation were just beginning to dawn upon her. However, the laugh had done her good; she felt less frightened than she had before. "I'll just show you how to do it," she said, rising briskly, "then you can do it all by yourself next time. Set them dishes back in the pantry, and pull the table out into the middle of the floor. Sarah Jane is particular about having it just in the middle of the room, because we get the breeze then from both windows, and are out of the way of the sunshine. Now bring the tablecloth from the lower shelf in the corner. Open it out, child, and spread it on nice and smooth. If there is anything Sarah Jane hates, it's a tablecloth put on crooked, and it does' look kind of miserable and lop-sided, I think myself. Now set four plates at each end and side. No, no! I don't mean four along in a row, but four in all; like this, you know," and she briskly arranged the plates. "Now you want knives and forks, and the salt. Put the salt in the middle of the table, so that we can all reach it. And the cups and saucers you want to fix to my place, so; now get a plate for bread and another for butter, and a pitcher for milk, and then set the dishes for potatoes and ham on this corner, so that I can reach them handy when I come to dish up the things. Why, child, you don't want a plate for potatoes. Sarah Jane hates to see potatoes in a plate. That there platter in the corner is what we put ham on. Oh! you'll learn after a while. I didn't think but what you knew all them things, of course. I supposed everybody did. Now I'll dish up, while you go out and call Steve and his father. Then you come in and set down at the table along with the rest of us. You can set over there, and we will have our dinner like folks."

Ten minutes more and Flora Ann sat down for the first time in her life to a civilized and reasonably well-appointed dinner-table. She was helped to a generous piece of the ham; she had the potatoes passed to her; she had a cup of tea poured for her, and sugared and creamed; she ate such butter and such bread as had never before fallen to her lot. It is true she took a potato from the dish with her own fork, and helped herself to butter with the knife that she had just taken from her own mouth; but so did all the others. She copied them carefully, and believed she was being as royally served, and sustaining herself as well in her new position as it was possible for a lady to do. As for the taste of the wholesome food, properly cooked, it would be difficult to explain what it was to this half-starved girl. I take it as a mark of progress in her education that she refused the third large potato, and obliged herself to be content with four slices of bread, although she could have easily eaten more. This was her concession to what seemed to be the customs of civilization.

It was a week for Flora Ann to remember. Every step she took in this plain little home was new and bewildering. It seemed to her that she washed her hands so many times that the skin would begin to wear out; it seemed to her that she used soap enough to have stocked the village store; it seemed to her that the dishes to be washed and dried, and put away in their places, were so many as to be beyond her counting; it seemed to her that supper-time came, and the table had to be arrayed in white again, almost as soon as she had gotten it cleared away, so swiftly did the hours pass.

"She does not know anything at all," Mrs. Mitchell confided to her husband in the privacy of their own room, at the close of the second day's trial. "She beats all that I ever heard of. Why, Josiah, it is a burning shame to think that in this country, and just a step away from us you may say, there's been living all these years a girl who knew so little. But then, what could I have expected? I have been there and seen how they lived. But I never thought there was folks that didn't sit down to a table and eat their victuals like human beings. She broke the blue bowl. I don't know what Sarah Jane will say to that; she set great store by the blue bowl; but, dear me! the girl was so scared that I couldn't say anything; she acted as if she expected me to knock her over the head with the broom I had in my hand."

"Like enough she did," said Mr. Mitchell. "That's about the way she has been treated, I guess. Old man Lucas isn't so ill-tempered when he has been drinking as some folks are; but that oldest boy of his beats all I ever heard of for raging around at such times, and the most of his time is 'such times.' They say he rules the whole family. Silas Springer was telling me to-day that it isn't more than a couple of weeks since he knocked this girl down and kicked her."

"Oh! for the land of pity," said Mrs. Mitchell; and her old face was white with sympathy. She had been a drunkard's wife, and it had been misery enough, though she had never been knocked down nor kicked. "Well," she said, after a moment's silence, "I declare, I will do what I can for the girl. I thought twenty times to-day I couldn't stand it. You see we are clean by nature, and she does lots of things that rile your stomach; but I'll make out. Did you see how nice she looked in that old dress of Sarah Jane's? We thought it wasn't fit for anything but the rag-bag; but I got it out to-day and mended it, and I declare, she looked real fixed up in it. Her own was so poison dirty that I just couldn't stand it. I am going to have her put it into the wash-tub the first thing to-morrow morning. Dear me, Josiah, I thought we were poor. But I have come to the conclusion that we must be rich."

As for Sarah Jane, who shall describe what this experience of life was to her? What a thing it was to occupy a room whose bed was spread in purest white, whose windows were curtained with white muslin, whose floor was covered with a neat and tasteful carpet, and whose dressing-table had the pretty little accessories of the toilet arranged upon it. Sarah Jane, as she stood before the mirror, and combed and arranged her abundant hair, felt at times almost bewildered with the thought that it was actually she herself who was living this charmed life.

She put on her pretty light calico dress in the early morning "just like any lady in the land," she told herself, and went down with Miss Ransom to look at the dew-washed flowers in the little garden under the dining-room windows, and wait there for the tinkle of the bell which should call them to breakfast. That breakfast-table! If the table appointments in the Mitchell home were a revelation to Flora Ann, what shall be said of those in the manse, and their effect upon Sarah Jane? Not that they were extravagant, or startling in any way. Miss Ransom would have felt only astonished had she known how they impressed her guest. The linen was fine, but not too fine for daily use. The dishes made no noise upon the table, for the hush-cloth underneath the linen was as much a matter of course to Miss Ransom as the tablecloth itself. Silver knives and forks and silver teaspoons, laid at each plate, were the common necessities of life to her; so, also, were the large, fine, carefully-ironed napkins, which Sarah Jane surveyed with awe. The pretty napkin ring, made only of fine cardboard and tied with ribbon, was also a work of art to the young woman before whose place it stood. Then there were the dainty butter-plates, and the individual salts, and the pretty breakfast service at Miss Ransom's place, and the fruit-plates of delicate pattern, and the vases of roses at either end — all simple, appropriate belongings to the hour, viewed from Miss Ransom's standpoint. Viewed from Sarah Jane's, it was a glimpse of Eden. Then the sewing-room, where she sat all day and sewed, with no unskillful fingers, was another revelation to her, of art. Simply furnished, with the conveniences which belonged to the work to be done there, but so dainty and fair, and free from dust and disorder, that Sarah Jane could hardly repress a little sigh of satisfaction whenever she let her eyes wander about. She worked well in the sewing-room, and the mistress of it rejoiced in the great strides in knowledge which her handmaiden was taking. For Miss Ransom, who did not like long seams and minute details, knew how to plait, and gather, and puff, and fold, and drape after the most approved fashion of the day. Better than that, after a refined taste of her own, and the cunning of her fingers Sarah Jane was quick to catch.

"I never could guess how it was done," she said exultantly, as she folded away a finished skirt, the drapery of which exactly suited its fastidious owner. "I studied them kind of skirts time and again, going out of church and walking along the street, and how they got them to hang just like that behind, and so smooth and straight before, I never could make out. But it's easy enough, now that you know how; I could make one just as well as not."

"Most things are easy after you know how," said Miss Ransom, smiling; "things of that kind, I mean. I sometimes wish that the rule applied to the other part of us as well."

"What other part? I don't know as I see what you mean."

"Why, I was thinking of soul education, instead of that which belongs to the fingers, and of how many things we know in that line which seem to be hard to apply. I know, for instance, how to be gentle and patient and long-suffering; but sometimes I find it very hard to put my knowledge into practice."

"I shouldn't think you did," said Sarah Jane, surveying her with undisguised admiration; "I think you know them things just as well as the others. I know I'd have been fit to fly to pieces fifty times, if I had had anybody to teach that was as stupid and awkward as I have been; and you have been just as patient as one of them lilies over there, all the time."

Miss Ransom laughed.

"My dear, I haven't found it hard to be patient with you. I succeed extremely well, I find, with people who really try to please — who mean to give me the best that is in them. I confess I was thinking of Nancy when I first spoke. She tries me very much; for instance, by sweeping in the middle of the room, and leaving the corners and under the bed, and all out-of-sight places, undisturbed — 'eye-service,' you know. I haven't learned the lesson of long-suffering with such failings. All of which reminds me to ask you if you would mind going downstairs to set the table for dinner. Nancy is belated again, and I have the dessert to look after. Can you take the arrangement of the table into your hands?"

"I should like it first-rate, if I could do it," said Sarah Jane, and her eyes shone with pleasure. She might be swift with her needle, but housekeeping was her forte, and her fingers had fairly longed to handle the pretty dishes and fine napery, and discover for their owner whether they knew exactly how to arrange everything. This was after she had been in her new sphere for nearly a week.

The truth is, Miss Ransom's handmaiden was a source of unfailing satisfaction to her. She had found her not only deft-handed, but keen-sighted and clear-brained, and possessing a resolute determination to make the best of every scrap of opportunity which fell within her reach.

The mistress watched, with a smile on her face, to see her arrange the cloth in its exact position, and then finger the pretty dishes lovingly, as she might have done with flowers. She arranged, and re-arranged, not forgetting the smallest detail of the well-appointed table, but making it in every particular as she had seen it before; and as she could not have seen it in her own home, nor in other homes to which she had had access, Miss Ransom decided, and told herself, for the hundredth time that week, that the girl was certainly unusual. She was not supposed to be on the watch, though she sat in the little alcove, curtained off from the dining-room, which was supplied with writing-desk and easy-chair. This was for the minister to lounge in, with the latest papers and magazines at his command; and was a corner dear to the heart of the young mistress of the manse.

"The average man, you know, cannot wait comfortably for five consecutive seconds after he has been summoned to the dining-room," wrote Miss Ransom to her mother, when she gave a description of her household arrangements; "and Max is no better than the rest of them, except that he pretends patience, pacing solemnly to and fro while he waits for the 'dishing-up;' so I have planned an arrangement by which he may have a retiring-place, with a book or paper to occupy him during the aforesaid five seconds. My experience has been that man is a peaceable animal under such circumstances. Some people might wonder why I called the masculine part of my family before the final dishing-up took place; but you, my dear mother, will have no such wonder; for you know, by a life-long experience, how utterly impossible it is for a man to come to breakfast or dinner when he is called. He is sure, on ninety-nine occasions, to have something important to do that shall detain him 'just a minute' after the bell rings. Do you think I will run such risks, and let my dinner cool? Oh! I am learning how to manage Max beautifully. I only hope I can have the opportunity of educating his wife before she comes into power."

At this writing-desk, therefore, sat Helen Ransom, transcribing briskly certain papers of her brother's which she knew he needed for that afternoon, but not so preoccupied that she could not rejoice over the work going on a few feet from her.

"Sarah," she presently said, pushing the portière a little aside that she might have a view of the girl's face, "can you cut the flowers, and arrange them for the table?"

Then did Sarah Jane's cheeks flush, and her eyes glow with pleasure. Miss Ransom was well aware that the girl loved flowers — the wildwood ones, in the broken-nosed pitcher on her mantel at home, had told that story. And the look, half of delight, half of awe, with which she regarded the roses and jessamine strewn lavishly about the manse, repeated it. Now the crowning delight of the hour had come to her. She was to go to the garden among the flowers, and select for herself those which should adorn the table.

"Why, I'm afraid" — she said, pausing irresolutely, sunbonnet in hand.

"Well," said her mistress, with a reassuring smile, "afraid of what?"

"How shall I know which you want picked, and which I must let alone?"

"It is not the question which I want picked, but which you want. I asked you to gather flowers such as pleased you. You are to use your own taste, with the garden before you. There are no restrictions placed upon any of the flowers. Gather enough for the two table vases, and arrange them, please."

"Oh! I don't know how to fix them," said Sarah Jane, her face redder than before; "I never fixed no flowers in my life; but I can bring them in to you."

"I am much too busy just now, Sarah. Mr. Ransom's papers, that I am copying, must be ready for him at dinner. I can trust you. Arrange the flowers as you like to see them, and it will be quite right."

CHAPTER XVII.

LAYING A TRACK.

SHE laughed softly over the vases when they were finally set in triumph in their places. Bright-colored autumn flowers were beginning in all their glory, and Sarah Jane had reveled in them. Crimsons and yellows and scarlets abounded, being placed in contrast to each other, as if in a sort of wild ecstasy they had rejoiced in the display which they could make. This, she found, applied to only one of the vases; the other surprised and touched her. It had been placed in front of her own plate, and held only a single white rose.

"It looks like you," said Sarah Jane, pointing to it. "All white things do, Miss Ransom."

"Thank you," said Miss Ransom, her voice breaking into a laugh, and her tears very near the surface. It began to touch her deeply, and, in a sense, to humiliate her, to see the almost worship which this ignorant girl bestowed upon her. "Simply because I have treated her like a human being," she said to herself. "How starved the poor creature's life must have been all these years! I wish I could make it up to her. I wish I could give her such a hold upon life — the true life — that she could never be starved any more."

The week was also an interesting one to the minister in his study. He worked over his sermon as he never had before. His list of words had puzzled him — written with Stephen's untrained hand — and the orthography was so remarkable that more than once had the reader, alone at his study-table, thrown back his head and indulged in a hearty laugh at the poor fellow's expense. But he did more than laugh; he entered into this thing with the zest of a teacher bent on winning his pupil. If from the list presented before him he could gather a theme which would speak to the soul of this young man, and awaken it to vigorous and healthful action, so that it should not only become a soul saved, but a soul at work for the redemption of others, that would be an object worth living for.

"I will work for a soul," he said exultantly to himself. He read the list, not only with care, but with prayer. He conjectured rightly that a boy who had been so much interested in words had probably learned his list fairly well by this time. What a thing it would be if he could weave a large number of them into his subject, and still keep the central aim in view. No, after careful thought, he would not try for a large number; that would confuse the uncultured brain. He would choose, say, half a dozen strong, vigorous words which would weave into the thought he had in mind, and make it so plain as to force the one who understood them to think of their connections. He went down the list, with pencil in hand, in search of a key-note, and marked it presently with a great deal of satisfaction. "Sun of Righteousness" — what idea had that phrase conveyed to the mind of Stephen Mitchell? Not much, certainly. He was not used to figurative language of that character. The minister determined that the "Sun of Righteousness" should be his central figure. After that his work was easy. The next word should be "surrender" — no, "rescue." A world in darkness — no, a soul in darkness — lost in an impenetrable fog; a storm gathering, and the Sun of Righteousness rising to dispel it, to rescue the soul. Then came the word "surrender." It was a necessity in order to the rescue. Even the glorious Sun of Righteousness could not dispel the midnight of the soul, unless that soul willed it to be so — free to choose to walk in the dark if he would; free to choose to revel forever in glorious light and liberty. Then there was "bondage." He would like to picture a soul in bondage — the darkness of it, the hopelessness of it, the dire necessity for rescue. "Obstacles?" Yes, he could use that word. There were undoubtedly obstacles in the way; when did

Satan ever see a soul trying to escape from bondage that he did not invent them?

In short, the minister was held to his study that week by a sermon such as he had imagined he would preach in the days which already seemed so far behind him, but which since he had fairly entered upon the work of the pastorate he had been unable to prepare.

"Well," he inquired, as he grasped Stephen Mitchell's hand, having overtaken him in the aisle at the close of the next Sabbath morning's service, "how did it work, my friend?"

"I found them," said Stephen briefly, but with a significance in his voice which meant something positive, though the minister could not quite decide what.

"I had a feeling that you were so interested in that list that no word belonging to it could escape you. Did I succeed at all in making their meaning plain?"

"Why, yes," said Stephen; "plain enough. A fellow would have to understand what you were driving at. Part of them I am, I guess."

"And the other part you need," said Mr. Ransom, catching the boy's meaning. "Undoubtedly you need rescue. No soul, save those who have been to the Sun of Righteousness for light, but what walks in darkness. Have you any idea how much I thought of you and prayed for you while I was preparing that sermon? If you have, you will think about this matter, if only for the sake of comforting me." This with a half-laugh that had a touch of sadness about it, and was altogether winning. But Stephen was not to be won. He was intensely interested in the sermon so far as it was connected with his list of words; he was interested in the minister — he wanted to see more of him, hear more of him, and to learn words. But no ray from the Sun of Righteousness had yet penetrated his heart. On the contrary, he felt in a sense disappointed because Mr. Ransom was trying to turn his thoughts in that direction.

"I don't know nothing about religion," he said, as he drove slowly homeward alone; Sarah Jane's work being not yet finished at the manse. "I don't know nothing about religion, and I don't want to know; not yet awhile. There is lots of other things to learn first; I just wish he wouldn't pitch it at a fellow. He ain't like the other ministers; none of them ever troubled me before. I like him the best of any of them, to be sure, but I don't want to know about them things. Queer, though, how he fitted in them words — six of 'em, and he acted just as though they were made to fit them places; he's a smart fellow. I wish't I knew just a little corner of what he does."

"O, Maxwell!" his sister said, as soon as they were together in the privacy of his study, "you preached a sermon for me this morning. The kind I want and have been watching for."

"I preached for a soul," he said eagerly; "I am fishing for a soul, Helen."

"I know — I was so glad to hear the ring of it; didn't you notice what a different impression it made upon the people? They went out ever so much more quietly than usual. Not a person told me 'what a lovely sermon that was.' But I heard Deacon Watson ask young Mr. Simmons if he could not begin to come to the prayer meeting again, now that the summer's hurry was over. Oh! depend upon it, Maxwell, such sermons will bear fruit."

Such words were pleasant to the young minister's ears; he had had many compliments for his preaching, which had been valued for what they were worth, and thought of afterward with a sigh, for they emphasized to him his failure. But to-day he had glowed with new energy; he had been working for results. And his prayer at family worship that evening was so earnest and pointed that his sister, at least, knew that some one soul was pressing upon his heart.

He gave himself with just as much earnestness to his study during the following week — only to be disappointed on the Sabbath. Stephen Mitchell, for whom he had prepared another sermon, did not appear in church. As soon after breakfast the next morning as he could accomplish it, Mr. Ransom was in his saddle on his way to the Mitchell farm.

"I have brought you a package of papers," he

said to Stephen, whom he had espied in the barnyard. "They have all sorts of farm articles in them; some of them, I should think, would be of practical interest to any one who was so fortunate as to own a farm. That horse of yours has a very intelligent face, and he is almost a match for mine in size, is he not?"

The two stood there together, talking about horses, and pigs, and other matters pertaining to farm life, until Stephen had recovered from his surprise and confusion; then Mr. Ransom came to the special object of his visit.

"I missed you yesterday, my friend; and it was a sore disappointment. My sermon was prepared with a special view to your list. I think I succeeded in making clear some words which would have interested you. I hope no one is ill at home?"

If Stephen had not been trying to be polite, he would have laughed. It occurred to him as a surprising thing — a thing which marked what Sarah Jane would have called a "difference" in their lives — to be cross-questioned in this way about his non-appearance in church. Certainly none of the family had been so regular in their attendance as to have their absence awaken surprise or anxiety. On the contrary, to have appeared there for two Sabbaths in succession might have astonished the congregation. Nevertheless, there stood the minister searching for a reason. Stephen cast about him for one honest enough to meet those keen, clear eyes which were studying him with evident interest.

"I'll tell you the downright truth," he said, suddenly; "I ain't been no hand to go to church, along back for a good many months. I said I wouldn't go no more; I didn't see no use in it. But last Sunday I was interested in my words, and I'd like to have come again; but I made up my mind it wasn't going to do. The fact is, I ain't got clothes that are respectable. We're harder up than usual this fall, somehow; or else the clothes are harder up" — with a grim smile — "they're wore out; I suppose that's the common sense of it. And I made up my mind, thinking it over, that it wasn't the fair thing to go to church and sit among nice-dressed people, looking like that, and I'd stay at home."

Mr. Ransom looked and felt bewildered. Himself brought up in a home where, if there was not much wealth, there certainly was not poverty, he had been able to have whatever seemed befitting his circumstances. He tried to imagine how it would feel not to have suitable clothes. He was not especially fond of clothes himself; at least, he did not know that he was — but he decided then and there that it would not be pleasant not to be suitably attired. He had not noticed Stephen's Sunday dress particularly; he tried to recall it now, and realized that it was shabby.

It was hardly worth while to counsel Stephen to rise above dress, and come to church in whatever he had. People further advanced in Christian knowledge than Stephen Mitchell, had not been able to rise above this thing; was it to be expected that he could? "People ought to have suitable clothes to wear to church," was this young man's conclusion. How could it be managed — not for the world at large, immediately, but for this one young person before him, in whom for the time being all his interests centered? If he could put his hand in his pocket and draw forth the sum needed to furnish the boy with an entire suit of respectable clothing, that would certainly be the easiest way out of the difficulty. But he looked at the strong-limbed, rugged-faced young man before him, noted the lines about the mouth — which on occasion could settle into firmness, or even obstinacy — remembered those flashes of feeling in the gray eyes which he had seen once or twice, and decided that such a course was not open to him. Poor, the Mitchell family certainly were; but it was a poverty which would have to be handled carefully.

Mr. Ransom made a comparatively short call, and galloped home without stopping at the Bascomes', although Fanny, who had seen him pass, dusted the parlor carefully, and put herself into her most becoming dress to wait for his return, certain that he would not pass them by without a call.

Fairly in his study, he summoned his sister to a council. "Come and help me, Helen; I'm fishing for a boy, and have struck a ponderous obstacle. I want that young Mitchell to come to church regularly; I am preaching sermons prepared especially for him; and he tells me he has no clothes to wear." He stopped over this sentence, and looked so perplexedly at his sister that she could but laugh.

"So that is your obstacle? It is a formidable one, I confess. One is always running against it in Christian work of almost any sort. Poor Stephen! I sympathize with him; his clothes really are dreadful. I thought he had a good deal of courage, or an almost unfortunate indifference to make him willing to come to church at all."

"Is that true? I remember he looked shabby, but I did not consider the matter very closely. It takes women to think of these things. What can we do, Helen? If I could send him to the tailor's, and order the bills sent to me, the matter would be easily settled. But that is out of the question. We must think of some way for him to earn them."

"Could he come here, Maxwell?"

The minister shook his head. "Too far away; he is needed at home all day; and after a day's work for himself and his horses, to think of driving into town and accomplishing anything, is not feasible. Suppose he could, what could I set him at?"

"Oh! there are things that might be thought of if we had him here. Could he copy anything for you, do you think?"

Mr. Ransom laughed. "I would show you his 'list,' Helen, if I did not think it would be a breach of confidence. He has shown great ingenuity in his manner of spelling words. No; copying is not to be thought of, yet awhile at least. But there must be some way in which we can hold out a helping hand to such a young fellow as that. I feel sure there is grand material to work upon; and whether there is or not, we are bound to do our best."

"Yes," said his sister, with a bright look for her brother. This was the brother she had been used to, and he had been lost for months; if it was the Mitchell family who had brought him back to hearty interest in human kind again, she owed them a debt of gratitude. Meantime, her eyes roved thoughtfully about the study, taking in the rows and rows of books, the shelves of pamphlets, the pigeon-holes lettered and numbered and filled. What was there in all their intellectual life which could be made to fit into the life of Stephen Mitchell? Suddenly her gaze rested upon a formidable pile of papers of miscellaneous character, which refused to be arranged in orderly shapes, but bulged out, and overflowed the box that was trying to hold them.

"Max, couldn't he cut out the marked articles

from those papers and place them in their envelopes? That doesn't require a very great deal of literary power, and it is of an intellectual nature; perhaps his orthography might possibly be improved by the process. There is a good deal of work crowded into that box; it would consume a number of his evenings, I fancy; and you keep me so busy with your numerous other schemes, that I don't know when I am to get to them."

Her brother turned quickly in the direction which she indicated. "The marked papers," he said, with a relieved air. "Helen, you are a genius. That is the very thing; nothing but scissors and patience are needed. I can supply the one, and it is my belief that he has the other, when there is something to be accomplished thereby. I can give him a package of envelopes marked like those in the scrap cabinet, and he can make files for me. Who knows but his eye may rest upon something while he works which may have an influence upon his whole after life. Living is very interesting, Helen " — he turned from his papers and gave her one of his bright looks. "It is so wonderful to think that the very next step one takes may influence a soul."

The next day but one, after this conversation took place, a very interesting tableau, to some people, might have been witnessed in the Mitchell kitchen. It was in after-supper order, neat and clean; the table was drawn into the middle of the room, and had two lamps burning on it. This in itself was an unusual luxury in the family; kerosene, like everything else, was used with sparing hand, and one small light was expected to supply the family needs, even during a long winter evening. But on this night there was rare work to be done, and Mrs. Mitchell herself had carefully filled and trimmed not only the kitchen lamp, but Sarah Jane's own, and set them both on the table.

"If Steve is going at scholar's work, he must have scholar's accommodations," she had said. "It's kind of wonderful, Josiah, that the minister should have picked him out of all the congregation, to help him; now, ain't it?"

Mr. Mitchell did not express his mind other than by an untranslatable sound in the throat, which apparently conveyed satisfaction to the mind of his wife. She went on with the work of putting the kitchen in extra array, then, with as careful a hand as if she were managing rare glass or china, she arranged the files of papers, the package of envelopes, the sharp, bright scissors, and set forward the best chair which the house contained, for Stephen to occupy. When the work was fairly commenced, Mr. Mitchell drew his chair out of the chimney corner, the better to watch his son; and Mrs. Mitchell made less progress at her patching than usual, because her eyes would constantly wander to see what "great big paper Stephen was looking at now."

CHAPTER XVIII.

COMPLICATIONS.

AS for Flora Ann, she hovered about the room in a restless way, unable to settle herself to anything, and unwilling, apparently, to leave the charmed region and climb up to her own small corner of the world. The fact is, Flora Ann deserves a paragraph by herself.

Almost three weeks of civilization had wrought a great change in her. It is doubtful whether her brothers and sisters, if they had come upon her suddenly in an unexpected place, would have recognized her. Sarah Jane's cast-off dress being washed, mended and altered to fit the younger girl, was such an immense improvement on anything she had worn heretofore, that, in her own estimation, it transformed her into a lady. Of her own will, after that, she combed and brushed and carefully fingered the reddish-brown curls. Also, there had been added to her dress a tiny line of white about the throat. "Sarah Jane always wears something white in her neck when she is dressed up," explained Mrs. Mitchell; "she says it makes her feel better." Flora Ann having examined herself after the addition, in Sarah Jane's mirror, understood the statement and agreed with it.

There is really nothing more exciting, if people understood it, than these transformations in life. Such little commonplace things had been done for the Lucas girl, yet they had started springs of hope and action within her of which she had not dreamed before, and which would lead no one could tell whither.

"She ain't Sarah Jane, not by a great ways," Mrs. Mitchell confided to her husband, "but she does real well, I must say; for a girl who knew nothing at all when she first came here, she has got along first-rate. She washes her hands now, without telling, whenever she is going to touch a dish; and she ain't run her fingers through her hair since I told her that Sarah Jane couldn't eat no dinner one day when she was sick, because Mrs. Jinks, who came in to help me, twisted up her hair when it fell down, and went to cut the bread without washing her hands. I told it to her just on purpose to see if it would learn her anything; 'cause she was always twisting her hair, and running her fingers through it. She is quick to learn; she colored up just like a peony, and she ain't fussed with her hair since. She's slower motioned than Sarah Jane and quieter like, but she gets things done somehow, and I must say I take to her as I didn't have any kind of a notion that I could. All the same, I'll be thankful to see Sarah Jane again, Josiah; I will that! There's lots of things she could teach Flora Ann."

I hope it will be understood and appreciated that Mrs. Mitchell had made a sacrifice in receiving this ill-kept, ill-taught, slatternly girl into her household. Mrs. Mitchell had been poorer in her life, even, than she was to-day. But she had never been other than neat and clean; and, as is natural with such people, dirt was her terror. Nothing but the minister's carefully dropped seed, that by receiving Flora Ann Lucas under her care she could help to cultivate a soul, had induced the mother to make the sacrifice. She would willingly have done without her help; she would gladly have saved the dollar a week which she paid her, but for this fact. It is pleasant to know that even thus early she was reaping her bit of reward. Flora Ann was copying her; was growing neat. She swept the kitchen in the corners as well as in the middle of the room; she was learning to rinse the dishes, as well as the dish towels, carefully; she was learning how to cook simple food and serve it decently.

"There is no telling," said Mrs. Mitchell to herself, "what good it may do her. It doesn't seem as though she could accomplish anything in that shanty where she lives, surrounded by them drunkards; and it doesn't seem as though she would ever have a home of her own. I don't know how anybody ever could take a notion to her enough to want to marry her; but then, things often happen queer in this world; I'll do my best."

So Flora Ann hovered about the neat kitchen, watching the bright scissors travel slowly down the black line which divided the columns.

"Couldn't I help?" she said presently, drawing near, and speaking very timidly. The magnitude of the proposition filled Mrs. Mitchell with dismay; but Stephen raised his eyes and surveyed the questioner thoughtfully. It was as if he had just noted the change in her. He said to himself that her eyes were even bigger than he had thought them.

"Do you know how to read?" he asked suddenly.

Flora Ann nodded her head eagerly. " I learned how to read when I went to school, up at the other place where we used to live. I could read real fast, and I was in the class with bigger girls than me."

"Read that," said Stephen, pointing with his finger to a paragraph which he had just cut from the paper. Flora Ann obeyed, her cheeks ablaze, her breath coming hard and fast, the words tumbling out on top of each other in a promiscuous heap without regard to pauses or pronunciation; but she proved her statement; she could "read," without doubt, and " very fast."

"Can you read writing?" Stephen interrupted the flow of words to ask the next question. Flora Ann paused for breath, and nodded again.

"Yes, I kin; I learned writing, too, at that school. I had a writing-book that I made full of letters and words; teacher said it was done real well, too. I can read them words just as plain as print." And she pointed to those written on the ends of the envelopes, in Mr. Ransom's round hand. They were really quite as plain as print, but Stephen was surprised that Flora Ann could compass them; perhaps, after all his looking down upon her, she knew more than he did. What a revelation that would be!

"Well," he said slowly, coming to his conclusion by careful steps, "I don't see why you shouldn't help do this, if you ain't got nothing else to do. Bring your chair and sit down here, and see if you can put these papers that I've cut out into the places that belong to them. Here is one about 'giving;' he said I would find the word 'giving' through the envelopes somewheres, and I was to put it in it; if you can find the word, you may as well do it."

Thus began a new era in the Lucas girl's life. With hands that trembled so she could scarcely hold the package, she searched eagerly for the word "giving" — and if she, sometime, finds, in searching through the years, a diamond lying in her path, I doubt if it will give her the thrill of exultant joy which came over her as she drew forth the envelope which had the word she was in search of at its top.

"Here it is," she said, in a tone of suppressed eagerness, "right straight here. I knowed I could find it. I ain't forgot them, though it is an awful while since I have seen any writing. It was when I was a little girl, you know. I ain't been to school this four year. But here is the word, sure enough."

Stephen leaned over and surveyed it. Yes; it was the word, and he watched Flora Ann's fingers seize the slip of paper and place it with great care in the envelope — dimly conscious the while of having gained a victory over self in thus summoning Flora Ann to his aid.

"You, being their near neighbors, can do more for them than any of the rest of us can," Mr. Ransom had said. Stephen was honestly trying to do something for the Lucas girl.

Evening after evening they sat together, over the papers and envelopes. It was long, slow work which had been given them to do. Stephen was slow in finding the marked places, and slow in using the scissors, which were unaccustomed instruments in his hands. Moreover, his eyes were often caught by a sentence which was not marked, and held spell-bound over it; and often he was in great bewilderment as to where certain slips really belonged. In cases where there was no definite heading, he had been told to decide by the statements made, where to place them; a tremendous piece of work was this last; it often necessitated his reading the clipping from beginning to end. Occasionally he read it aloud, and speculated over it; and Mr. Mitchell found himself listening and giving his opinion; and on two or three occasions Flora Ann had given hers, with such success that the clipping had been consigned to the envelope which she chose. All these things took time — and another Sunday came, and passed, before they were half-through with the first great package.

Long before this, however, both Stephen and his helper had grown intensely interested in the work. It was becoming the custom, now, to read out the small bits of special interest, and to enter into a discussion concerning them; not only as to where they belonged, but as to the statements made. In short, the Mitchell family, with the addition of the Lucas girl, were becoming a reading circle. It would be difficult to tell how much it increased Stephen's interest to discover, from time to time, certain words which were in his list, and to find that their connection threw great light upon their probable meaning.

One evening, he and Flora Ann settled to their work before the father and mother appeared. Mr. Mitchell had gone to the cellar to examine something which needed his care, and Mrs. Mitchell was in her bedroom looking through the depths of a great bandbox for certain pieces which she needed to use. It was Flora Ann's opportunity to ask a question which had been haunting her all day :

"Steve, do you suppose all them things can be true that you have clipped out?"

"Of course," said Stephen indignantly; "he ain't a man that would want to cut up papers and keep a lot of things that wasn't true ; and he knows what he's about — there's lots of things he ain't marked, you see."

"Well, I wish I could believe them all."

This was followed by a sigh so heart-felt that Stephen looked at her curiously.

"What do you care?" he asked, in a voice which, though gruff, was not unkind.

"'Cause I do ; I read one of them I put up last night, and it has just been following me round all day ; I can't get it out of my head. It was about a man who drinked ; an awful drunkard he was, and he swore awful. Just as much like our Jake as could be. He had a little girl who went to Sunday-school, and she took to praying for him every day — after a while he gave up drinking ; and he got kind, and he went to work, and was just as good as he could be. And it was all along of the little girl's praying, so it said. Do you believe that?"

"I s'pose so ; folks that know about such things seem to believe in praying ; and, of course, if there is any use in it, things get done by that means."

"Steve Mitchell, do you believe that if anybody should pray for Jake, say — pray day in and day out, like that little girl did — that he would ever get good in this world?"

Here was a question in theology which might well have puzzled wiser heads than Stephen Mitchell's. He laid down his scissors, and ran his right hand thoughtfully through his hair, and considered what it would be best to say. In his heart he knew he had very little hope for Jake Lucas.

"I don't know, I'm sure. If we could find the little girl who was willing to try it, we might prove whether there was anything in it or not. Maybe there's some that might be got a-hold of in that way, and maybe there's some that can't. I don't know about them things. I should think Jake was about as hard a one to try on as any of 'em."

"Yes," said Flora Ann earnestly; "he is that! He is enough sight worse than the others; but I was thinking if the thing was true, I might try it. I ain't a little girl, and he ain't my father, but I wouldn't think that could make a difference, would it? There's father; I might try with him; but he ain't bad, you know. He drinks, but he don't knock folks around and swear; and he's kind of good natured always, and I don't feel that hard about father that I do about Jake. It wouldn't make so much difference, either, if father would give it up, but Jake, O, my! If Jake should come in sober, I guess mother would just about die. You see, Steve, mother cares more for Jake than she does for the rest of us. He's the oldest, you know, and she had him to think about when she was young. She has got some of the clothes he wore when he was a baby — cries over them, if you will believe it. She says he was a good little boy, and just as pretty as a picture. Folks used to stop on the street and watch her go by with him, when she got him all fixed up nice. She didn't have as good times with any of the rest of us, because we was so horrid poor and low down after a spell; but with Jake she had real nice times. She loves him this minute, for all he knocks her around and is horrid. I'm just a-mind to try it, anyhow; it couldn't do no harm, if it didn't do no good." She spoke the last sentence in lower tone, and looked up timidly at her auditor as if to discover what he thought of it.

"Well," said Stephen, after a silence which could have been felt, "I don't know why you shouldn't, I'm sure. I don't know much about them things, but folks do pray, and they pray for folks, and they believe in it; the minister believes in it, and thinks it ought to be done."

"Would he believe in praying for Jake, and me doing it?"

"Why, I s'pose so. I tell you I don't know anything about it, but I can't see why not — if there is anything in it. If Jake would let the drink alone, I s'pose he could learn to be decent; and there are folks that do give it up after they have been at it a good while." Stephen thought of his father, but not for worlds would he have mentioned his name in this connection.

"Well," said Flora Ann, with a little catch of the breath which was peculiar to her, and betokened great and suppressed excitement, "I have been thinking about it all day, and wondering if I couldn't; and I just made up my mind I would ask you what you thought. I could use them same words, only, instead of 'father,' I could say 'Jake.' It was real short: 'O, Lord! please save my father.' That is all she said — she was a little bit of a girl, you know — and I could say, 'O, Lord! please save Jake.' It couldn't do no harm, now, could it, if it didn't do no good?"

"I should say not," said Stephen, low-voiced and troubled. Already was Flora Ann, "one of the Lucas set," getting ahead of him — asking questions that were too far above him for him to give intelligent answers. He ought to know how to answer her. He ought to be able to assure her, and that from his own experience, that prayer was exactly what Jake needed. He ought to be able to say to her that he would join her in praying. His conscience told him all these things. The minister's sermon two weeks before had been very plain. He did not dare do other than advise

Flora Ann to carry out her purpose. He was not willing to confess to her that he knew he ought to begin, himself, to pray; he was not willing to begin. It is true he had no realizing sense of the power of prayer; it is true he had not the slightest hope, or rather expectation, that any prayer which Flora Ann, or, for that matter, which anybody else could offer, would make any difference with Jake Lucas; but he did believe that praying for her brother would, in some mysterious manner which he did not understand, make a difference in Flora Ann herself. So far as this his knowledge of theology reached: that he recognized a certain element of power in prayer, but that it would help in the direction in which he was reaching, he did not understand.

The little church to which Maxwell Ransom ministered had a sensation the next Sabbath. The congregation was made up of people who, to a marked extent, were posted as to their neighbors' affairs. They knew, for instance, to the fraction of a dollar what each new garment cost in which any of their number chanced to appear, and where it was purchased. The minister's sister was an exception and an excitement. They did not know where her things were bought, nor what she paid for them. There was a shrewd suspicion abroad that she had a great deal of money, else how could she manage such elegant costumes? For the community was largely made up of the class of young people who suppose elegance and refinement to have only a money value. They were by no means through with the discussion of Helen Ransom's attire, and various speculations concerning the probable cost of certain articles were still rife, when Sarah Jane Mitchell helped to cause the new sensation. Back of this is a story, a bit of which you ought to hear.

There was, hanging in Miss Ransom's wardrobe, a dress of soft cashmere, delicate in color and fine in texture, but in the making of which one of those trying blunders had occurred which sometimes happens even among good workers. The dress was a trial to Miss Ransom. She had sighed over it as ill-fitting and uncomfortable, and yet managed to wear it more or less, as many suffering sisters have done before her. Of late, as often as her eyes had fallen on the dress, she had thought of Sarah Jane, and mentally measured her height and shape.

"I believe it would fit her to perfection," she told herself; "how very pretty she would look in it. She has just the complexion which fits that shade of goods, and has never discovered it. I would like to see her in it and a bonnet of the same color, with the slightest touch of pale pink about them both; what a revelation it might make to her. I wonder if I couldn't manage to give her the dress? She needs a new one, and I have sacrificed my comfort to this long enough. I will talk to Max about it." And "Max" had shown a lively interest in the whole matter. In fact, as he laughingly told his sister, he had adopted the Mitchell family, and meant to induce them to adopt the Lucas family, "and between us we will civilize the whole of them." Then his face had grown sweetly grave, as he added : " We may do more and better for them than that ; perhaps we can bring them into intimate companionship with Jesus Christ himself. Helen, I am getting in love with life again ; there are such possibilities for souls."

And Helen had gone away glad ; and resolved that the gray dress should be presented that very day.

CHAPTER XIX.

PROGRESS.

SHE had no such puzzling road to travel as Mr. Ransom had had with Stephen; there was a sense in which Sarah Jane was above her brother.

The girl had been with her now for more than three weeks. They had sat and sewed together through the long days, and in some respects had come very near to each other. Miss Ransom knew that she was looked upon as a friend, and that Sarah Jane had a frank, sunny nature, which could receive joyously and gratefully any tokens of kindness which she might choose to bestow. She had no hesitancy in saying to her, as she did an hour after her decision was reached: "Here is a dress which I have borne with for some time; it doesn't fit me, and I don't like it, and as I do not need it this fall, I am going to give it to you if you will accept it. I think that with very little alteration it will fit you, and I know it is just the color to suit your face."

Sarah Jane's face had been a lovely color just then, and her bright eyes had grown brighter as she looked at the soft, pretty folds of gray, lying over Miss Ransom's arm.

"O, goodness me!" she said. "Ain't it too fine a dress for me? I never see anything prettier; and it is just as soft as feathers."

"It is not expensive goods," Miss Ransom had explained, nor was it from her standpoint. "And it wears well, and washes nicely. It will make you a very pretty dress; and it is just the right shade to go with those bits of velvet I was showing you. A piece of the cashmere trimmed with the velvet will make you a pretty bonnet. Suppose we spend this evening in seeing what we can do in the millinery line? I was considered skillful at home, in that direction; I have made hats for my mother, and for the girls, who are both older and younger than myself, for several years. I quite like the business. But, Sarah, there is a question I want to ask; would you like to have me begin my sentences with goodness me?"

"Goodness, no!" began Sarah Jane; then she stopped and sat down in a chair near at hand, and laughed. It was a pleasant feature of the girl's character that she could laugh where others might have cried, and felt insulted. "No, Miss Ransom; I would not like it at all; it wouldn't be you, you see. But then it's me, and all them things — I mean those things — seem to belong to me."

"No, my dear, they do not; they are weeds which have grown up in soil where they do not belong, and they need to be rooted out. Our 'goodness' has nothing to do with a great many things for which we call it to account. If we should say 'my badness,' there would really be more sense to it. You and I have taken the Bible for our guide-book, you know, and there is a verse in the Bible about it."

"Oh! my"—began Sarah Jane, and stopped. "You don't mean, Miss Ransom, that there is a verse in the Bible about talking?"

"Yes, indeed, there are a great many verses about talking; but the one in particular of which I am just now reminded, is a very simple rule, which, if remembered, would help. You will find it in the fifth chapter of Matthew, the thirty-seventh verse."

That afternoon, while she arranged her hair and made herself neat for the pretty work which was the order of the hour, Sarah Jane pondered over the words: "But let your speech be yea, yea; nay, nay. And whatsoever is more than these, is of the evil one."

It will be understood that Sarah Jane had taken great strides during the three weeks which she had spent at the manse. To those who have not worked among people with a view to helping them, it will seem incredible that such a change of manner and views as had come to her could be reached in so short a space of time. But what the grace of God can accomplish in a human heart, even in a few days, is very little understood by those who are not looking out for harvests. The seed had been dropped in good soil; Sarah Jane had lived thus far an honest, earnest sort of life. She had busied herself eagerly with the only things which in her starved surroundings she could find — the making and keeping in order of the few garments she had to wear, and keeping the few rooms with which she had to do, neat and clean. She had been taught severe neatness and cleanliness by a careful mother. She had had no books to read, and no opportunities for study. She simply had not thought to read the Bible; and why should she? None of the people with whom she came in contact seemed to read it much; at least, they never referred to it in conversation, and when she came into the atmosphere of Helen Ransom's life, it was a revelation to her. Here were two people, at least, who evidently ordered their lives by the Bible; who referred to it familiarly, read it together morning and evening, and stopped over the verses to talk of their meaning in a simple and interesting manner which she could understand and appreciate. And when, after two or three days' acquaintance, Helen Ransom had said to her, "Sarah, you ought to be living for Christ, working for him; you have splendid opportunities for service — why have you not begun?" she was simply bewildered.

"Me, opportunities for service! Me live for

Christ!" She did not understand what was meant, and said so. The conversation which followed would have astonished many a minister of the Gospel in the habit of using only theological terms; of talking about "conversion" and "regeneration" as though they were understood as matters of course. Helen Ransom, who had been accustomed to teaching young people, found that she had to choose her words with care, and go back over her sentences and simplify; but she had a listener who meant to understand, if it was within the range of possibility.

There came an hour when her eyes seemed to grow luminous with a new thought which had taken possession of her. The work she was doing dropped from her hands into her lap, and she sat with parted lips, as if about to speak, yet hesitating for words, and looked at Helen in a way which thrilled that young woman. At last she said:

"Why, Miss Ransom, that almost scares me. It sounds as if I could have it for the asking."

"You can, my dear," said Helen, moved exceedingly by this way of receiving the call. "It is His own desire. His 'Come unto me' means all this, and infinitely more; means daily and hourly companionship and guidance, and such depths of love, and tenderness, and patience, as you will have to learn about from Him, for no mortal tongue can tell it."

And Sarah Jane had received the thought with the same directness and frankness with which she had received her invitation to come and sew at the manse. That had been a wonderful opening to her, and she had accepted it as such. Now here was another; something, it seems, which she might have had all her life, and she never understood it before.

"There has been a lot of wasted time," she had said, decidedly, a little while after this conversation. "I wish't I had known it a long time ago, Miss Ransom, and I wish Steve had known it; it would have made a difference. But I will do my part now, whatever it is. I don't understand it, of course, but I'll do my level best to find it out."

In this straightforward manner her Christian life had begun. Her first conscious prayer on her knees might have startled you, it was so unlike the ordinary forms of prayer, so simple and direct: "O, Lord Jesus, I have just heard that you wanted me for a friend. Folks have said so in sermons, I s'pose, and it has always been in Bible verses that I knew, some of them; but I never understood it — I don't know why. Now, Lord, I feel in my heart that it is true, and I want to belong; and do just what you want me to."

So, in their separate ways, Sarah Jane Mitchell and Flora Ann Lucas, all unknown to each other, had begun to pray. Sarah Jane's Christian life from that moment was a vigorous plant. What she undertook she meant to perform; she was as resolute about her Christianity as she had been about ripping, and turning, and remodeling her dresses. She took the Bible as a literalist, with no hesitancy about its meaning just what it said; and when she did not understand what it said, she went to Helen Ransom for light. Also she went daily on her knees for help from Him who is the light of the world, and who has pledged to give wisdom liberally, and who upbraideth not. Does any one who understands Him need to be told that such living as this meant steady and rapid growth? She took the verse about "yea and nay" to Miss Ransom in the sewing-room.

"I don't think I understand it," she said. "It can't mean that we are never to say anything but yes and no?"

Then there followed a conversation upon care in the use of language, and upon the value of simple words which meant just what they said, and were not marred by extravagances of any sort. Sarah Jane's attention being called to it, she confessed that she should not like to hear Mr. Ransom say "My gracious!" or "Goodness me!" or "Oh! my land." Of course the more serious meaning of the verse in question was explained to her, but she was quick-witted enough to catch its adaptation to ordinary habits of conversation, and to apply its principles rigidly to herself.

All these things being taken into consideration,

it is perhaps not surprising that the young girl had greatly changed, both outwardly and inwardly, in that short space of time. Three weeks of constant intercourse with refined and cultivated people had done much, and who shall undertake to say what companionship with Jesus Christ had done for her? Yet Sarah Jane was not a little startled over the picture which was presented to her in the mirror on the Sabbath morning when she first put on the gray dress and bonnet.

Limited in her choice of colors as she had been all her life; obliged always to wear that which she chanced to have, whether suited with it or not, she had had no opportunity for studying harmony of color, even if she had understood how to do it. But she would have had to be blind indeed not to discover that the young girl arrayed in soft gray cashmere, with a neat little bonnet of the same delicate tint, made in the prevailing style, and brightened with the faintest touch of pale pink, was a very different looking person from any "Sarah Jane" that she had ever seen before. When she came downstairs to wait for Miss Ransom, the minister added unwittingly his note of commendation, by pausing with an air of surprise and bewilderment at sight of a stranger in the hall, but recovered himself in a moment to say cordially: "Why, Miss Mitchell, is it you? I didn't know you at first."

"I am glad of it," murmured Sarah Jane to

herself, as the door closed after him. "I would like to begin all over again, and not to have anybody know me. I would like to be somebody else; Miss Jones, or Miss Jenkins, or somebody, and just start afresh. Things are different, and I would like to have them different all through; but then Steve wouldn't be my brother, I suppose, and there would be mother and father — no, I guess I like to be Sarah Jane Mitchell, but a different one all the way through. My! how different I will have things when I get home."

She had almost said "My goodness!" but had caught her breath in time, and even felt mortified over the misused pronoun. She had taken to her inmost heart the direction: "Let your speech be yea, yea; nay, nay;" she was struggling with the habit of her lifetime, which had been to use expletives with every breath. She had even cultivated this habit; for did not Fanny Bascome and girls of her set talk in that way, and had they not been heretofore Sarah Jane's ideals?

I hope you fully appreciate the sensation which this young woman made, seated in the pastor's pew — the finishing touch to her wardrobe added by a pair of kid gloves which matched her bonnet. The gloves had been Helen Ransom's birthday gift to her, presented at that time because she could not resist the temptation to study their effect. There was another figure near the door which required more or less study. This was none other than Stephen Mitchell himself in a new suit. The papers, having been clipped and arranged in their various envelopes, had been brought home two days before, Stephen interrupting the hearty commendations which his work had received, to say, with the air of one determined to be honest at all hazards:

"It ain't fair for me to get all the thanks. That Lucas girl working at our house, she helped me lots. She's a better reader than I be, a good deal, and she put the things in their places and kept them straight. I don't know as I could have got through with them if it hadn't been for her."

"I am glad of it," said the minister heartily. "If you were able to set her to work and interest her in doing it, you accomplished more than the work itself. It is worth a great deal for a young girl like her to have her evenings employed for her in such a safe and helpful manner. So she can read and write? That is good. Perhaps she would like to study. Why don't you start a school, Stephen, while she is with you — you and she?"

"Humph!" said Stephen, with infinite sarcasm, "and me be the teacher, I s'pose."

"Yes; unless you would like me for a teacher. Suppose I furnish the books and the suggestions, and you and she do the work? Perhaps you will give her a start which will save her to a respectable life. Why not try it? But now to business. You have not told me what this work is worth that you have done for me, and as I have some more of the same kind that I would like to have done, I have a plan to talk over with you." Then with great care he had presented his plan, which was to have Stephen go with him on the following morning to the city, which was only twenty miles away, and select from the clothing-store a neat suit of clothes, such as would be proper to wear to church all winter; the minister to pay the bill, and Stephen to do such work for him during the winter evenings as he could furnish, chiefly in the line in which he had been working for the past weeks. There had been a good deal of conversation, and some opposition. Stephen was quick-witted enough to know that it would take a great deal of work such as he had been doing to cover the expense of a suit of clothes; but the minister explained that he meant to furnish a great deal of work. Matters of that kind had been accumulating in his study ever since he began his college course, waiting for leisure hours which had never come. And that he should be extremely glad to get his study put into systematic order. "You can give an evening to me here, perhaps," he added, "which will be very helpful in several ways. In short, it is as reasonable a business transaction as I ever made. I could pay you in money, of course, and let you wait for the clothes until it accumulated, but I would a great deal rather have it as I have proposed. I like to see you in church. You are a help to me there, and I want you in my Bible class. I am working up a class, and I want recruits from your neighborhood, and I want you to get them for me. I have an ambition to have all three of those Lucas boys in my Bible class."

He laughed at Stephen's dismayed exclamation, but labored to impress him with the fact that it might be done; that stranger things even than that had been done in the world. He went to his library shelf and got down the great encyclopædia of illustrations, and turned to one or two startling facts illustrative of the power of God over depraved, and apparently lost, human lives.

Stephen's reply was one that the minister least expected to hear: "Flora Ann Lucas would like to hear them stories."

"Would she? Why?" Then Stephen, somewhat to his own regret, had to repeat the conversation which he had had with her, and her resolution to "begin that very night" to pray for Jake. "It's queer praying, I suppose," he added, with a little chuckle. "She knows as much about that as I do, I guess. But it can't do no harm, I reckon."

"We cannot tell, neither you nor I, what it may do," said Mr. Ransom, and there was such a ring of gladness in his voice that Stephen looked at him in wonder — almost in pity. What could he expect Flora Ann Lucas to accomplish by saying over a half a dozen words about her brother Jake?

"You don't know Jake Lucas as well as I do," he said. " He is low down, I can tell you. He's enough sight worse than the other two; hateful and cruel, you know, when he is drunk; bad to everybody; kicking and knocking things around that ain't doing him no harm, and swearing just awful. They are all afraid of him, the whole set. The girls will hide for hours to keep out of his sight; and his mother, she's afraid of him, too; she don't dare to speak while he is in the house, unless he takes a notion to let her. I think it will take more than praying to make a decent fellow out of him. If he could get put into jail somewhere, and have to stay there, maybe something could be done for the rest of the family. There's Flora Ann, now; she has been to our house three weeks; she is afraid to go home, because she knows Jake will go on so. He hates her worse than the rest of them somehow, and yet she's a-praying for him. I kind of think something decent might be made out of her, if somebody would take hold of it that knew how to do it."

There was more conversation, about this and several matters, but it ended in the minister carrying off his prize in triumph the next morning to the clothing-store. The result was even more bewildering than in Sarah Jane's case; for Stephen had had no ability to make the best of his own poor wardrobe. The change from the worn and patched and outgrown garments, in which he had figured so long, to a suit of clothes which fitted him from head to foot, made a transformation which cannot be described in words. Stephen himself had felt its power, though he had no mirror to look into; there was a little eight-inch glass in Sarah Jane's room, and he had been tempted to slip in there before he went down. But, after reaching the door, he had turned away with a shamefaced air, calling himself a fool, and gone downstairs. Here his mother had been sufficient mirror, reflecting his image in her own delighted eyes, and having not the slightest hesitancy in expressing her views.

CHAPTER XX.

TRYING TO CATCH UP.

"WELL, if ever I saw the like in all my days! Why, Steve Mitchell, I wouldn't know you if I should meet you on the street. I'll tell you who I'd think you were, Steve; you look just like your father did as much as thirty years ago. O, my! but he was a handsome young man. I never knew you favored him so much. O, dear boy! I'm just too glad to think of your being all dressed up, as you ought to be, and going to church." Whereupon her emotions rose above the reserve or timidity of years, and she wound both arms around his neck, and kissed his tanned red cheeks again and again.

"Huh!" he said, struggling a little, yet pleased in spite of himself. "What a fuss you do make, mother, over a fellow's new clothes."

"'Tain't the clothes, altogether," said his mother. "It's the feeling, Steve, that that's the kind of clothes you ought to wear, and that we meant our boy should wear, didn't we, Josiah? Only look at him. Isn't he a handsome fellow, now?"

Mr. Mitchell, thus appealed to, turned and surveyed his tall, broad-shouldered son from head to foot, and presently nodded his head with great satisfaction. "I guess he'll do, mother — if he behaves as well as he looks, and I reckon he will. The fact is, he has always behaved pretty well, hasn't he? Only the clothes haven't matched. Maybe you can keep things matched now, Steve; times seem to be a-changing with us somehow."

It was really the first hearty commendation that the boy had ever received from his father in his life. He turned and went out of the room suddenly, a choking feeling in his throat. It was a new sensation to be approved. On the instant his conscience arose, telling him of hundreds of things that he could have done to have made the lives of father and mother easier.

"And I'll do it," he murmured; "I'll learn more than words. If father will trust me, I'll try to make things different on this old farm. I'll do the very best I know how, and I'll learn how, in ways I don't know about now. He'll help me." (The pronoun always referred to Mr. Ransom.) "He said he would; and them papers will help me. I'll show father yet what kind of a boy he has got."

It was this spirit which he took to church on the day when he helped to create a sensation. I am bound to confess that he did not listen to the sermon as Mr. Ransom hoped he would. There were portions of it to which he listened intently, but this was when he recognized some of his words, as he still called those on the list. But between times his thoughts wandered frequently to a distant pew, where sat Miss Ransom and a strange young lady. I am sorry to say that this strange young woman filled him with discouragement. He thought he recognized in her a being of another sphere. "'Tain't clothes," he said to himself, disconsolately, "and it ain't knowing words. I don't know what it is. Sarah Jane, now, might know all the words on the list, and a lot more, and so might Flora Ann, and they wouldn't either of them look like that girl no more than I look like the minister, though I've got on new clothes and do look different. Maybe it's knowing words, and wearing that kind of clothes all your life, that makes the difference; and folks that hasn't had them never get it."

Thus, from the state of exaltation in which he had entered the church, he sank into the depths, all because of the strange lady from another sphere. I hope you will be able to put yourself, to a degree, in his place, and feel the shock of amazement which thrilled through him, as, almost with the "Amen" of the benediction, the strange young woman turned her head and let her eyes move eagerly over the church, evidently in search of some one. Behold! the eyes belonged to Sarah Jane. Stephen stood perfectly still, lost to every idea but that.

It was clothes, then, or knowing words, or it was being with the minister's family for three weeks — perhaps all three combined. How did girls manage it to make themselves so different in such a little while? He stared at Sarah Jane, his amazement growing steadily. She caught a glimpse of him, and her pleasant face broke into smiles as she nodded appreciatively. Manifestly she also saw a "difference."

"She is pretty," said Stephen to himself; "as pretty as a picture. She ain't like the other one, but she is most as pretty. I never see the like. I reckon she's learned lots of things. I wonder when she is coming home?"

"Dear me!" said Fanny Bascome, "if you'll believe it, Sarah Jane, I didn't know you at all when you first came into church. What a difference fixing up makes, doesn't it? Is that one of Miss Ransom's dresses? I never did see a woman who has as many dresses as she has. I should think if her father was a poor minister, she'd have used up all his salary long ago. But it is very becoming, Sarah Jane; so is your hat. Did she give that to you?"

And Sarah Jane was jarred. The verse which the minister had recited at family worship that morning was: "Let the words of my mouth and the meditations of my heart be acceptable in thy sight, O Lord, my strength and my Redeemer." He had made a little talk about the kind of words the Lord would naturally like to hear in his house, and contrasted them with what he must often have to hear. The seed had sunk deeply in Sarah Jane's heart. Remember, she was trying to order her life by the Bible; and her conscience was tender. She looked about her in a startled way to note whether Mr. Ransom had heard the unfitting words, then blushed to think she should care first for Mr. Ransom instead of for Him to whom they were to be made acceptable. But she had no answer whatever for Fanny Bascome, and liked her less than usual that morning. Nothing daunted, however, by her silence, Fanny hurried out her questions.

"Are you going to stay there all winter, Sarah Jane? What do you do, anyhow? Housework? I didn't know you was willing to do housework. Ma would have liked your help many a time if she had known it.

"How d' do, Steve?" for they were moving down the aisle, and Stephen had taken a few steps forward to meet his sister. "I declare, Steve, if you and Sarah Jane keep on getting fixed up, we'll need spy-glasses in order to recognize you." She laughed at her own silly words. "I never knew before that clothes could make such a difference. Yours are brand-new, aren't they, Steve? No made-over about them. O, Mr. Pettibone!" raising her voice as that gentleman slipped from a seat just ahead of her, "wait a

STEPHEN CAME FORWARD TO MEET HIS SISTER.

minute, won't you? I want to see you about the sociable;" and Stephen and Sarah Jane were released.

"Who is that young fellow coming down the other aisle near the door?" inquired Mr. Bascome of his pastor. "I never saw him here before."

"O, yes! he has been here several times. That is young Mitchell, from the Hilton Hill neighborhood, you know."

"Is it possible that that is Steve? I didn't recognize him. Why, he looks very much changed."

"Does he?" asked the minister, smiling, and he passed on in haste to reach the door, that he might have a word with Stephen.

The Mitchell family were thoroughly discussed that day at the Bascome dinner-table.

"I must say," began Fanny, "I never saw any one so changed in all my life by a little finery, as Sarah Jane Mitchell. Half the people in the church didn't know her. Mrs. Smith nudged me while the first hymn was being sung, and asked me who that pretty girl was in the minister's pew. She's quite stuck up, too; I couldn't get anything out of her after church. I believe I asked her a dozen questions, and she didn't answer one of them."

"Steve has blossomed out too," said Mr. Bascome; "I didn't know the fellow. I asked Mr. Ransom who he was."

"Yes. Stephen was in a spick-and-span new

suit. I wonder where he got them? Mr. Ransom must have given them to him. Dear me! How they are going on. I don't see what they find in the Mitchells to attract them. Steve has always seemed like the stupidest fellow. Sarah Jane is smart enough about some things, but she don't know anything that other girls do. Why, the Mitchells are nobodies, we all know — and have been for years and years. I must say Helen Ransom looks high for her friends."

The talk flowed on uninterruptedly for some time, until not only the Mitchell family, but various other persons who were in church, or were conspicuous by their absence, were discussed. Not a word was said of the sermon, on which the minister had put not only hours of study, but hours of prayer; not a word was spoken that indicated in any way that this family were pledged, all of them, to make "the words of their lips and the meditations of their hearts acceptable in His sight," nor that this day of days was theirs to help them into nearer fellowship with Him.

Sarah Jane went home by the middle of the following week, Miss Ransom having detained her until, as she told her brother, there was not even the semblance of an excuse for keeping her another day. And though he meekly suggested shirts and other masculine articles, which might be made for use in the indefinite future, she only laughed and shook her head, assuring him that there were limitations even to her and Sarah Jane's ingenuity, and that shirts, she must confess, were beyond her. Then they discussed, from various standpoints, the condition of the family in which they had become so deeply interested, seeking possible ways of helping them.

"We must help them," said Helen earnestly. "It would be a shame to leave them to themselves now. Sarah is a very unusual girl. If she had had even the ordinary opportunities of life, she would have shown her exceptional ability, but she has been dwarfed on every side. Really, Max, there seems to have been no one, in the church or out of it, who has thought of their neighborhood, and tried to reach it in any way. I did not know there were such let-alone portions of country, in this State at least."

"There ought to be some kind of a Sabbath service out there," said the minister, thoughtfully. "There is that Lucas family to reach, and several others of like kind in the outlying neighborhood. I wonder if I couldn't compass an afternoon service? It is quite a distance to go, but we might ride there. Could you go, Helen, and sing, and teach, and do all sorts of things, if we could wake up an interest there?"

It certainly was not Helen Ransom's fault that the idea got no further than the minister's "ought." He was a young man, and there were so many "oughts" pressing upon him. He did speak of the plan once to Mr. Bascome and one or two others, who assured him that there was no place in that neighborhood for holding meetings, and that the people would not attend if there were.

Meantime, Mrs. Mitchell went about her home like one bewildered. Sarah Jane had returned, brisk, bright, full of the same breezy energy which had been a part of her life, and yet different; every hour of the day the mother noted and studied over the difference. What mysterious something was it which had gotten hold of the girl? Not only the mother, but the father, noted it; and most of all, Stephen. In a hundred ways her life indicated that its center was changed. Ways which perhaps it would not be easy to define, yet which could be distinctly felt. It was not her new ideas about setting the table and arranging the furniture, nor her new ways of expressing herself, though these were marked enough. It was something back of all these changes, and superior to them all. Mrs. Mitchell fathomed it to its source one day

"I don't know what has come over you, Sarah Jane," she had said, looking at her in that bewildered, wistful way; "you seem so dreadful different, somehow."

Sarah Jane laughed cheerily. "Don't I seem nice, mother?"

"O, nice, child! That is no word for it. If you knew how glad I was to have you home again. Not but what Flora Ann did her best, poor thing!

and she did a great sight better than I expected her to, and I am sorry for her having to go back there to live like the pigs, as they do. She cried about it dreadful hard, poor thing, the last day, but then — O, my ! — Sarah Jane, I done my best for her the three weeks she was here ; but she never was, and never will be, you. No ; it isn't that you have changed in any way for the worse, child. You was always industrious and faithful, and all that, and you was always good natured and never grumbled nor found fault, and yet it seems some way as if nowadays the sun was shining all the time where you are. And you look out more than usual for other folks, though you never was selfish. I don't know what it is. Don't you feel it yourself, child?"

Sarah Jane laughed again ; a bright, sweet laugh.

"Yes," she said, "I feel it myself. It is true, mother, I have got some sunshine in my heart that I never had there before. I suppose if you come squarely down to it, I have been converted ; though Mr. Ransom didn't use that word, and she didn't ; but I was reading a book he gave me yesterday ; he said it would explain some things to me that maybe I didn't understand, and it has. As near as I can make out, I have been what they call 'converted.' At first I was almost scared to think that anything so wonderful could have happened to me ; but I guess it has. The more I think about it, the more I believe so."

"Bless the Lord!" said Mrs. Mitchell softly; "here I have been praying for this thing every day of my life since you was born, and yet I didn't seem to expect it, somehow; and I am just as astonished as I can be."

Sarah Jane turned from the pan of potatoes she was carefully paring, and gave her mother a curious, half-wistful glance.

"Have you really, mother?" she said. "I wish I had known that you were praying for me. When I think about it, it does seem too everlasting foolish that I have wasted so many years. It seems to me sometimes that if I had known about it I would have attended to it right off. But maybe I wouldn't. I suppose I knew enough all the time, if I had ever done any thinking."

"It is likely my fault," said the mother meekly; "I never was brought up to talk about them things, and I didn't know how. I was always afraid of doing harm. It is my opinion that Satan gets hold of a lot of people that way. Many a time I have wished that I knew how to say something to you, and I thought I couldn't do it right. But you've got it now, Sarah Jane; that just explains it; it's religion, bless the Lord!"

She pressed her old tired hands together in a sort of ecstasy of delight. And her worn, homely face would at that moment have made a study for an artist.

Still it must be confessed that, as the winter

closed in upon them Sarah Jane found it very hard to settle down to her meager life. She was not unhappy; she was simply restless; full of an intense desire to reach out. The contrast between her days and those that she had spent at the manse were too vivid. She wanted books; she wanted to study; she wanted a hundred things which she could not compass. It was not that she did not have enough to do — her days were by no means spent in idleness; there was the usual routine of farm work of which she relieved her mother now almost entirely, and there were many little touches which she had learned that, while they made life much pleasanter in the little old house, certainly took more time. There were long evenings which were full of interest now, for both Sarah Jane and her brother. They gave faithful study to the few books which the minister had put into their hands — among them was a dictionary; and there was no let up to the interest with which the now famous list of words was studied. But these glimpses into the world of knowledge served to make them both realize more fully what they had lost, and how much of a journey they must take before they "caught up," as Sarah Jane briefly phrased it. She never explained in words who the persons were with whom she was trying to catch up, but they were certainly not the Bascomes.

Helen Ransom had by no means forgotten her

protégé. Not a week passed but that a book or paper, with a choice paragraph marked, or a text-card with an important verse on it, or perhaps only a ruffle or bit of ribbon, found its way through the mail to Sarah Jane. She began to watch eagerly for a chance to send to the post-office; and Stephen, though he did not wish to own it in words, was as much interested in the coming of the little parcels as she was herself, and was ingenious in planning ways and means to secure them.

Nor did Helen Ransom's interest end here; she was constantly planning how to help her friend. The Mitchell family was the subject of frequent and earnest conversations in the manse during those early weeks of winter. Many projects for furthering their interests were brought forward, considered · carefully, and abandoned as impracticable. Frequently, during the conversations, Helen would remark: "I wish there was some way for them to keep boarders. I cannot help feeling that Sarah is talented in that direction. The mother is very neat, you know, and understands good, wholesome cookery. And Sarah would be as dainty as any lady in a home of her own, if she had the means to do with. Think what a pleasant country home it could be made into for tired city people. If we only knew just the right sort to gather about them, and it were only summer."

Her brother laughed pleasantly over this statement, and said: "It seems to me, my good sister, that you have several important 'ifs' in your plans. Since it is not summer, and we have no winter boarders to suggest to them, the question is: What can we do to help them more than we are doing now? I confess I like the boarding scheme immensely, if it could be brought to pass, for the reason that I see in it a way to reach the Lucas family. I suspect that the Mitchell home was paradise to that poor Flora Ann, who, on the whole, is the most hopeful one in that household. I wish very much she might be kept under Mrs. Mitchell's teaching for a time."

CHAPTER XXI.

TRANSFERRED.

"Do you know, Max, I believe Hilary would come to the Mitchells' to board if she understood the situation? The thought came to me last night like an inspiration. I mean to write to her this morning, and explain all the circumstances. I wonder that I had not thought of it before."

Her brother's laugh was compassionate this time, but the only reply he made in words was, "So that is your latest scheme, is it?"

She answered the laugh, rather than the words. "You do not approve of it, do you?"

"Oh! as to approval," he said, smiling kindly on her, "of course I have nothing to say. But as to the feasibility of the plan, you will pardon me for being skeptical. Did you not tell me she was settled in New York for the winter — and very comfortably settled? By what process of reasoning can you expect her to break up her home and come out to a very uninteresting and dreary portion of the country, among total strangers, and take up her abode in a farmhouse? If she were to be near you, that might be an inducement; but the road to the Mitchell farm is not particularly inviting in the winter. I can fancy nothing more dreary, for one accustomed to city life, than to be set down there, and shut in, often by storm or cold, from getting away."

"Ah! but, you see," answered Helen, eagerly, "you do not know Hilary. If you did, a great many of those statements would go for naught; given the fact that she believed she could accomplish results."

His smile was still compassionate, and superior. This young man of twenty-six believed that he knew the world, especially the world of women, much better than did his sister; so much had Gertrude Temple accomplished for him. By his process of reasoning, Gertrude Temple had not been weak and false above others; but all women were weak by nature; shrank from unpleasant situations or uncomfortable surroundings. He had quite as much faith in Hilary Colchester as he had in any woman, but, as he had said to Helen, what could be her motive?

"Hilary does not think of herself," explained Helen. "She never belonged to the class of people who put self first. That there is work to be done for the Master, which possibly she may be able to accomplish, will be motive enough for her."

"But, my dear sister, there is work everywhere

to be done. She will not have occasion to let her talents in that direction run to waste while in New York. I cannot see why she should feel called upon to put herself in unpleasant surroundings in order to work."

"Not if the thought was really an inspiration, Maxwell? If it was, the Lord Jesus intends that it shall be carried out."

Now his smile was sweet to see; there was not a cynical line in it. "By all means make the attempt," he said gently, "if you feel impressed in that way, it will do no harm to try. The trying will work good to your own soul at least."

But he went away from the table with so little faith in the coming of Hilary Colchester, and so little interest in the matter, that he forgot it entirely, although during his leisure moments that day he revolved several projects in his mind, any one of which, if it could be brought about, might be helpful to the Mitchells. And Helen Ransom wrote her letter.

In the course of a very few days came a reply which was so characteristic of Hilary Colchester, that you shall have it complete :

My Dear Helen: — It was a joy to hear from you again and, it was good in you to write me so long a letter. I am deeply interested in your friends. I both laughed and cried over "Sarah Jane" and "Steve," and that poor "Flora Ann" touches my heart. But your scheme fairly took my breath away for a few minutes; it was so unexpected. Were you entirely frank in your picture, my dear? Are the surroundings as dreary as you made them?

If so, what a forlorn life it must have been for Sarah all these years. I will be glad to help her out of it; no, I mean help her in it, if I may. You are right. I am fond of the country — just as fond of it as I ever was; though I am fond of city life also, and I am pleasantly situated here, but not really at work yet. There seems to have been no open door that I could quite enter. I wonder if it was because I was needed elsewhere? I shall so interpret it, if your friends will receive me. Make all arrangements for me if you can, and I will leave New York as soon as I receive your letter directing me to do so.

I am writing to catch the next mail out, after receiving yours, so there is no time for long stories, nor is there need. I have nothing to tell save the old story: that the Lord is good, and that his tender mercies have been great toward me. A wonderful story, truly; but you know it by heart. Of course the joy over the thought of possibly seeing you soon is great.

The minister arched his eyebrows in evident surprise over the contents of the letter, and made only this comment as he gave it back: " It is very direct and to the point; but I confess I am astonished at the result. Of course you know, Helen, that I hope it will work out according to your desires."

"But you have no faith in it, nevertheless, nor in her," was his sister's mental comment. "You believe that all women, except mother, and possibly myself, are built after the fashion of your shattered idol, and amount to very little in the aggregate. I hope your eyes may be opened sometime."

Perhaps there was a little resentful sparkle in her eyes as she indulged in these thoughts. It really was hard, with the prospect of Hilary so near her, to have so unsympathetic and unappreciative a brother.

A word of explanation is necessary as to why this beloved friend of her youth had never come in contact with her brother. Hilary West had been Helen Ransom's roommate during her entire four years' course at a boarding-school, which was distant several hundred miles from her home. From almost the first day of their companionship they had been friends; congenial in tastes and pursuits. Wonderfully unlike in outward appearance, but wonderfully alike at heart, they had grown toward each other through all these years. Of course the home people had heard a great deal about Helen's school friend, and many plans had been made in regard to her coming to spend some weeks with Helen; but various household matters in both families had intervened to prevent this, and at last Hilary West had graduated, married, and sailed for India with her husband, without ever having met any of her friend's family. Up to that point, life had been continued sunlight with her. The only child in a lovely home, surrounded by all the beauty and culture that wealth and refined taste could secure, consecrated from her early childhood by Christian parents to the service of the Master, whithersoever he would call her, she had been given to the far-away work in India, with tears, it is true, but with tender tears in which smiles intermingled. Father and mother felt their hearts breaking at the thought of parting with her, yet were proud and glad to part with her for such a cause. She had made a safe, pleasant journey to her far-away home, and begun what she thought was her lifework, under circumstances the most hopeful for success.

Then the shadows began to fall. The first news from home brought word that the father had been called from them without a moment's warning. This had left the mother and the little sister, only seven years old, desolate.

"It almost seems as though mother needed me now," the young wife had said with trembling lips, looking up at her husband; but he had bent to kiss the lips which trembled so, and to say tenderly:

"The Lord knows, my darling. Did he not send you out here to work among those who need you?"

So she had thought, and her faith upheld her during the mysteries of that dark hour. She had need for faith; for the darkness thickened about her. Before he had mastered the language so that he could preach even one sermon to the benighted souls he came to reach — though not before he had, by his kindly ways and skillful ministrations to those in physical need, won some hearts — the young missionary succumbed to the disease which makes victims of so many in that land, and the six-months-old bride was a widow. Now, indeed, there was nothing to hinder her from going back to the mother whom she had thought needed her; for the customs and superstitions in that heathen land are such as to make a widow all but useless as a missionary. So, as soon as Mrs. Colchester could arrange her affairs, she sailed alone for America.

A long, weary, dangerous voyage; detained by storm, almost shipwrecked, "in perils often by land and sea," she reached New York only to learn, as the first item of news given to her after she trod her native soil, that her mother, too, had gone home to God. Father and mother and husband in less than one year gathered home! Would it have been any wonder if the young spirit, whose life had been heretofore so bright, had been almost crushed? I confess that such a result would not have seemed wonderful, but to know that the faith of this young woman was equal to the strain, and that after the first shock of the added sorrow was over — nay, even while the first hours of it were still upon her — she cried out, "Though he slay me, yet will I trust in him;" and, after a little, with lips that quivered and smiled: "It is all right. He knows;" — that is, I confess, to me almost a mystery. But, thank God, there are on record many such grand triumphs of faith over sorrow.

Helen Ransom had gone at once to her friend, upon her arrival in this country, and had brought her to spend two precious weeks with her in her father's home, before she went to take up what was now her lifework — the care and training of her little sister Nina. But young Ransom had been hard at work in the second year of his seminary course at the time, and had not met his sister's friend. Truth to tell, he had very little interest in meeting her.

"All girls have friendships," he told his mother, in that oracular fashion in which young men are wont to talk, "and they are always perfect, while it lasts. Helen's dearest is perfect, of course; and in a few years she will not even write to her. I don't think young men have such exclusive friendships. They are more sensible in their arrangements, and think enough of a good many nice fellows, and let it go at that. If Helen corresponds with this paragon of perfection in five years from now, I shall have some curiosity to see her."

This had been in response to a suggestion from his mother, while he was at home for the short vacation, that he should go out of his way on his journey back, a two hours' ride, in order to make the acquaintance of Mrs. Colchester. There was just one young woman at that time whom he considered worthy of taking a two hours' ride to meet, and that was Gertrude Temple. To his mother's hint that his sister's friend was a missionary, and therefore worthy of all the respect that could be paid her, he answered:

"Certainly, my dear mother, if it were going to

do her or the missionary cause any good in life, I would take an extra journey at the risk of the breaking up of a week, in order to shake hands with her; but we must remember that she can have quite as little desire to see me as I have to see her; so it is an unnecessary sacrifice. She has my respect and my sympathy, of course. Her threefold sorrow must have almost crushed the life out of her, and indeed I honestly think that the best thing strangers can do for her at such a time is to let her alone."

That was two years before; and still they had not met. Neither, it must be confessed, was Mr. Ransom any more anxious to meet this woman than he had been in the past. In fact, he shrank from the ordeal in dismay; had he felt that there was the slightest prospect of Helen being able to carry out her scheme, he would have urged against it. A sad-faced, broken-spirited woman was not the one he would have chosen to have come in contact with the Mitchell family, in any effort to help them. Moreover, what did she know of life, from such a standpoint? It was all very well to be a missionary, and it required a certain form of sacrifice, which he admired and respected. But she had gone out to India from a home of wealth and elegance; she had come back from India to inherit the large fortune which her father had left her, and was able to surround herself with elegance still. What had she in common with such a life as she would have to live? Helen was wild, he told himself, half-irritably.

"She thinks that because a girl has spent six months in India as a missionary, she is ready to take up home mission work of this sort; nothing is more absurd. She will be miserable herself, and will make their lives miserable. I gave her credit for some degree of common sense when she declined Helen's invitation to be her guest at my house, but she must have taken leave of it now. As for Helen, I am amazed. The whole scheme is as unlike her usual good sense as possible."

On the whole, the minister was very much perturbed. The improbable had happened. An attack of melancholy, he thought, had induced the rich young widow to turn her steps toward martyrdom. "To the great discomfiture of all concerned, I have no doubt," he muttered, and was perverse enough to feel relieved when, all arrangements having been made, on the day appointed for the stranger's arrival, he was summoned by telegraph to a distant town, where an old college friend lay ill. Circumstances connected with the friend's illness and death necessitated a Sabbath's absence from home, and an exchange of pulpits for the Sabbath following. So that, in point of fact, Mrs. Colchester had been domiciled in the Mitchell homestead for nearly two weeks, and yet Mr. Ransom had not seen her.

When at last her brother reached home, he was

so entirely indifferent to the new-comer that Helen felt piqued, and half-resolved to wait until he himself proposed a call. However, after four days' waiting, she meekly suggested one morning that they improve the pleasant weather and hard roads by riding out to the Mitchell farm. The minister assented with a grave countenance, as if he were resigning himself to a necessity; of course it was a call which must be made some time, and really ought, in courtesy, to have been made before.

Flora Ann, who had been installed as "help," admitted them, much flurried thereby, and left them standing in the hall while she went to receive directions. Calls were not common at the Mitchells', and Flora Ann's reign had been too recent for her to learn what was proper under existing circumstances. She had no sooner disappeared from view than Sarah Jane's head was to be seen leaning over the baluster.

"O, Miss Ransom!" she said; "is it you? Could you come upstairs just a minute? And would Mr. Ransom wait there a few minutes? I will come down just as quick as I can."

Mr. Ransom cordially signified his willingness to "wait there" any length of time, and Helen disappeared. The door leading into the Mitchell parlor stood invitingly open, and the minister, gazing into it abstractedly, not realizing that he was gazing, became suddenly aware that it had undergone a change. He had been in this dreary room several times during the early fall, but the glimpse which he had of it now gave an impression utterly different from that which had lingered in his memory. It dawned upon him that the parlor must have been given up to the boarder. No sooner had he settled this, than the occupant of the room appeared before him. He remembered afterward just how she looked. Quite unlike the mental picture he had unconsciously made of her. That person was tall, and had steely blue eyes, and fluffs of yellow hair about her forehead. He could not have told why; no personal description of the woman for whom he had conceived an unreasoning dislike, had ever been given him.

This woman was perhaps below the medium height, and the arrangement of her hair was very unlike the prevailing style, but fitted the face to perfection. Her eyes were brown, like her hair, and there was a healthy color on cheek and lips. A young, fair, pleasant-faced woman, in a plain black dress. She came swiftly toward the stranger as soon as she caught sight of him, her face breaking into a smile of recognition.

"Is not this the pastor?"

She spoke the title as though there needed nothing else to win recognition and respect. As he half-confusedly bowed assent, she held out her hand cordially.

"I thought so; Helen resembles you. Come in, Mr. Ransom; we receive our friends in this room."

CHAPTER XXII.

A NEW ENGINEER.

YES, the room had undergone a transformation. It was one of those old-fashioned, long, low rooms, which are capable of being made so pleasant. There was an alcove at the further end, formed by some repairs made long ago when a hall room containing one window had been let into the room. If this parlor were to be made into a sleeping-room, the natural place for the bed was in that corner, and there it had been set; at least the minister learned afterward that such was the case. No suggestion of the kind presented itself to him that afternoon. There were heavy curtains hung before the alcove, shutting it out entirely and making the room cosier thereby. There was a fireplace in which at this moment burned a great pine knot that threw a ruddy glow over every somber thing; there was a large table, wheeled into the center of the room, which had about it that air, if one may coin a phrase, of systematic disorder, which betokens constant and intelligent use of books and papers, pens and paper-weights, and all the various belongings of a well-furnished study-table. There was a bookcase occupying a niche near the south window, and behind its glass doors the book-loving eyes of the minister caught the names of treasures. The very common ingrain carpet, dulled by age and worn threadbare in spots, was almost covered from sight by rich rugs, which lay in soft luxuriance at either side of the study-table, in front of the book-case, in front of the fireplace, everywhere indeed that an excuse could be found for laying a rug. There was an old-fashioned lounge or "settee," as it used to be called, which had been in the Mitchell family for generations, but it had been completely transformed simply by having a brilliant afghan, long and wide and soft, thrown over it, and sofa pillows piled high at one end ready for use. Two or three straightbacked, high, uncomfortable chairs still lingered in obscure corners of the room, ready for emergencies, but a study-chair, of peculiar shape and design, a couple of low rockers and a wide-seated arm-chair, occupied the comfortable spaces. To complete the picture of a home, instead of being merely a room, there was a tiny table with a chair of like dimensions set beside it, and near the chair a dolly's crib, on which reposed at the moment the great, fair-faced dolly herself. A little row of shelves occupied the corner, filled with all sorts of treasures dear to a child's heart. There were vases on the old-fashioned mantel, and potted plants in the window, filling the room at that moment with bloom and fragrance. In short, the specklessly clean, but very dreary room, which Mr. Ransom remembered and which he was always sorry to be ushered into, preferring the kitchen by far, had become instinct with beauty and comfort. And the lady, who motioned him to the highbacked chair, and dropped herself into the low rocker, seemed to fit her surroundings extremely well. The very first sentence she spoke was decidedly unconventional.

"Mr. Ransom, do you know I believe Flora Ann has become a Christian?" There was not the slightest bit of affectation in her tone, not a hint that she understood herself to be saying anything out of the ordinary course of conversation with a stranger; instead, there was a quiet assuming of the fact that he was interested in Flora Ann, as a matter of course. Having given his life to the work of soul-saving, he was to be recognized as interested in that theme above all others. In fact, the tone was so natural, and the statement so surprising and interesting, that Mr. Ransom forgot conventionality — forgot that he did not quite approve of the lady who was talking to him, forgot the lady herself, indeed, and thought only of Flora Ann.

"Is it possible!" he said, with eager voice and hearty sympathy; "I did not know the poor girl understood what such a term meant."

"I am not sure that she does. Is there not such a thing as being a Christian without knowing it? Does not the mysterious change come sometimes to ignorant hearts, who do not recognize its name? This girl is very ignorant. I have never met one who was more so. She has no recognition of Christ as a personal Saviour, so far as I understand her, but she has heard of him as a Saviour, and she trusts him, and prays to him daily, hourly; not for herself, you understand, she seems not to have thought of herself at all, but for her miserable brother."

"Jake?" inquired Mr. Ransom, his mind going at once to the reports which Helen had brought him concerning the horrors of the Lucas home when Jake was present.

"Yes, Jake. Humanly speaking, the most hopeless of all that family. The poor girl seems to have grasped the fact that the Lord Jesus Christ is able to save even him, and for this she cries to him constantly."

"This is very strange," said Mr. Ransom, "and very touching. How did she get this much knowledge, Mrs." —— and then he paused, remembering for the first time that he had never been introduced to this lady.

"Mrs. Colchester," she said simply. "I beg your pardon. I took it for granted that you knew my name, because you were Helen's brother."

"I did know it," he said humbly, ashamed of

conventionality before this bright-faced, earnest woman, who had a subject of so great importance to talk about. She did not wait to be led back to it, but answered his question promptly.

"That part of it is very strange to me, too; what information she has secured seems to have come to her through Stephen."

"Stephen! I did not think he possessed enough knowledge to impart any. You do not think he has found the way?"

"Not for himself, but he has pointed it out to another. I think he knows the way, Mr. Ransom, but does not choose to walk therein — like so many of his brothers and sisters. But Flora Ann is different; she is simply sublimely unselfish. Hearing of Jesus Christ and his power to save, her faith has sprung entirely past herself, and laid hold upon Him for her brother. I wanted you to know about it," she added, simply, "because the poor girl ought to be helped, ought to be instructed; and it is such a peculiar case; she is so entirely ignorant, and yet so intensely in earnest, that I have not known how to teach her; have not dared to touch it, indeed. And Sarah feels much the same; Sarah is a very lovely Christian, Mr. Ransom, but a beginner, you know; and therefore — well, I am not a beginner; I have been personally acquainted with Jesus for a great many years; but I confess I do not know what to say to this young girl. And, besides, Mr. Ransom, there are others.

Not only that entire Lucas family, but other families not far away from us, who need help so very much. Could we not have a meeting? A regular evening service here, until we get hold of the people, and induce them to take the trouble to go to church? Indeed, some of them are too far away, and too feeble or too poor, to make church practicable just now. But could we not have a service? Are you too busy to undertake it?"

"Not at all," he said, with the enthusiasm of one who was ready to meet any effort half-way. "I have wanted to undertake it. One difficulty has been to find a place. Helen and I have talked it over, and suggested and abandoned several plans already."

Mrs. Colchester glanced about her pretty room.

"Could we not have them here, Mr. Ransom? Wouldn't that do for a time? Or, perhaps, in the dining-room; that is a large room; a real old-fashioned, farmhouse room, very cheery and comfortable. I am sure Mr. and Mrs. Mitchell would gladly lend it for an evening service. And Sarah and I could trim it with evergreens, and make it bright and inviting. Then, my piano is on its way; if it could be moved into that wide old hall once a week, I could lead the music. Oh! I hope something of the sort is feasible."

"I am sure it is," said the minister heartily. "You are making it so."

Then there was a sound of flying feet on the

stairs, and Sarah Jane came in, her face flushed with haste and excitement.

"I was hurrying down to introduce you," she said, looking from her boarder to her guest. "But I guess you don't need it."

"No," said Mr. Ransom, smiling; "I think we are introduced."

Then he stepped aside for Helen to greet her friend, as she greeted no other woman. He looked on with curious interest while the two women, so nearly of an age, so unlike in all other respects, exchanged greetings. How fond they were of each other. He had known that for years, but it had never seemed entirely reasonable until that moment.

"She is very different from other people," he told himself, as he watched the two. This "missionary woman," as he had called her, not taking the trouble to remember her name, had known the neighborhood but a few days, yet she said "we," and "us," and "our," like one who had adopted the people, and meant to center her interests and her influence among them. He had known her but a few moments, yet they had carried on a conversation about the most important concern that belongs to human kind, with the manner of those who were friends, as a matter of course, and one in sympathy. Well, were they not? Had she not evidently the interests of the Master at heart? And was not his work in the world the same as hers? It would be foolish not to enjoy such a woman; not to meet her frankly on her own ground, and take freely and gratefully the help she was so freely offering. Certainly work ought to be begun in that neighborhood, if there were none but the Lucas and Mitchell families; were they not worth reaching after? He ought to be ashamed of himself for having been so slow. He would take hold of the matter now with vigor. He dimly realized that a certain amount of vigor was being breathed into him by the atmosphere which surrounded him. He would show Mrs. Colchester that her confidence was not misplaced; that he was as deeply interested in this work as she had thought him to be.

"Nay," he said to himself, with humility, "I will prove to the Lord Jesus Christ, by my life, that I am interested in souls above all things else. That I am ready to work anywhere, with anybody; to take the lead, or be led, as He shall direct. I thought I was roused some weeks ago, but I am afraid there are portions of the work that I have been shirking. If I know my own heart, I mean utter self-surrender now. And personal fancies or distastes shall have nothing to do with it. There is power enough in Jesus Christ to save even Jake Lucas, though I have not been able to realize it before."

Thoughts somewhat like these surged rapidly through his mind, but there was all the while an undertone of consciousness that it would not be disagreeable to work in this portion of the vineyard.

They had intended to make a call of reasonable length, and have time to call at the Bascomes on their way home; but, as a matter of fact, they spent the afternoon — staid to tea, indeed, and Sarah Jane, in a flutter of excited delight, served them in her best style: had her table set in napery of the whitest, and ironed until it shone; had a vase, which Mrs. Colchester had given her, crowned with a single flower that Helen had brought her, in the center of the table; had gems of rare puffiness, which she had learned to make while at the manse; had strawberries of her mother's own canning — and Mrs. Mitchell knew how to can strawberries; had new-laid eggs, poached as even the minister rarely had opportunity to see them, for there were some things Sarah Jane did well, because she had what her mother called "knack." In short, I suppose there was rarely a tea-table enjoyed as much as that one at the Mitchell farmhouse.

Stephen, who had expected to be embarrassed before Mrs. Colchester, and who had but half-liked the scheme at any time, had forgotten to be afraid of her after the first day, and was learning to handle even his napkin with ease, and a certain degree of satisfaction. As for little Nina, about whom I see I have said nothing at all, she was simply the sweetest, most winsome child of eight that ever made sunshine in a home. She had centered herself with one bound in Mr. Mitchell's heart — called him "grandpa," and bestowed all the pretty little attentions and courtesies upon him which a child of eight can give to a man who looks as though he were nearly seventy; though, in point of fact, Mr. Mitchell was not so old by years as he looked; but he had lived too hard and fast in his youth to have a genial or appropriate middle age.

Truth to tell, Mr. Mitchell had dreaded the invasion into his home as no other member of the family had done. It might have been hard for Stephen, but it was martyrdom for his father; yet he had surrendered his heart to Nina, and already began to feel as though the house would be a desolate place without her.

Flora Ann, who sat at the table with the rest, according to the customs of the locality, kept herself in absolute quiet, but with eyes alert for anything that might be wanted of her, and at the same time with ears attent for anything which might be said that could help her in the consuming desire of her heart. For a feeling, which was almost a passion, had taken hold of her, in regard to her brother. He was daily becoming more of a terror in his home, and her prayers were daily becoming more intense and importunate. Mr. Ransom noticed the watchful eyes of the girl, and, remembering what Mrs. Colchester had said, shaped some of his conversation with a view to encouraging the desire of her heart.

"Mr. Mitchell," he said, "do you know the man they call 'Old Roger?' He lives about a mile from town; a shoemaker by trade."

"O, yes!" said Mr. Mitchell; "I know Old Roger; Smithson his name is, though you don't often hear the last name. He used to work for the Harding Brothers until they discharged him. Since that time he hasn't done much but drink and swear. He is a hard old case."

"That describes the character he has earned; and he has sustained it well for the last five or six years, they tell me; but the description won't answer any longer, sir — Old Roger is made over. People will be calling him 'Mr. Smithson' soon."

"Is that so?" exclaimed Mr. Mitchell. "Why, I haven't heard anything like that. What has happened to him?"

"The Lord Jesus Christ has met and saved him," said the minister earnestly, with an involuntary glance toward Flora Ann, whose eyes seemed to fairly glow. "He went to the city some time ago, got intoxicated there, and quarrelsome, and was arrested; he spent the night in the lockup — spent two days there, in fact. It seems a curious place in which to reform, but that is exactly what Roger did. He came in contact with some Christian workers, who succeeded in making him acquainted with Jesus Christ, the only one who can save. He has been true to his word once more, and Roger is saved. That is the story in brief. Is it not a marvelous thing that the Lord can take hold of such wrecks as that, and make men of them?"

Mr. Mitchell was absolutely silent. He was thinking that there were people who gave up the drink without the help of the Lord Jesus Christ. But did it make men of them? He had all his life felt bowed down under the weight of his early evil-doing. He had carried about with him a discouraged, disappointed heart, and had told himself that he had wrecked not only his own prospects, but those of his children, and that there was no help for him; yet it was years since he had drank a drop of liquor. His wife, who had not studied his face for a quarter of a century without understanding it, knew something of what he was thinking, and ventured her timid response to the minister's words:

"But folks do sometimes give up the drink without His doing it for them, don't they?"

Mr. Ransom turned toward her in surprise. He did not know Mr. Mitchell's story. Why should she be anxious to emphasize that side of the question?

"There is a sense in which He never does it for them," he said; "that is, there is a part which they must do for themselves. They must yield their wills to the power which is trying to save them. But I question whether a man is ever saved from liquor, or from any other evil habit, except by the power of Jesus Christ. He may not recognize that power; he may not give himself afterward to the service of Christ; but by so much has he been freed from Satan's power, if he is freed from the curse of liquor, and the only one who is stronger than Satan is Jesus Christ."

"Then he ought to love Jesus just for that."

It was Nina's clear, child-like voice which took up the story.

"Yes," said the minister emphatically; "he ought. He is only half a man who can receive such help as that from the Saviour of the world, and yet fail to own it, or to give Him thankful service in return."

"Grandpa wouldn't be such a man as that, would you, Grandpa?"

Mrs. Mitchell's face flushed, and her eyes took an anxious look; and Stephen's hand trembled so that he almost dropped the cup he was lifting to his lips. None of the rest knew cause for special anxiety; but Mr. Mitchell put out his wrinkled hand and touched tenderly the golden curls clustered around Nina's neck, and said not a word.

CHAPTER XXIII.

BLOCKING THE TRACK.

BEFORE they went home that night, it had been arranged that there should be, on the following Friday evening, a religious service in the Mitchell dining-room, and Stephen had promised to tell any neighbor who passed that way, or with whom he came in contact, and give the invitation.

"It is out of my line," he said, with an awkward smile, avoiding the minister's earnest eyes as he spoke, "but then I s'pose I can do it."

"I do not wonder that you are fond of Mrs. Colchester, Helen," the minister said, as they rode home in the moonlight; "she is very pleasant and winning in her manner."

And Helen, like the wise woman that she was, resisted the temptation to say, "I thought you would discover that there were other women in the world beside Gertrude Temple," and held her peace.

The winter, which a few months before had seemed to stretch endlessly ahead of Mr. Ransom, passed as if by magic. He was so absorbed in his work, and there was so much work to be done, that he had no time to regret the holidays when they were fairly upon him, although he had regretted them much in anticipation, because of the contrast in his life with that of a year ago. He even forgot the date of the last letter he wrote to Gertrude Temple, and was so absorbed in preparations for the Christmas-tree for the Hilton Hill Sunday-school that he forgot to recall how he was occupied just a year before, till some chance remark of Helen's suggested that time, and then he smiled, somewhat sadly, it is true, over what he had taught himself to call his blighted past, but the next minute he responded to Stephen Mitchell's call for help in fastening up the evergreen over the west window, and forgot all about it.

By this time you know that a Sunday-school was started in the Hilton Hill neighborhood, and I may as well tell you now that it was a success. Even Sarah Jane Mitchell, who thought she knew the neighborhood well, declared one day that she didn't see where the children came from. They seemed to spring up in the night. As for the meetings started in the Mitchell dining-room, who shall tell what they had wrought?

"From the very first," Mr. Ransom said, speaking of them with deep feeling to an intimate friend long afterward: "from the very first the Lord seemed to smile upon that effort. Do you remember how surprised we were over the number who came the first night? And what a joy it was to hear Mrs. Mitchell break the timid silence of years, and pray before them all! And how wonderful it was when Flora Ann came to a knowledge of herself and gave the wealth of her heart's love to Jesus."

Oh! they were weeks to remember. And the interest, instead of dying out as the spring drew near, seemed steadily to increase. Not only had the Sunday-school been started, but a reading-circle was organized and a young people's club that had the temperance pledge for its center, which pledge was signed by some who were least expected to take that stand.

In short, as Fanny Bascome put it: "That stony old Hilton Hill neighborhood has become the fashion. If you don't go out there to their prayer-meetings and clubs, and I don't know what all, you don't amount to anything."

But despite all the good that had been wrought, there was no denying the fact that some who had been prayed for most earnestly, and reached after with most persistent effort, failed to be moved. Among these was Stephen Mitchell, the minister's special care and anxiety.

"I am greatly disappointed," Mr. Ransom said to Mrs. Colchester; "in fact, I may as well own that my faith has gotten a setback. I confidently looked for him as a first fruit. He interested me from the first time that I ever spoke with him, and seemed fairly started on the road toward a better life, even then."

"He is improving very rapidly," said Mrs. Colchester. "Sarah makes good progress, and so indeed does Flora, but they are both slow compared with him. You would be surprised, Mr. Ransom, to see how rapidly he acquires that which he has set his mind upon learning, which is, by the way, the explanation of your disappointment. He has set his mind and heart upon acquiring knowledge in certain directions. Something, or some one, has roused in him the determination to become a skilled farmer, and everything agricultural, or anything which will tend toward agricultural knowledge, is seized upon with avidity. If the book or the person, whoever it was, who started him in this direction, could have laid the other foundation first, Stephen would have been won for Christ before now."

Then the minister looked at her in a startled, troubled way. He remembered his first walk with Stephen when they went "across lots" to the Lucas place. He remembered distinctly the conversation which had been carried on. A few words he spoke for Christ at that time, surely he did. But he recalled with humiliation and pain that his special effort had been to arouse in Stephen an ambition to reconstruct the old farm, which had been for years so nearly a failure. The foundation work had been his. He knew he was responsible for having started Stephen in the direction in which he was pressing. He tried to find comfort in the thought of the sermon which he had preached, using Stephen's words. Certainly then he had tried very hard to lead the young man to a sense of his need of Jesus Christ, and the importance of making that the first work. Yes; but the first impression was evidently the stronger. And the first impression had been made in another direction.

That evening the minister went home troubled at heart. But if Stephen Mitchell had been called as a witness, and had been honest with himself, he would have owned that enough had been said to lead him to understand fully the importance of choosing Christ as his leader, in the new life-journey he meant to take.

He is simply another illustration of the power which is at work in this world, keeping people away from the road which they ought to travel; setting their wills against the decision which they ought to make. Stephen Mitchell could not have explained, even to his own satisfaction, why he was so persistent in his determination to avoid all decisions of this kind. Why he should listen to Mr. Ransom's sermons with a view to getting every bit of information out of them which they could give, and shut his heart determinately against any call to himself. Why he accepted, at Mrs.

Colchester's gracious hand, assistance in writing, in reading, in the study of words, in the construction of sentences, and was grateful for it all, but turned from her almost rudely the moment she attempted to speak a word for the Master whom she served. Why he met Sarah Jane half-way in all her improvements in the home, and in her plans for future development, but told her gruffly "not to preach," when she asked him if he had read the verse on the card which she had given him, and if he didn't think it was about something which ought to be looked after. Nay, he even turned coldly away from his mother one night, after she had prayed for her children in the prayer meeting, and told her heartlessly, when she questioned him as to what was the matter, that he "didn't care about being prayed at; he thought folks better keep such things to themselves."

Oh! there was no question but that Stephen's conscience was enlightened enough, and was being very much wrought upon; it was his stubborn will which was blocking the track.

"I don't understand him," said Sarah Jane frankly, to Miss Ransom. "He isn't a bit as I thought he would be. Why, the first time the thing dawned upon me that I could have the Lord Jesus Christ for my friend, I was happy enough to shout. Do you remember when it was? I was at your house, that first three weeks, and I wanted to come home right away, and tell Steve about it. I thought I would only have to tell him how it was, and he would take hold of it. I never once thought that he would hang back from such a chance as that."

There was another who "hung back" from all the chances which might have redeemed his wrecked life; that was Jake Lucas. Despite all their invitations and appeals, he had not once attended the neighborhood prayer meetings, nor been inside the little red schoolhouse after the Sunday services were established there. Others of the Lucas family had been reached, and in a measure helped. The little girls came regularly to Sabbath school, and were learning outward propriety of behavior, at least. Miranda was quite a frequent attendant at the afternoon service, and occasionally came to the midweek prayer-meeting, and was at least respectful when spoken to as to her personal interest, or responsibility; Mrs. Colchester felt sure that she was thinking.

Even poor, worthless Jim had lounged in once or twice of a Sunday afternoon, when he was less intoxicated than usual, and had admitted to Flora Ann that the singing was "fine," and that maybe some time or other, when he felt like it, he would come again. And the poor old mother, weighed down with the sorrows of many years of disappointment and ill treatment, found a refuge at last, and crept into it like a bruised soul in dire need of shelter; but Jake would have none of it.

Would not even answer when asked to the meeting; growled at his mother, and swore at Miranda for having anything to do with the "canting hypocrites," and threatened at last to "knock the breath out" of Flora Ann's body, if she ever "opened her head to him about any of them things again," and, in short, steadily grew worse and worse. As the spring opened, it seemed folly to invite him to come to the meetings, for he was rarely ever sober enough for them to have been of any avail.

"I am afraid," said the minister, with a long-drawn sigh, "I am afraid Jake is a hopeless case. That miserable Jim and the other one may possibly be reached. They are better natured, naturally, than Jake. I have even hopes, at times, of the old sot of a father; but I confess that it requires more faith to pray for Jake than I seem able to exercise."

"There is one who will pray for him as long as she has breath, I think," Helen said, with a grave smile. "The tenacity with which she holds on to that worthless brother is remarkable. He is more cruel to her than he is to any of the others. Mrs. Mitchell confided to me last week that she 'hated' to have the girl go home, because her brother abused her so."

It was all true. Flora Ann's bloodshot eye or bruised arm often told silently and eloquently the story of her wrongs, yet she prayed on.

Perhaps there was hardly one of the group for

whom the winter had done more than it had for Flora. She was wonderfully changed. Wholesome food, and enough of it, eaten at regular intervals, had rounded out her form and made her less hollow-eyed and hungry looking. Then her dress, though very poor and plain, of course, was always scrupulously neat nowadays, and Mrs. Colchester began to see to it that on Sundays and extra days there were little brightening touches put to it, which made a wonderful difference in the girl's appearance. She had become skilled in many little household ways, meantime; and Mrs. Mitchell did not hesitate to pronounce her "real downright good help; enough sight better than I had any kind of notion she ever would be. She is willing to learn, and that's half the battle."

She was still very quiet and reserved, speaking plainly her thoughts and feelings to no one but Stephen, whom she always looked upon as her first friend, the one who had protected her unexpectedly from Jake on that terrible midnight of her mother's sickness. Perhaps Stephen listened to her more patiently than to any of the others, because she never spoke to him of himself. Never seemed to realize, indeed, but that he was in all respects what he should be. It was about Jake that she poured out her anxieties.

"Why don't you let him alone?" Steve asked her roughly, though not unkindly. "He kicks you about as if you was a toad. I wouldn't stand it; he is just a worthless fellow, too; why not let him go?"

"Oh! I can't, Steve, I can't! There is something here"—laying her hand on her heart—"which tells me to pray for him, and pray, and pray. I guess if I knew he was going to kill me, I should pray right on. Steve, it is just an awful thing not to have him saved. He is so bad—worse than the rest, you know—worse than anybody around. I heard a man say last night, coming home behind me, that Jake Lucas was the worst fellow in the neighborhood for miles around; and it is so, and he ought to be saved, Steve. He could be so easy, if he only would."

Stephen did not believe this. In his heart he even sneered at the idea of any one caring whether Jake Lucas was saved or not, and as to it being "easy" to make a changed man of him, nothing seemed more improbable.

"Humph!" he said in reply, "I wouldn't pester him about religion, if I were you. If the fellow would get sense enough to give up his whiskey and be half-way decent, it would be all I would ask, and enough sight more than I expect," he added in muttered undertone as he strode away.

Nevertheless, his conscience troubled him. Had he not been called a "champion" of the Lucas family? What was he doing to further their interests? For Flora Ann he had begun to have a very friendly, brotherly sort of feeling. He aided her in her laborious studies to the best of his ability, and his ability was steadily growing. Still, he was well aware that Mrs. Colchester, and the minister and his sister, and even Sarah Jane herself, were doing more for Flora Ann than he could. As for the others of the family, he was letting them severely alone. What if he should induce Jake to reform! not to "get religion" — he had no confidence in that for Jake — but to sign the pledge, and let whiskey alone. "Father did it," he muttered to himself when in severest solitude ; father has let it alone this many a year, and he didn't sign a pledge, either. Jake could stop if he was a mind to, of course. What if there should be a way that I could coax him to do it? and he half-formed a purpose to try, at the next opportunity; not without an undertone wish that the opportunity might be long in coming. And this state of mind perhaps any of us, who have been hard pressed by conscience, can understand, but opportunities are not very hard to find, and very often they come unsought. Stephen's did. Not two hours after the conversation last recorded, Jake came lumbering over from the cabin to borrow a hoe. He was more nearly sober than the morning often found him, and he had a vague intention of trying to behave in a respectable manner to people who did not belong to his own family. But if Stephen had been skilled in the study of the human face, he would have known that Jake was very cross; that every nerve was tingling with a desire for the liquor which he had no means of getting. The only thing of which Stephen thought was that here was his chance, a rarer one than had come to him for months, so far as Jake was concerned. If he actually meant business, it ought to be improved. He looked over toward the window of the upper back room which Flora Ann occupied, and strengthened his resolution by remembering the prayer which had floated in to him from the cracks in the wall only that morning: "O, Lord Jesus, do please save Jake. You know you can if he will let you. Do please do something to make him let you."

"Yes," said Stephen, "you can have the hoe if you will bring it back; I want to use it this afternoon. And look here, Jake, if I was you, it appears to me I would turn over a new leaf; now is as good a time as any."

Jake turned upon him the most astonished pair of bloodshot eyes that he had ever seen; but was apparently dumb with amazement. So, taking heart at the silence, Stephen went on:

"If you would let whiskey alone, Jake, you could be a decent fellow. People would help you, and would help your folks; they need it bad enough, the land knows. It is just because people are discouraged about you that they don't try to do things for the family. There is your mother, with her sick spells coming oftener, Flora Ann says;

she will go in one of them spells yet, and then how will you feel?"

Certainly Stephen had made an effort; had done what was his best. Jake still stared at him, but found voice at last to speak distinctly:

"If I was you, I would mind my everlasting own business. You are a miserable little puppy that ain't worth the salt you eat on your potatoes, and that get your very clothes out of other folks; begging and fawning and whining around preachers, and their set. And then you undertake to turn preacher yourself. You just mind your own business, will you, every time?" And he shouldered the hoe and strode off; none too soon, perhaps, for there was a fierce light in Stephen's eyes, and his muscles were strong and firm. If Jake had known it, his would-be helper had exercised a mighty self-control to keep from knocking him down. As it was, he trembled under the excitement of temptation. He looked after Jake with dangerous eyes, but took no step to follow him. In fact, he stood perfectly still until the excitement had somewhat subsided, then he said aloud and firmly:

"Well, I have done it; done my level best, and it is the last time. Flora Ann can pray forever, if she is such a fool as to do it, for all I shall try to help — she might as well pray for that stump out there to split itself up into kindling-wood. It would never do it, and he will never reform; he don't want to, nor mean to. I have washed my hands of the whole of them."

No; he didn't mean Flora Ann; there was a mental reservation concerning her. The truth is he was separating her in his mind as far as possible from the Lucas family. She was beginning to be classed with the Mitchell family. Then this illogical young man took an axe, and proceeded with strong, powerful strokes to demolish and make into kindling-wood the very stump which had served him as an illustration. If he had only understood enough of theology to realize the force of his own worked-out illustration. It was true that the great stump could never make itself into kindling-wood; but a power outside of and superior to itself, could and did.

CHAPTER XXIV.

THE WRONG ROAD.

WITHIN the week something occurred which brought Flora Ann home from a visit to her father's cabin, red eyed and miserable.

"Jake's gone," she said to the first person she met as she entered the house, and that person happened to be Stephen. "Jake has gone off; he never came home last night, nor the night before; and Bill says some of the boys saw him get on the train; and he's tooken his things, and he never did that before. He never staid from home a whole night in his life. Ma says so, and she says her heart is just broke." Whereupon Flora Ann sat down in an utterly forlorn heap on one of the kitchen chairs, and buried her head in her hands, and cried.

"A good riddance, I think," said Stephen, brusquely; "I wouldn't take on about it, if I were you. Maybe it will be the saving of your mother's life; she couldn't have stood the way he is going on much longer. Didn't you tell me yourself that he kicked her only the last time you were home?

And that was the very day that I"— Then Stephen stopped abruptly. He was not going to own, even before Flora Ann, that he had made an effort and failed. "If any fellow had kicked my mother, I reckon I wouldn't cry because he had taken himself off. Look at your wrist there, all black-and-blue this minute, because he twisted it so the last time you saw him, when you was trying to keep him from kicking your mother, and yet you cry about him being gone. I would have more spirit."

"It ain't that," said Flora Ann, between the sobs. "But I thought, you see — I thought he would be different; and now he has run away. And the last thing he did was to kick mother, and hurt me, and swear at the little girls. Oh! it is just too awful to think of him gone."

"Oh! but he hasn't gone away from God." It was Nina's clear, astonished voice which made this startling announcement. She had come into the kitchen with her velvet tread, a few minutes before, and stopping in dismay to see Flora Ann in tears, had been absorbed in her story. Flora raised her eyes and looked at the child, the misery in her face slowly dying out.

"That is as true as a Bible verse," she said, at last. "We can't get away from God, can we? I thank you for that, Miss Nina. I will go right straight on praying for him."

"I will pray for him, too," said Nina, her own

eyes full of sympathetic tears. Then Stephen went out, slamming the door a little as he did so. He was vexed with Flora Ann for being "such a fool."

It was the evening for prayer meeting in the Mitchell dining-room; and Mrs. Colchester, who had heard the story of Jake's disappearance, and Flora's grief, from little Nina, presented his case for special prayer. It was a prayer meeting to remember; Mrs. Mitchell, having once found voice, had such joy in this prayer circle, that it was ceasing to be a cross to spread her wants before the Lord in words which her friends could hear. And she prayed for Jake that night so that his mother's heart, at least, would have been touched, had she heard it. Miranda was there, and cried softly behind the corner of Flora Ann's neat white apron, which had been lent to her to cover certain disreputable portions of her dress. Then Mrs. Colchester prayed, and Helen Ransom, and the minister — all for Jake. Then little Nina, as simply and naturally as though she had been kneeling by her own bedside, bowed her head on her folded hands, and said, "Dear Lord Jesus, please find Jake to-night, and save him, and take care of him for his mother and Flora."

It was then that Flora Ann's heart broke entirely, and she sobbed out her cry to the Lord, for the first time in the hearing of human ears:

"O, Lord, please do save him; we know you

can if he will let you. Oh! do please do something to make him let you."

Mr. Mitchell coughed a good many times that evening, and used his handkerchief as often for his eyes as he did in any other way. He shook his head when Nina brought him the book for the closing hymn; when she looked wondering and regretful, he bent down and whispered to her that he couldn't sing to-night. Just as the minister was about to offer the closing prayer, an electric thrill went through the hearts of the little company, for Mr. Mitchell was rising to his feet. He took hold of Nina's hand as he said: "Friends, this little girl wants me to tell you to-night that I have begun to pray, too, and that I join you in praying for Jake. I have been a good many years finding out that it was the Lord who helped me, but the little girl has shown me the way to him at last; and my poor service, such as it is, I am going to give him for the rest of my days. I thank him to-night for all the way he has led me, though I was blind, and didn't know I was being led."

Stephen was not there to hear his father's voice. He had taken his lamp early and gone up to his own room, shaking his head in response to Sarah Jane's petition that he would come down in time for the meeting; replying gruffly that he hadn't "time for meetings;" he had got a "tough lesson to get out." In the midst of Sarah Jane's joy over her father was a sigh for her brother. She was very anxious for this young man, who, everybody said, was improving so rapidly. Her daily prayer for him, though perhaps not so heart-rending, was as earnest as Flora Ann's for her brother.

The night was a beautiful moonlight one, and as the minister and his sister rode home they talked about the blessed meeting they had had, and the changes which even a short time had wrought in the Hilton Hill neighborhood.

"It is truly astonishing," said the minister, "that we have all been asleep so long; why, the fields were white for the harvest. Those people listen as if for their lives. I am sure there were many consciences wrought upon to-night; the stand that Mr. Mitchell has taken is worth a great deal. It is a wonderful thing to see a man of his years come out squarely for the Lord. We have now another proof of the truth that 'a little child shall lead them.'"

"Hilary has been watching for this for some days," said Helen. "She told me two weeks ago that Nina was not going to be satisfied until 'grandpa' prayed. They have had long talks together, he and Nina; he has asked her a great many puzzling questions which she has brought to Hilary, of course; and, I suppose, has been carefully taught how to answer them; though Hilary says she has been taught of God."

"I do not doubt it," said the minister heartily. "Her sister evidently is; I think she is peculiarly a woman who is led by the Spirit."

Then the talk drifted toward Jake, and the wonderful prayers which had been offered for him that night, and they wondered where on the broad earth he was.

"Only the Listener to our prayers knows," said the minister. "Isn't it wonderful to think that he carries the sins and sorrows of this great old world on his heart, and hears the cry of every child of his, and treasures up their requests, and brings to pass, through them, human impossibilities? I have faith for even Jake to-night. I don't know how many years it will be before the Lord will find him, but it does seem to me as though those prayers to-night have been answered, and that Jake is to be saved."

"That is just what Hilary said," was Helen's jubilant response. "In the hall she put her arms around me and whispered, 'Do you know, I expect to meet Jake in Heaven?'"

"Did she?" said the minister; and there was a very satisfied note in his voice. It gave him, to say the least, a not unpleasant sensation to learn that he and Mrs. Colchester had thought alike.

In the meantime, what of Jake? If those who prayed could have seen him at that particular moment, I do not know but their faith would have almost failed them. He was distant three hundred miles from his home, on one of the dangerous streets of a large city. He was partially sober, for the simple reason that he had failed in securing any liquor since morning. He was cold and hungry and utterly miserable. He had been intoxicated when he left his home, and had continued so during the hours in which he had begged and stolen his way to this point. What his plans had been in going away, even he never knew. A vague idea that sometime he would run away, and get rid of "the whole pack," as he called his family ties, had possessed him for months; why he had not carried it into execution before, he could not have explained. Why he selected that particular night for starting, only He who overrules all events can tell. Half an hour before the moment in which we introduce him to you he had occupied a corner of a down-town omnibus. It was what we call a chance incident which had given him the opportunity. He had been standing at the street corner, more utterly dreary and desolate than he had ever felt in his life. A burning thirst for liquor in his throat, not a penny with which to gratify that thirst; not a spot to go to warm his half-frozen body; not a place where he could get a mouthful of food or a chance to sleep. Perhaps for the first time in his life, he had a dim impression that even the wretched home from which he had run away was worth something. Two ladies descended from an omnibus which had drawn up very near the curbstones. As they did so, the string, which confined two or three bundles in the hand of one of them, broke, and the bundles rolled. It was a wonder that Jake Lucas thought to stoop and pick them up, or, thinking, cared to take the trouble. Perhaps he had in his heart a hope that they would reward him; at least, he gathered the packages, brushed off the filth of the street as well as he could, and carried them to their owner.

"Poor fellow!" she said compassionately, as she offered her thanks; "I haven't a cent of change. Will an omnibus ticket do you any good?"

He had smiled cynically as he took the offered ticket. What good would an omnibus ticket do him? But the lady was not out of sight before he decided to make it useful. Why should he not have a ride in an omnibus, since there was nothing else for him to do? It must at least be warmer there than on the street corner, and by the time it had reached the end of its route, it might land him in a part of the city where he could somehow manage to get something to drink. So he hailed a passing omnibus, and seated himself in the corner, drawing his hat well over his face. He paid little or no attention to the constantly-changing passengers, not even glancing at a middle-aged, well-dressed man, who was quietly, from time to time, passing little slips of printed paper to one and another. He had halted before Jake once or twice, and looked at him doubtfully, but, seeming to decide that the man was too much intoxicated to be approached, had turned away. He was about to leave the omnibus as a couple entered it — a young and elegantly-dressed lady, accompanied by a gentleman. The stranger offered his slips of paper to both of these.

"What is it?" asked the lady, as they seated themselves, and the seat she had taken was beside Jake. The gentleman laughed.

"It is an invitation to the midnight mission, Gertrude. Shall we go?"

"O, dear!" said the lady, echoing the laugh. "Do you suppose he thought us suspicious-looking characters? I wonder if mine is the same? Yes; it is. 'Come to the mission to-night, and hear the song, "I was lost, but Jesus found me."'

"That does mean us, Charlie; we have been lost, you know. Are you sure you can find your way home now? We are certainly in a part of the city that I have never seen before. O, Charlie! mine is a tract on the other side; the most solemn talk you ever heard of. The idea of giving such things out in a public omnibus. What in the world made me take it? I don't want a tract. Do you suppose they ever do any good in that way, Charlie? I believe I will try it. Here, my good fellow, don't you want a tract? You look as though you needed something of that sort."

"My dear," said "Charlie," in warning undertone, as the pretty gloved hand was reached over toward Jake, "don't speak to the fellow; he is intoxicated."

"Never mind; he won't hurt me. Take it, my man. If you will read it, and do as it says, I have no doubt you will be improved. O, Charlie! we are passing the Twenty-third Street Theater. Now I know where we are. We must take the green line of cars at this corner."

And Gertrude Temple gathered her handsome robes about her, and followed her escort from the omnibus, leaving the little tract in Jake Lucas's hand.

He had not accepted it; he had simply let it lie passive on his arm, where it had dropped, while he remained lost in astonishment over being addressed by an elegant woman. Presently he took the tract in his thumb and finger, and held it up to the light. When Jake was a little boy the Lucas family had been almost respectable, and his early educational opportunities had been passable. He could read much better than Flora Ann. The words on the tract were very distinct to him:

Come to the Mission on Wilmoth Street to-night, and hear the song, "I was lost, but Jesus found me," and get a bowl of hot soup and a good night's rest.

Here, then, was his opportunity. The singing he cared nothing for; there was no objection, of course, to their throwing it in, if they were fools enough to do so; but the bowl of hot soup was not to be despised, since he could not get whiskey; and the thought of a place to sleep, to a man who had wandered homeless for three nights, was certainly inviting. He wondered vaguely where Wilmoth Street was, and how he was expected to find it. He even muttered a curse on the people who hadn't brains enough to define the locality. Then he turned the tract over, and glanced contemptuously down the other side, where the words were which Gertrude Temple had pronounced "solemn." While he was looking at it, the omnibus driver put his head in at the little window, and called, "Wilmoth Street; change cars for Green Avenue," and Jake started up at the sound of the name, and lumbered out again into the night, Gertrude Temple's tract still between his thumb and finger. Now he was in the lowest and most crowded portion of the city. Saloons, gambling-houses, and all kindred places of evil resort, seemed to have headquarters here. The air was throbbing with the fumes of vile tobacco, and viler whiskey. The air was pulsing with oaths. Jake Lucas, only half-sober, burning with the desire for whiskey, stumbled on, looking in at the brightly-lighted soul-traps — the only cheery spots on all that dismal street; they allured him with sight, and sound, and smell. He was kept from entering only by the thought that he had no money, and by the knowledge of the fact that such as he would be unceremoniously kicked out of all such places, unless money in some form could be produced. He cursed the tract he still clutched in his hand, because he could not hope to turn it into whiskey, and stumbled on.

CHAPTER XXV.

REVIEWING THE ROAD.

IN due course of time, summer came again to the Hilton Hill neighborhood; and if summer were that sentient creature which poets would have us believe, she would undoubtedly have looked about her in wonder, over the changes which one brief year had wrought. There were hints of change all through the neighborhood, but nowhere were they so marked as on the Mitchell farm. Stephen himself, in the midst of his busy life, occasionally took time to look about him with admiring surprise, and contrast it all with but the June before. Not for a single day had Stephen Mitchell lost sight of the new idea which had taken possession of him during that first walk to the Lucas cabin. It was on the way back, while the minister was trying to press upon his attention other and more important concerns, that he had resolved to put all his strength into the old farm, and see " what would come of it." He possessed certain admirable qualities for grappling with such a task. He had always, from childhood, persevered in his undertakings; the main difficulty in his life having been that he had rarely been offered sufficient inducement to undertake. He possessed, also, an almost exhaustless patience; so, when he was roused and energized by encouraging words, he had put himself into the effort. It had been hard work at first; yet very soon it grew interesting simply to note how many opportunities for acquiring knowledge seemed to open before him. He began to listen to the chance talk which he heard among farmers from time to time, and to discover therefrom how many things could be done on the old farm, which had been left undone. It surprised him to learn how many of these things lay within the scope of his own strength. Once realizing that he was worth something in the world, and that he could "make a difference" in life about him, he bent all his awakened energies to the work. The result was not large in any way, nor remarkable, except to people who had for years let strength run to waste; it meant simply a mended fence here; a mended hinge there; a few lights of glass set in a certain window; a coat of whitewash in some places, a coat of paint in others; a general picking up and clearing up about barnyard and farmyard, and a surprising "difference" began to manifest itself. People driving by remarked upon it. "The Mitchell place is coming up," they said, one to another.

As spring opened, and work began with such

earnestness as the fields had not known for years, the ever-ready ground responded; the dew and the rain, and the sunshine of Heaven, blossomed things into beauty; and people said: "What has happened to the Mitchells? Their fields haven't looked like this for years." Then there were new things: a strawberry bed, over which both Stephen and Sarah Jane — to say nothing of one scarcely less interested, Flora Ann Lucas — had worked, and read, and studied, early and late; the result was, ripe strawberries before any others were heard of in the neighborhood; potatoes fresh from the ground were on the Mitchell dinner-table before their neighbors had thought of its being time to try theirs. Green peas, of a very early, and very choice variety were the next sensation. At a surprisingly early date the Mitchell farm wagon was filled to its utmost capacity with fresh fruits, fresh vegetables, even fresh flowers, and started on its way to the summer encampment grounds.

It is an interesting thing to watch people adjust themselves to altered circumstances and positions. Stephen was only a year older than when he took that ride before, but it seemed to him that he had lived half a lifetime since; so marked were the contrasts. He scarcely knew when it was that his father, instead of saying with authoritative voice and manner: "Go here" or "there;" "Do this" or "that" — the order always followed by a sigh for his own physical limitations, and a groan over probable results — had adopted the fashion of asking: "Shall we get at the potatoes to-day, do you think?" or "How had we better plan for the south meadow?" or "What is your idea about that fence on the west side?" Only the day before, he had heard the father explain to a neighbor, "Steve thinks we better change the crop entirely on this lot another year; he says the ground needs the change; that it is worn out for the other crop. I don't know how he finds out, but he appears to know about a great many things that I never heard of, and his plans turn out all right. There was a man looking at his strawberry patch yesterday, and he said he didn't know any such strawberries in the country."

Doll and Dobbin may not have approved of all the changes, though nothing in their manner hinted at such a thought. They were taken better care of than ever before, more faithfully fed and groomed, but they certainly had to work faster; and loitering, on reasonably good stretches of road, was not permitted in these days.

Stephen's start for the encampment was early, and his entire air was the alert one of a man of business. He looked around him curiously as he drove through the enchanted land, fully as beautiful as it had been the year before; and was rather pleased than otherwise, to learn that the all-important Mr. Baker could not be seen until noon.

This gave him a chance to go around to that remarkable spot where he had first secured his list of words. Apparently the same crowd was there, at least a like crowd in numbers. The platform was occupied, not by the speaker he had heard, but by one who seemed to use language with equal ease. Stephen secured a seat, by dint of a little effort, and gave close attention. It chanced — as we are fond of using language — that this was "Agricultural Day," at the encampment, and the subject of the platform address was one which had an absorbing interest for the young farmer. It was in a line in which he had been reading and studying; and no more earnest or intelligent listener was in that large audience, than Stephen Mitchell. Very early in the hour, he took notebook and pencil from his pocket, not this time to secure lists of flying words, but to note down certain points which were quite new to him; as he did so he made the mental resolution to "study them up, to see if that fellow was right."

Oh! there was no denying that Stephen had made wonderful progress. He let his mind dwell a good deal upon contrasts, this summer day; all the experiences of his first visit were such vivid memories. As he drove homeward his thoughts were busy. Perhaps no small thing marked the changes more forcefully than his stop at the corner store, where the same Mr. Pettibone still simpered behind the counter. Stephen did not like him any better than he had the summer before, but he was by no means so afraid of him. He had discovered that Mr. Pettibone was not so grand a gentleman as he had supposed him to be; and that his opinion of persons and things was of comparatively little consequence. He gave his orders with an ease and glibness which contrasted strongly with the "green braid" experience. Mr. Pettibone's manner was also changed.

"How are you, Mitchell?" he had said with friendly familiarity, as Stephen entered the store; and as he attended his customer's commissions, he asked if he had been out to the encampment, and whether there were crowds there, and if there was anything "nice" going on evenings.

Then, to sharpen the sense of contrast, Miss Ransom entered the store; and her eyes brightened with welcome as Stephen turned to meet her.

"How fortunate!" she said. "You are just the one I wanted to see. Can you call at the house a moment? I am anxious to send Sarah a package; and my brother has a package for you, I think; some illustrated papers, which he says make plain those plans for the trellises of which you and he were talking."

Stephen even had to call at the Bascomes' — not this time to borrow a pattern; Sarah Jane had no need of Bascome patterns in these days; instead, they were delighted to borrow of her — but to leave a book which Mrs. Colchester had promised Fanny.

When he had passed in the morning it had been too early for the Bascomes; their house was closed and silent. Fanny was on the piazza when he returned, and her manner pointed the contrast again. She had decided to be very friendly with Stephen Mitchell — was he not on intimate terms at the manse, much more at home there than she was herself? And there was that elegant Mrs. Colchester; he seemed to be really intimate with her; and Steve really was a nice-looking fellow, now that he wore good clothes, and had found out what to do with his hands and feet. Moreover, she had heard Judge Parsons say that young Mitchell was a smart fellow; destined to make a man.

She gave him most cordial greeting, and tried to be very cordial; sent her love to Sarah Jane, and her thanks to Mrs. Colchester, and asked if he wouldn't bring them both out some day to see her flowers; she had some flowers that she knew Mrs. Colchester would admire. It was not so much what she said, as the way she said it, that reminded Stephen forcefully once more of the year before. His smile was half-amused, half-cynical as he sprang into his farm wagon, and made haste homeward.

"She is willing to stand Sarah Jane and me, if she can have Mrs. Colchester thrown in once in a while," he said to himself; "but she wouldn't speak to Flora Ann, not for a farm;" by which you will discover that Stephen Mitchell, though he had learned many things, had not learned to like Fanny Bascome.

It might have been a vague feeling that Flora Ann had been slighted, which made Stephen unusually kind to her that evening. He looked at her thoughtfully as she moved around the dining-room, putting the finishing touches to the table, which she had learned to do quite as neatly as Sarah Jane herself. He was still in the mood for contrasts; he contrasted Flora Ann not only with the Bascomes, but with the many girls he had seen that day.

"She is a pretty girl," was his grave conclusion, "and she is a good girl, and she's going to be a smart girl. In some things she goes ahead of Sarah Jane."

It was at thàt particular moment that the subject of his thoughts stopped in front of the window near which he sat, and looked wistfully down the road.

"It will be nice moonlight," she said; "if I can get off early enough, I mean to go home. I am kind of worried about mother. She looked as though she was going to have one of her poor turns the last time I was there; and I haven't seen any of them for more than a week. I could stay all night, you know, and come home real early in the morning."

"There is no need for that," said Stephen kindly.

"I will go over with you. I would just as soon go as not; I haven't been working to-day."

Within another hour they were walking briskly down the moonlighted road, talking cheerily together. The two had many subjects in common. As a scholar, Flora Ann managed to keep very good pace with Stephen, and she had original ideas upon many subjects, which surprised and interested him. His sister did her best to be interested in agricultural studies, but her tastes evidently did not lie in that direction.

"She is quick as lightning at grammar," Stephen had explained one day to Mrs. Colchester, "and she is willing to study half the night about flowers; but when it comes to turnips, and beets, and cabbages, why, you can see she only reads because she thinks it ought to be read. She doesn't take to farming. Now Flora, if she had a chance, would make a first-rate farmer. She has ideas that surprise me."

Mrs. Colchester smiled, and explained that that was an experience common to students; each had his or her specialty; and she reminded him that if all the world "took to farming," there would be no teachers, or merchants, or preachers. She was always pleased when Stephen said "Flora" and "Sarah," which he was learning to do. She never spoke of the two girls by their full names herself, nor did Nina; and the force of example was asserting itself in the household, even in this respect.

"It is very still around here," said Flora, as they neared her father's cabin. "I don't think the boys can be at home; or else " —

She had no need to finish the sentence; Stephen understood it only too well. The boys, now that Jake was not there to frighten them into silence, were rarely quiet. They were not fierce, or dangerous, as Jake had been, but hilarious, in a way which was sometimes harder for Flora Ann to bear than Jake's blows had been. She never neared the door of this sorrowful home without thinking of "poor Jake." She always spoke of him now with that adjective before his name; but she spoke of him frequently, and made it evident that she had by no means forgotten him. She still spoke more freely to Stephen than to any other person; still apparently continued to believe that of course he felt as she did.

"Poor Jake!" she said, her thoughts going from the boys to him. "I am praying for him right along steady, Steve; I always will, you know, till I hear he is where he don't need it. Wouldn't it be nice to know that he had got into the right way, and God had taken him where he wouldn't be tempted any more? I would be willing for that — I guess for mother's sake I would be glad for it; because, Steve, mother mourns for Jake all the time. She can't get along without him as the others can. I never go home but she talks about him, and cries, and says she wishes she had borne with him better. Poor thing! she used to bear with him always, only she won't believe it. It was the rest of us that used to be cross to him."

"I guess you was never cross to him," said Stephen. "I never saw anything like it."

"Well, I wasn't much of anything to him. I was afraid; that was the trouble. It was silly in me to be such a coward; he wouldn't have killed me, I guess, if I had tried to help him more. I wish I had."

Then she opened the door leading into the family room, and they went in. It was surprisingly still; the boys were not there; the father was sitting in his chair, drowsing, and partially intoxicated. The little girls had huddled themselves into a corner, and were occupied in staring at a neatly-dressed stranger, who sat with his back to the door.

"There's Flora Ann!" exclaimed the children, as the door opened; and the stranger arose and came toward them. Behold! it was Jake. Jake, with his shock of black hair neatly combed — Flora Ann never remembered to have seen it combed before — and not only were his clothes whole and neat, but he had on a collar and a necktie. Moreover, his eyes, which had always been bloodshot, were clear and smiling.

"How do you do?" he said, holding out his hand, as Flora Ann still stood staring at him. "Surely you have not forgotten me?"

"He's come home," exclaimed his mother, unable to keep silence any longer. "He come this afternoon. I told 'em we ought to send for you; but there wasn't nobody to send; the boys ain't come yet. Don't he look nice? I wouldn't have knowed him if I'd met him in the street. O, yes! I would. I'd know my Jake anywheres. Ain't it wonderful?"

But Flora Ann had no words. She was overwhelmed. This to be Jake! This man with a smile on his face!

"Things don't match, do they?" he said, the smile deepening. "I don't think they ever will again. I am Jake, and yet I am not Jake. No; I'll tell you how it is: I am a new Jake."

Then he turned to Stephen.

"How do you do, Stephen? I remember being downright hateful, the last words I spoke to you; and I was getting a favor from you at the same time. That was the old Jake; I know you don't lay up anything against him. The new Jake is ashamed of him."

Stephen shook the offered hand heartily, but was as silent as Flora Ann. This seemed to him in very deed to be a new Jake, or rather not Jake at all. Remember, he had never seen him when he was not more or less under the influence of liquor. Now there was no sign or smell of it about him; he was thin and pale, and the marks of his hard life showed on his face; but he was quiet, with the quietness of one who had been in the battle, and been wounded, but had come off conqueror.

They sat late in the evening, listening to his story. He told it from the beginning; described the ride in the omnibus, and the gayly-dressed, silver-voiced young lady who laid the tract in his hand. Told how he got out into the night and the darkness, and on what sort of a corner he stopped, cursing the tract because it could not be turned into whiskey. Told how the little tract had seemed to lure him on, pointing out soup and a bed — although he would have given the prospect of both for one drink of whiskey. Told how at last he found the mission, and the soup. How he was offered a chance to wash, and was given some decent clothes, and invited in to hear the singing. It was a wonderful story, though it could be put into a few sentences; and the same story is being lived over every night in our large cities.

There were men and women connected with that mission, who held on to Jake, even though he tried his stupid best to slip away from them, and more than once fell back into the very gutter, only to be sought after, and reached after, and lured back to the shelter of their care. There were miserable weeks, during which Jake came afterward to realize that the workers in the mission had not lost sight of him for one full day.

Elude them as he would, and manage in some cunning way to get enough liquor to fire his brain, and make him angry at them all, yet would they follow him up and bring him back to that one spot where things were clean and pure; and where food was wholesome, and faces were kind.

"I cannot tell you about it," said Jake, breaking off in the middle of a sentence. "I don't know how to tell it. I didn't understand what made them hang on to me so; I hadn't a bit of faith in myself. I thought I was about as worthless a fellow as they could find, even in that city; and I saw some hard looking fellows too; but I looked, to myself, worse than any of them. And I felt worse. I haven't had a very high opinion of myself for a good many years, and I thought it was too late for me to be anything else."

But they wanted to hear his story; they plied him with questions, and heard how at last the outraged body and brain refused to endure any more; fever and delirium followed, during which poor Jake raved and cursed and groaned; and was watched over, and cared for every day and night, faithfully, skillfully, tenderly. Following the fever were long weeks of prostration, during which he lay as helpless as a child. Then he slowly, very slowly, crept back to life and strength again.

CHAPTER XXVI.

OTHER TRAVELERS.

"AND the rest of it," said Jake, breaking off again, a light on his face such as they had never seen there before — " I don't know how to tell. I haven't found any words yet that tell it. There was one day when I felt so low down and miserable that it seemed to me a terrible pity that I had lived. I couldn't see how I was to be of any use to myself or anybody else. I thought I would be just a blot on the earth. I thought of mother, here; and it seemed to me that the best news that could have come to her would have been that I was dead and buried. I thought of all of you here at home, and I felt as though there would be more hope for you if I was gone; I didn't see why I had lived; I didn't have a bit of hope for myself; I knew there wasn't any use in trying to be anything but a drunken wretch; spite of all I had been through, the sickness, and everything, there was nothing I wanted so much as whiskey, and I knew that just as soon as I got out on the street where it was to be had, I would find a way to get it. I don't know what made me think of Flora Ann just then, but I did. You see, I knew about her praying for me, and it used to make me mad — but all of a sudden it came over me that there was a God, and that he must have made me, and that I had a sister who had talked to Him a good deal about me. I didn't suppose that I believed in prayer, but I seemed to, all of a sudden; I was alone, sitting on the side of the bed, and I just slipped down on my knees, and I said, 'O, Lord' — that is every living word I said." To have seen the look of awe on Jake's face as he repeated the word would have been a lesson in reverence. "And the reason I can't tell the rest of it is because I don't know what happened; only He came, and took hold of me, and — well, I knew that I wasn't Jake Lucas inside any more. But how can a man tell a thing like that?"

Yet Jake must have understood that his face and voice and manner told the story eloquently. He was not even Jake Lucas outside any more.

There were other details; he had been very slow in regaining his strength. He had been very much afraid of the streets at first — until he had discovered that the Power which had taken hold of him, would "go along with him through the streets." Having come to himself—or rather having come to God — his next fixed thought was for his mother. But along with the desire to see her, came to him an ambition to present himself before her in such garb as would fit the new man he felt himself to be. With this for an incentive, he had gone to work, almost before his strength was equal to the demand, and had worked faithfully until he had earned a suit of clothes, and a little money in his pocket. Then he had started homeward, working his way as he came, stopping at point after point, as the necessity for doing so arose; working at anything he could find to do — so that his small sum of money, instead of decreasing, steadily increased.

"And so," he said at last, "I've got home."

"Yes," his mother broke in eagerly at that point, "and the first thing he did was to buy some tea for me. And he bought crackers, and a piece of meat, and brought them home. Just to think of my Jake coming, and bringing me tea."

Flora and Stephen made almost one third of the distance home in total silence, that evening. They seemed unable to find words for their thoughts. At last Flora broke the silence:

"It seems too wonderful to believe, doesn't it, Steve? But I don't understand why I should feel so; you see, I have been praying and praying for him, and wanting him to come home; yet it seems I didn't expect it. When I found him sitting there all dressed up, and talking so nice, and being good to mother, why, I just felt as though I should scream. And one time things got all black in the room, and I was dizzy like, just because I was so astonished. I find I didn't expect any such thing."

"I don't wonder," said Stephen. "I wouldn't have been more astonished, it seems to me, if a stick of wood from the woodpile had walked in and sat and talked with us. It is a most amazing thing. It doesn't seem as if he could be Jake Lucas."

"He isn't," said Flora Ann, with quiet exultation. "He is made over; folks aren't the same after they begin to pray, Steve; I know that by myself. I'm not the same girl I used to be, at all. Folks don't know it, but I'm not. I don't think the same things about people, nor places, nor doings of any kind you know. Oh! I ain't a bit the same; I can't describe it, as Jake says, but I understand just what he means; it is all different — still there is more difference for Jake than for any of us. O, my! Think of Jake coming to prayer meeting, and praying. Do you suppose he will? I am just afraid I will faint, then, and miss hearing the words, and I wouldn't for anything."

It was fully as wonderful and bewildering as Flora Ann had foreseen. The first time that Jake Lucas came to prayer meeting, the Mitchell dining-room was crowded to its utmost capacity, and the hall was full; even the stairs were full up to the very landing. It was such a strange sight for the neighborhood to see one who had been its terror, sitting among them, "clothed, and in his right mind." He not only prayed, but sang, and talked, standing up boldly for the One who, as he always reverently expressed it, had "made him over."

"You can all see, friends, that I ain't the same," he said earnestly. "I don't think the same thoughts, nor do the same things; not by a great sight, I don't. I know what has been the matter with me; I have belonged to the Devil for a good many years, and I have served him faithfully, nobody will deny that; now I have changed owners — no, it isn't that; *I* didn't do it; another owner has got me somehow. I don't know how He got me away from the Devil, but you can see for yourselves that He has done it; and from this time forth I belong to Him, and it makes a difference."

As he sat down, Helen Ransom's clear voice took up the story:

> "I was lost, but Jesus found me,
>   Found the sheep that went astray;
> Threw his loving arms around me,
>   Drew me back into his way.
> I was bruised, but Jesus healed me;
>   Faint was I from many a fall;
> Sight was gone, and fears possessed me,
>   But He freed me from them all."

The minister came into the manse sitting-room one afternoon, and found Sarah Jane in earnest conversation with his sister.

"Sarah has an application for board," explained

Miss Ransom, when her caller had been duly greeted.

"Indeed!" said the minister, with polite interest. "Who is that?"

"A Mrs. Sedgwick," said Sarah. "I have a letter from her; she wants to come for the summer, and have her husband come Saturday nights when he can. She says sometimes he cannot get away. She wants to get into the country for her health, and to be near the city where her husband's business is; she offers a very nice price for her board."

"That is a good recommendation for her," said the minister, smiling. "How did she hear of you, Sarah?"

"She says a friend of hers is a friend of Mrs. Colchester, and told her where she was staying."

"What does Mrs. Colchester say?" asked the minister, rousing to deeper interest. "Would she like to have this boarder come?"

"I do not think she is anxious to have more company," said Sarah. "She is very busy all the time, and never seems lonesome; but she says of course she wants us to earn all the money we can; and she thinks there is no reason why we should not have this lady come, if our rooms will suit her."

There followed a detailed discussion of plans, carried on by Miss Ransom and her guest; the minister lingered, and offered a suggestion now and then; but he chiefly interested himself in the study of Sarah Jane, contrasting her with a girl by that name who had come to them only a year before. He decided that she was a somewhat remarkable study; and felt that he had not realized heretofore that a human being could take such strides in a year's time.

"She is a pretty, lady-like girl," he said to himself, "neatly and becomingly dressed. Helen has certainly done wonders for her. She is more changed than her brother, in some respects. When one thinks of those four people — Sarah, Stephen, Flora, and that marvelous Jake — it is enough to intoxicate one with life. To realize what human effort, supplemented by the almighty power of God, can do for souls, even here on earth, gives one a faint conception of what an eternity of Heaven, and the companionship of Jesus Christ, may be able to do for us all."

By the time he had reached this concluding thought, Sarah's arrangements were perfected.

In due course of time, the new boarder came to them.

"A sickly-looking, fashionable girl," Helen said, describing the new-comer to her brother. "She does not look at all like a married woman, nor act like one. I can hardly understand what the attraction could have been in this direction. She impresses me as one who would be able to cordially hate the country; and there is no more affinity between her and Mrs. Colchester than there is — between Sarah and Fannie Bascome."

She closed the sentence with a laugh; for both brother and sister realized that comparison could go no farther.

"Well," said the minister with a sigh, "if she pays the price for her board, of which Sarah spoke, there will be some compensation, at least."

The sigh was for a thought which he had — that it would not be so pleasant at the Mitchell farmhouse as it had been. Up to the date when the new boarder was heard of, he had felt that no scheme of Helen's had been happier than this one of setting Sarah Jane to keeping boarders. Since that time he had been occasionally troubled with doubts as to its wisdom.

It was two weeks before he made the acquaintance of Mrs. Sedgwick. She had come on the Wednesday following the Tuesday evening prayer meeting, which had now become an institution in the Hilton Hill neighborhood. The following Sunday had proved rainy in the extreme, and although Mrs. Sedgwick was said to have expressed a strong curiosity to attend church, she was not inclined to brave a six-mile ride in the storm in order to do so. On the following Tuesday evening the minister was called miles away in another direction, to visit a sick parishioner, and the prayer meeting had to get on without him. In this way two weeks had passed.

It was on Saturday evening that he came to Helen with a proposition to ride out to the farmhouse.

"I have been working very hard," he said, "and I think a canter would do me good. Besides, I hardly ought to let another Sabbath pass without calling on the stranger. We can make a short call, and get home in good season."

Sarah Jane saw and recognized them in the distance, and came to the gate to meet them.

"I never was so glad to see any one in my life," she said earnestly. "I have just been praying that Mr. Ransom would come; I didn't know what else to do."

"What is the matter?" asked Mr. Ransom hastily, recognizing more than cordial greeting in her anxious tone.

She made her story brief: Mr. Sedgwick had arrived that afternoon, very much under the influence of liquor when he reached there, and was growing more so every moment, having brought a plentiful supply in his traveling bag. Sarah Jane's eyes were wide with terror.

"He has been singing, and shouting, and acting like a crazy man for the last hour," she explained; "and now he is getting cross. They are in the dining-room, and he won't go away himself, nor let her. I think she is scared at him; and he keeps getting so much worse, we don't know what to do. If Mrs. Colchester were here I think she could do something with him; she can with almost everybody; but she went with Flora out to her house. And Steve hasn't got home from the village; so we are just alone. Father don't know anything to do, and he won't go in there at all. He says he would just as soon see a wild tiger as a drunken man. I never saw father act as he does about this."

And Sarah Mitchell never understood why her father "acted" as he did. The loyal wife and son kept always silent about that chapter in his life.

"Mrs. Colchester's help should not be expected under such circumstances," said the minister, with more severity than Sarah Jane had ever heard him speak. "Where drunken men are, is no place for her. I will go in at once, and see what can be done."

What he succeeded in doing was presently apparent. His sister and Sarah, waiting outside, heard their voices; the drunken man's loud and hilarious, the minister's firm and commanding. Presently they heard the footsteps of the two, making their way upstairs, the drunken man's unsteady and trembling; evidently he was being half-carried, and the minister was speaking quiet, authoritative words:

"Put your foot there, Mr. Sedgwick; so! You will not fall; I will see to that. No; you are not coming back; the place for you at present is in your room. You are to get to bed as speedily as possible. Yes, you can; I will help you. Yes; I understand," interrupting the man in his maudlin attempts at explaining that he had been "s-sud-sud-'nly ta-'on ver-ver'- s-s-sick."

"I understand it perfectly, sir; you need not explain."

And by this time they had reached the landing above. Sarah Jane drew a long breath of relief.

"What a man he is!" she said, meaning the minister, for there was admiration in her tones. "He is like Mrs. Colchester, Miss Ransom; he can do anything with people; they both can. I don't believe he will have a bit of trouble in getting him to bed. And she just coaxed and begged him to go. Miss Ransom, he swore at her. O, dear! such a time as we have had. And I was afraid Jake Lucas would come in every minute. It would have been awful for Jake to see a drunken man, don't you think so? Miss Ransom, will you go in and see Mrs. Sedgwick? Maybe you can comfort the poor thing. I suppose her heart is almost broken."

"Perhaps she would rather not see a stranger just now," said Miss Ransom, holding back, and wondering what it would be possible to say that would comfort the wife of a drunkard.

At that moment the door opened, and Mrs. Sedgwick's pale, pretty face appeared.

CHAPTER XXVII.

DANGER SIGNALS.

"GOOD evening," she said to Miss Ransom. "Wasn't it awful? He never was so bad as that before; he has been with some of those fast men in town, who have such a bad influence over him. Isn't it dreadful to think that men will drink, and make such awful nuisances of themselves? But they all do it; I don't believe my husband has an acquaintance who doesn't take a glass when he feels like it. They are not drunkards, you know, of course; but once in a while they are overcome. I am sure I wish my husband didn't drink at all; but I suppose he would have to be a minister in that case; I believe they are the only men who do not indulge. You are fortunate in having one for a brother. I think girls ought to look out for such men for husbands. It is a hard life, but there are compensations, it seems."

And she actually laughed, this silly little woman! Helen looked at her in dumb dismay. She made no attempt to comfort; she would as soon have tried to comfort a parrot.

"I suppose I would better go upstairs," said the wife. "Or would you wait down here until Mr. Ransom gets him to bed? I am sure I have had enough of him for one night. But he will be all right as soon as he gets to bed, and has had his first sleep. He will waken in the morning very much vexed with himself, poor fellow! He does dislike making a scene. I assure you, Miss Ransom, this is really a rare occurrence. Gentlemen stay in their clubs in town, you know, when they find themselves overcome with liquor; but in the country, of course, there is nothing for them but to brave the embarrassment. Sarah, I believe I will go up to your room, if you will let me, and wait until Mr. Ransom comes out."

And she gathered her silken robes about her, and climbed up the old-fashioned staircase, Sarah and Miss Ransom looking after her, the one almost as much bewildered as the other.

Mr. Ransom came down presently, pallid to a degree that startled and frightened his sister, and grave almost to sternness. He was in haste to start homeward; he would not go into the dining-room, which, between meals, had now become the family sitting-room. He declined waiting to see Mr. and Mrs. Mitchell, who had fled to the kitchen from the presence of the drunkard. He could not wait for the return of Mrs. Colchester and Flora, nor even to see Stephen, with whom he was supposed to have an errand. "Another time would do," he said; he must get home at once; he and Helen had only come out for the exercise.

He hurried Helen's last words with Sarah, and in a few minutes they were out, mounted on their horses, and galloping toward home. The minister rode at almost break-neck speed, and in the moonlight his face showed pallid still, and his mouth was set in stern lines. Helen wondered, and was silent. He had seen drunken men before; why was he so moved by this exhibition? Was it sympathy for the foolish little wife, who did not seem to deserve to have such feeling wasted upon her?

"But she must just have talked at random," Helen said repentingly to herself; "talked to cover embarrassment and pain. She wanted me to think that nothing very terrible had happened, and talked on, perhaps, without realizing what she said. She probably lost her unnatural self-control when she got upstairs. I wish Maxwell would talk. How miserable he looked! If he is going to carry other people's burdens in this intense way, he will wear out long before his time."

They were within two miles of home before the minister spoke, other than to ask his sister if they were riding too fast, and if she were comfortable. But at last he slackened rein, and turned toward her. The first words he spoke struck his sister **dumb.**

"Helen, Mrs. Sedgwick is Gertrude Temple."

It was even so; the pretty city boarder, who had been willing to bury herself in the country, and to offer an extremely liberal price for the privilege of doing so, was the woman who, for one well-remembered year, Mr. Ransom had looked upon as his promised wife.

His sister, who had not felt drawn toward the stranger, but rather repelled, and who had struggled with the feeling, and chided herself for it as unworthy, now began to study the woman with a strange mingling of feelings, and was obliged to pray much for grace to keep her not only from saying that which might be an injury to others, but also from thinking uncharitable thoughts. Still the curious problem would present itself: What motive could Mrs. Sedgwick have for coming away from all her home surroundings and home friends, miles into the country? Unquestionably it was not the love of nature that had brought her; nature, in its most lovely forms, seemed to be only endured by her; and when it put on its unlovely face, was positively repulsive.

Perhaps it was hardly to be expected that a woman like Helen Ransom should have understood a woman like Gertrude Sedgwick; nothing could be much farther apart than the moral vision of the two. Yet to those who have come in contact with this type of human nature, Mrs. Sedgwick's motive will be readily apprehended. From very babyhood, she had pleased herself; she had been a creature of whims and fancies; she had not for one quiet hour in her life looked ahead and studied the consequences of her acts from the moral side of her being. Results which might be disagreeable to herself, she could to a degree apprehend — though even for herself she was very short-sighted. She had married, the winter before, the man whose attentions had first inclined her to feel that she was not fitted to be the wife of a minister. Had Maxwell Ransom been preparing for the bar, or had he been a gentleman of wealth and leisure, she would have decided for him, instead of for Charlie Sedgwick. But since she could not move him from his purpose, and since she was able to realize that his profession would demand certain duties from her which would be irksome, the scale had finally turned in favor of the man who was her husband. She was fond of him in her way, but as compared with her pleasure — even the passing pleasure of an hour — he was altogether secondary. She had lived fast, after her marriage; without regard to the laws of health, or to any laws save those which her fancy dictated. She had treated her body as a mere machine whose business it was to do her bidding. Of course it had taken but a few months to break down a body which was never strong, at the best. When the physician had ordered rest, and entire freedom from the requirements of fashionable life, Mrs. Sedgwick had looked about her for some entertainment; and in doing so, had heard of Mrs. Colchester's departure from the city.

"Have you heard of our beautiful young widow's latest freak?" That was the way the news was communicated. "It has suited her fancy to go to the country in mid-winter, and bury herself and her little sister in a farmhouse."

"There is some special attraction, you may depend upon it," Mrs. Sedgwick had said as soon as she heard this story. "Mark my words, Mrs. Sylvester, you will hear of some interesting young man stranded in the vicinity of that country farmhouse, before the season is over."

This explanation was met with approval by some of the circle, and with indignation by others. A thorough discussion of Mrs. Colchester's affairs had followed. But Mrs. Sedgwick, caring not in the least for either side, had forgotten all about it, until the conversation was recalled to her a few days later by Mrs. Sylvester.

"You were evidently right about Mrs. Colchester, my dear Mrs. Sedgwick. I am told there is a brilliant young clergyman where she has gone, who has one or two *protégés* in the aforesaid farmhouse, and is therefore a frequent visitor. One may always trust young widows to keep their eyes wide open."

"It speaks well for her husband, that she is willing to choose another from the same profession," was Mrs. Sedgwick's gay rejoinder. "What is the name of the clergyman who is brilliant enough to hold people in the country through March?"

"Why, that is an interesting part of the story. His name is Ransom, Maxwell Ransom; he is a nephew of the famous professor by the same name, and has inherited all his uncle's talent, I am told."

Mrs. Sedgwick had received this piece of information in utter silence; but had pondered over it to such purpose, that later in the season when she was ordered to the country, she could think of no part of the world where she could be induced to go save to the Mitchell farmhouse. No; you are not to think of her as the wickedest woman on the face of the earth, but simply as a weak, vain woman, who desired to amuse herself. She could not help feeling that it would be amusing to come in contact with Maxwell Ransom, and bring her fascinations to bear upon him once more. It would really be very exciting to meet him again and talk over old times; even sigh a little over the memories of the past. Where was the harm? They had had delightful times together. She frankly admitted to herself that in some respects he was "Charlie's" superior; she had always thought so. There had been times when she had frankly told "Charlie" that if she had married Maxwell Ransom, he would never so far have forgotten himself as to drink enough liquor to make him either silly or cross. No; it was entertainment, pure and simple, which Mrs. Sedgwick was after. She felt herself somewhat defrauded of entertainment at times, for her husband's temptations were such as to make her more or less nervous in society, and now her failing health had come to add to the inconveniences of life. It was but fair that she should get what enjoyment she could out of banishment; and where could more be found than in the society of a young man whom she knew so well, and with whom she could talk freely, and associate familiarly without being misunderstood? For he was a clergyman, and she was a married woman.

This was really the extent to which her shallow little brain had planned; and Helen Ransom, in studying her, did not do her justice. Perhaps one of her nature was not able to do justice to so small an amount of brain as had been given to Gertrude Sedgwick.

The minister, as soon as he reached home, went directly to his study, and was seen no more that night. The next morning he was himself again; possibly a trifle paler than usual; he admitted to his sister that he was late in retiring. But he was as deeply interested in his work as he had been the day before, and entered upon it with energy. Nor did he change his habits in the slightest degree in regard to the Hilton Hill neighborhood. He went regularly to the meetings, and made his regular calls quite as usual. Helen, who always accompanied him on these trips, watched with anxious eyes, but could not see that he treated Mrs. Sedgwick in the slightest degree differently from what he would any stranger, whom chance had brought in his vicinity. As the weeks passed, Mrs. Sedgwick also made this discovery, and it is unnecessary to confess that it annoyed her. Mr. Ransom as a theological student had been wont to flush and pale under her influence; to try in every way in his power to please her; to put himself out to gratify her whims. But it was only too apparent that this Mr. Ransom, while perfectly courteous at all times, was also perfectly indifferent as regarded herself. He neither sought her society nor shunned it; and the weak little woman who liked her husband less, and Mr. Ransom more, every time she saw him, and who knew, or thought she knew, that it was Mrs. Colchester who had "come between" them, as she expressed it to herself, grew every day more determined to win the attention she coveted. Or, failing in that, at least she would prevent their enjoyment of each other. It was not in Gertrude Sedgwick's nature to stand tamely by and see Mrs. Colchester accomplish what she could not.

It was a lovely afternoon in early autumn, and the Mitchell farmhouse, which had taken on many improvements during the summer, was bright with sunshine, and gay with many autumn flowers. In Mrs. Colchester's room, that lady, with Helen

Ransom and her brother and Sarah Jane, were having what the latter called "a first-rate visit." It was Tuesday, and Mr. Ransom and Helen had come out early, as they always did on that day, to make a call or two in the neighborhood, take tea at the Mitchell farm, and get ready for the evening meeting; which meeting was so growing in interest and power since Jake Lucas had taken hold of it, that people drove for miles in various directions in order to see and hear this marvelous specimen of what God could do. He was so earnest in securing allies for his new Master that he let no opportunity pass without urging upon people "just to try Him, and find out for themselves."

They had been talking together about Mrs. Sedgwick. "I invite her to my room as often as I can," Mrs. Colchester had said, "because I am very sorry for her; she is an unhappy woman. She is not gaining in health, and her husband is not improving in his habits. He was worse at his last visit than we have ever seen him. Of course she feels very anxious about him, with an anxiety which cannot be spoken of. It seems to make her nervous even to hear his name mentioned. I don't know how she bears her burden; and she is trying to bear it all alone. I know," in response to Helen's inquiring look, "she is a member of the Church, but I think the first principles of vital Christianity are yet to be learned by her. And she is so hard to reach, because she takes it for granted that she is on safe ground, of course; — hasn't she been a church member in good and regular standing ever since she was fourteen ? — I am afraid for such people; it seems to me they are in far greater danger than those who reckon themselves outsiders."

CHAPTER XXVIII.

THE THROUGH LINE AT LAST.

IT was at that moment that Mrs. Sedgwick had entered the room, and Mr. Ransom, who had been a listener to this talk — which was rather between Helen and Mrs. Colchester — after greeting the new-comer, had moved away and taken up a book; not to read, but as a cover for his thoughts. Was it his duty to assume more friendly relations with Mrs. Sedgwick, in order to try to lead her into the right way? He admitted to himself that probably Mrs. Colchester was right, and there was little hope that this woman, whom he had once thought such a lovely Christian, understood the first principles of personal religion. Was it his duty to try to help her? Would he not be misunderstood? But even if he were, would that relieve him from his duty?

And the minister's mind was in chaos. It ended by his joining the little circle, summoned thither by a question which Mrs. Sedgwick called out to him. For a few moments the conversation was general; then Sarah, being called from the room, presently returned and petitioned Miss Ransom to come out to the dining-room a few minutes; and the three were left together. Whether the spirit of maliciousness took hold of Mrs. Sedgwick to an unusual degree that afternoon, will not be known; certainly she became very personal in her words.

"This is almost like old times, isn't it, Max? Dear me! what a little time ago it seems when you and I used to be very much pleased when people were called out of the room. Do you remember that Friday evening at the seminary, when the girls would all stay down in the parlor? I suppose I ought to say 'Mr. Ransom,' but it sounds very much more natural to me to call you by the name I am used to. Mrs. Colchester, we are amazing you, are we not, by our reminiscences? You did not know that Mr. Ransom and I were very, very old friends, did you?"

"I am a very new friend of Mr. Ransom," said Mrs. Colchester, with a quiet smile; "and therefore have no knowledge of his friendships of long standing, of course."

"No; and our friendship was not of a character to be published, was it, Max?"

"I know no reason, Mrs. Sedgwick, why you should not state to any one whom you choose, that we were formerly very intimate friends, if it please you to do so."

The minister's tone was cold as ice, and his

manner dignity personified. It made Mrs. Sedgwick feel more wicked still. Evidently she was not gaining any influence over him; then she would sacrifice him to her jealous disappointment.

It had been disappointment from the very first; she had gone angrily over it in her mind only that day, and told herself what a fool she had been for her pains. How carefully she had guarded the secret of her former acquaintance with Mr. Ransom, on her first arrival, in order that she might enjoy the excitement of his and their surprise when they should learn who she was; and behold! the first meeting had been when he came to help her drunken husband to bed. How hard, even after that, she had striven to get a little excitement out of it, by being only an innocent child before Helen Ransom, in the belief that her brother had been too much overcome to explain who she was! It had been but another disappointment.

"Certainly I know you were once Miss Temple," Helen Ransom had said one day when Gertrude had resolved to make the revelation. "I have known you since the first evening my brother called here after you came. It was quite natural, of course, that he should mention it." And she had spoken as though it were a matter which had no interest for her, or for her brother. At that time the lady had concluded that her story was well known to Mrs. Colchester — for of course Helen Ransom had told it — this was Mrs. Sedgwick's idea of friendship; but later, when she came to know Helen better, she had a shrewd suspicion that utmost silence concerning her had been maintained. When she made the resolve to sacrifice Mr. Ransom, she rejoiced over this. She laughed the little girlish laugh that used to be so sweet to Mr. Ransom's ears.

"Dear me, Max, don't be so fearfully dignified! What is the use? You remind me forcibly of the times when some escapade of mine used to disturb you; I have received many a curtain lecture from him, Mrs. Colchester; I used to be a sad trial to him, I suspect. He owes me a vote of thanks for refusing to victimize him all his life. What a queer minister's wife I should have made! Can you imagine me for one minute in such a position, Mrs. Colchester?"

"No," said that lady, with a grave smile; "not with your present views of life."

"That is just the trouble; my views of life were always at variance with the life which was planned for me; and they are yet, for that matter — I think life has treated me in a very niggardly fashion. Here I am an old married woman, sick and miserable, when I ought to be just a girl, enjoying myself. But I will try to do my duty, Mrs. Colchester, and I warn you that this gentleman is very set in his ways. He is a slave to a creature which he calls 'Duty,' but which is really only another name for self-will. He will not hesitate to sacrifice any and everything which comes in the way of it. Oh! don't I know all about it? I am one of the sacrifices. But, my dear, I don't think you need to blush so over my revelations. Having been a married woman, you know men of course. They are all alike — fickle, I dare say. Some of them think more of books, it is true, than they do of any woman, even before marriage — but I assure you Mr. Ransom is quite attentive for him. Of course it is most apparent that you are the attraction to this old farmhouse, and you may as well enjoy it while it lasts; that is the only way to get along with life."

Said Mrs. Colchester: " Nina dear, do not try to get out of the swing alone; wait — I will come to you." And she stepped from the doorway near which she stood, out on the piazza, and moved swiftly off toward the swing under the great old trees. Mr. Ransom was left alone with Gertrude Temple. She lifted her eyes to him, and actually they were full of tears.

"O, Max!" she said, and her voice had the old childish quiver in it which used to move him, "have I offended you? Have I been very hateful? I did not mean to be. I do not know what I say half of the time; I talk lightly to other people, but really, Max, life is very hard upon me; you do not know what I have to suffer, and it hurts me so to think that you who used to be so entirely my friend, should seem to "— then she stopped, her beautiful eyes all dim with tears. She might as well have attempted to move a marble statue with tears and tremulousness. Mr. Ransom had risen from his chair the moment Mrs. Colchester left the room, and moved to the doorway through which she had passed. His voice was cold and stern.

"You have done no harm I imagine, Mrs. Sedgwick, except to yourself. A woman who can forget herself and her husband, and speak as you have done just now, is to be pitied perhaps, even more than she is to be blamed."

Then he, too, went through that open doorway, and walked deliberately out to the swing under the old trees. In the near distance was Stephen Mitchell, riding in from the field on a load of corn; he shouted to Nina, and she ran gayly away to ride up the long lane by his side. Her sister stood looking after her, her fingers engaged the while in breaking little twigs from the great tree, her face averted from Mr. Ransom, and her whole manner showing that she was struggling for an outward calm which would have belied the tumult at her heart.

"Mrs. Colchester," the minister said, speaking in quick, firm tones, "you have heard several truths this afternoon; you may not be interested in any of them, yet it becomes me as a man to own them as truths. I was engaged to be married to Mrs. Sedgwick, as she has intimated. I did not desert her as she hints; instead, she deserted me. I would have been true to what I thought she was had she given me opportunity. It is a long story, which you may not care to hear; it rests with you to say whether you care or not. She spoke other words which are also true; among them, that I am drawn to this house in order to see you; I have known it for some time. I have hoped that the time might come when you would let me tell you so; when you would let me explain everything which has to do with my life; I had not meant to come to you in this abrupt, almost rude fashion, and assuredly I had not meant to subject you to insult because of me. As it is, I hardly know what I ought to do next. You would be justified in wishing me to leave you, yet I can not feel willing to do so without an effort at explanation. I am so hurt and grieved that through any influence of mine, however remote, you should have been exposed to the venom of a cruel tongue, that I find myself unable to decide what would be the least offensive course for me to pursue under such strange circumstances."

There was silence under the trees for what seemed to the minister hours of time, although it was in reality but moments. Then Mrs. Colchester gave him a view of a very sweet face, and eyes that smiled. He had never heard a gentler voice than the one which said: "My trust in you is not shaken, Mr. Ransom. I give you leave to tell me as much or as little of your past as you choose, whenever you will. And I am not angry at that poor woman — it is as she said: Life has used her hard — or rather she has used it hard; and there is bitterness in store for her. When I think of the contrast between her life and mine" — her voice broke, and it was a moment before she added, "I have only pity for her, Mr. Ransom."

They lingered under the trees, sitting down together on the rustic seat which Stephen had made. Nina danced back from her ride, and finding them unsatisfactory company, flitted away again, and went to help Sarah and Flora arrange a most delightful-looking tea table. In her room upstairs, Mrs. Sedgwick watched the two under the trees with angry eyes, and brushed away from time to time certain miserable tears, and said to herself over and over again: "What a wretched idiot I have been all my life!"

Downstairs, Helen Ransom sat alone, taking neat stitches in the bit of work she was doing, and giving satisfied glances occasionally, out of the window — she liked the picture under the trees. In due course of time Nina summoned them all to that delightful tea table.

"Helen," Mr. Ransom said, as they rode home that evening after prayer meeting, "did you ever tell Mrs. Colchester anything concerning Mrs. Sedgwick and myself?"

"Maxwell!"

It was the only answer he received; but he needed no other, and made haste to respond: "I beg your pardon, Helen — but you are friends of such long standing, and so very intimate, I thought possibly " —

"Max, do you think that long and very intimate friendship justifies breaches of confidences made by other friends?"

"Certainly not; forgive me. I have never thought that you did or could do other than that which was true and noble. It was only my awkward way of introducing the subject. I have told her myself, the entire story — and I have something to tell you. Not about Mrs. Sedgwick — poor creature! — I find I can feel only pity for her. I have not even the heart to be indignant with her to-night — though assuredly she gave me cause this afternoon. Helen, I know it will make you glad, but will it surprise you very much to hear that your friend has promised to be your sister?"

It was three months afterward, on a moonlighted winter evening, that Stephen Mitchell and his pastor were walking across lots from the Lucas home, where they had been spending the evening together under circumstances the most solemn that human experience knows. "Old man Lucas," as he had been known in that neighborhood for so many years, had but just exchanged worlds.

The marvel of marvels had taken place once more. The old, worn body, dimmed of sight, dulled of hearing, poisoned with rum and tobacco, abused and wasted beyond repair, had been left behind. The soul, stained so many years with sin, having breathed out through lips of clay curses innumerable upon its Maker; having done almost all that a soul can do to make wreck of its possibilities, had toward the closing of that solemn "eleventh hour" given heed at last to the Voice which had steadily called after it. Those waiting around the old man's bed had heard the sin-stained lips speak marvelous words, even these: "God, for Jesus Christ's sake, has forgiven my sins." At the very last, when they had thought him done with earth, the dimmed eyes had opened again and looked upward for a moment; the thin, pale lips had taken on the majesty of a smile, and once more formed the words, "God, for Christ's sake — Amen," and old man Lucas had gone.

"What a wonderful experience!" said Mr. Ransom, as he crushed the frosted snow under his feet. "What a privilege has been ours to-night! Think what an infinite Saviour is ours, to take that man with his load of seventy years of sin upon him, and put a new song in his mouth, and stamp the clay that he has left behind with such a look of a conqueror that his children stand about it in awe, saying, 'Can that be father?' What a thing it must be for that man to enter Heaven."

They were crossing the Mitchell farm now; it lay under the snow, but both men thought as they trod, of the golden harvest that had waved there but a short time before; of the golden returns, very unusual both in quality and quantity therefrom. Stephen Mitchell was going to be a farmer; nobody questioned it now. Even in so short a time he had made his mark; even in so short a time his father had learned to say: "Ask Steve about it; he does the planning. Steve knows what he is about." Even in so short a time they had learned at the market in the city to ask for berries and early vegetables — yes, and even flowers from the Mitchell farm. O, yes! Stephen's heart was in it. The way he worked, and the way he studied, and the way he planned, proved that. But the minister thought of it all sadly; he remembered their first walk together across these fields, and the mistake he was convinced he had made. Why had he started Stephen Mitchell's energies, ambitions, hopes and plans all earthward? Even while he thought and sighed, Stephen broke the silence.

"Mr. Ransom, something else has happened to-day that you don't know about yet. I have boarded the right train at last, sir."

"What is that, Stephen? What do you mean?"

"I mean that I have been running on a side track for the last year or so; it has been a pretty good road, as you know, in some respects, but you haven't been satisfied with it; I know that; and I haven't been real downright satisfied myself, though I tried to think it first-class. But I have changed roads now; I am on the main line at last, and am bound for home. I'm not a passenger, either, but a stockholder."

"The Lord be praised!" said the minister, the joy in his heart ringing in his voice as the full meaning of this quaint language dawned upon him, and he grasped Stephen's hand. "I have waited and prayed for this so long, Stephen. Do you mind telling me the story — what started you on the right road at last?"

"Well," said Stephen, clearing his throat, "I have been thinking about it a good deal more than any of you know; but I really suppose it was Jake Lucas at the last who got me on the main track. It seemed so remarkable for him to board the lightning express, as you may say, and me, with the long start I had ahead of him, to be left behind. Then he was determined I should travel with him; it seemed as though nothing less would satisfy him. Then — perhaps you remember that list of words which started me in the first place?"

"I certainly do," said the minister promptly.

"Well, I keep studying them. I made up my mind, you know, to master them, and they brought me square up against the Bible one day, and made me go at that if I meant to be honest."

There was a moment's pause, then Stephen

cleared his throat and continued: "There's another thing, to be downright honest. I found out that Flora had taken me in place of her brother, and was praying for me every day, in the same way she used to for him before he started; and she has had such a hard life, one way and another, I couldn't seem to want to disappoint her."

The minister told this story over to Mrs. Colchester not long afterward.

"So it was Jake, and the list of words, and Flora Ann who reached him, you see," he concluded, and there was the faintest little sigh in his heart as he said the words. He had prayed so long, and worked so earnestly for Stephen Mitchell. "Well, what matters it?" he added, "so that he is on the main line at last; it is of very little consequence who took him to the train." Then, after a moment's silence, he laughed. "I remember he told me once he thought something might be made of 'that Flora Ann,' if the right person could only get a-hold of her; and I really think, Hilary, the right person to help her all through her life has been found."

www.ingramcontent.com/pod-product-compliance
Lightning Source LLC
Chambersburg PA
CBHW030259240426
43673CB00040B/1010